GENDER, WORK AND MEDICINE

GENDER, WORK AND MEDICINE

Women and the Medical Division of Labour

edited by
Elianne Riska and Katarina Wegar

SAGE Studies in International Sociology 44
Sponsored by the International Sociological Association/ISA

610.82 RIS

First published 1993

SAGE Publications Ltd
6 Bonhill Street
London EC2A 4PU

SAGE Publications Inc
2455 Teller Road
Newbury Park, California 91320

SAGE Publications India Pvt Ltd
32, M-Block Market
Greater Kailash – I
New Delhi 110 048

British Library Cataloguing in Publication data

Gender, Work and Medicine: Women and the
Medical Division of Labour. – (Sage
Studies in International Sociology;
Vol. 44)
  I. Riska, Elianne.   II. Wegar, Katarina
  III. Series
  610.696082

ISBN 0–8039–8902–4
ISBN 0–8039–8903–2 (pbk)

Library of Congress catalog card number 93–083603

Typeset by Type Study, Scarborough
Printed in Great Britain by Biddles Ltd, Guildford, Surrey

Contents

Notes on contributors   vii

Acknowledgements   ix

PART I   INTRODUCTION

Elianne Riska   1

PART II   THE MEDICAL PROFESSION

1   Sex stereotypes in women doctors' contribution to medicine: India
S. Muthu Chidambaram   13

2   Women doctors in a changing profession: the case of
Britain
Mary Ann Elston   27

3   Why women physicians will never be true equals in the
American medical profession
Judith Lorber   62

4   Women physicians: a new force in medicine?
Elianne Riska and *Katarina Wegar*   77

PART III   OTHER HEALTH PROFESSIONALS

5   The subordination of nurses in health care: towards a
social divisions approach
Mick Carpenter   95

6   A cross-national view of the status of midwives
Raymond G. DeVries   131

7   Health-manpower planning or gender relations? The
obvious and the oblique
Arminée Kazanjian   147

PART IV   CONCLUSIONS

Katarina Wegar   173

Index   189

Notes on contributors

Mick Carpenter trained as a general nurse before entering higher education. He is now a senior lecturer in the Department of Applied Social Studies, University of Warwick, Coventry. He is the author of the official history of the Confederation on Health Service Employees – *Working for Health* (1988) and has published widely in the fields of industrial relations in the health services and the politics of health.

S. Muthu Chidambaram is a lecturer in sociology at Mother Teresa Women's University in Madras, India. She has published a number of papers in various international journals, her main research interests being the sociology of occupations and professions and women's studies. She is also involved in extension activities pertaining to women and won the Tamil Nadu State Award for her work in this field.

Raymond G. DeVries is Associate Professor of Sociology at St Olaf College in Northfield, Minnesota and author of *Regulating Birth: Midwives, Medicine and the Law*. His study of midwifery is part of a larger concern with the influence of law and professionalization on health care. His current research includes an examination of the history and current status of midwives in the Netherlands and an investigation of the new speciality area, 'medical ethics'.

Mary Ann Elston is a lecturer in sociology in the Department of Social Policy and Social Science at Royal Holloway University of London. Her main interests are in medical sociology, the social history of medicine and the sociology of gender. She has undertaken research in the history of women's work in British medicine, contemporary medical careers and the organization of biomedical research.

Arminée Kazanjian is the Associate Director, Center for Health Services and Policy Research, and Assistant Professor, Department of Health Care and Epidemiology, The University of British

Columbia, Canada. Her research has focused on models to assist in the management of health human resources and in the development of appropriate policies. Technology diffusion and its assessment for the provision of appropriate services is another area of her research interests.

Judith Lorber is Professor of Sociology at Brooklyn College and The Graduate School, City University of New York, where she was also Coordinator of the Women's Studies Certificate Program from 1988–91. She is the author of *Women Physicians: Careers, Status and Power* (1984), and of *Paradoxes of Gender* (forthcoming, 1994). She was the founding editor of *Gender & Society*, official publication of Sociologists for Women in Society, and, with Susan A. Farrell, co-edited a collection of papers from that journal under the title, *The Social Construction of Gender* (1991).

Elianne Riska is Professor of Sociology and Director of the Institute of Women's Studies at Åbo Akademi University, Finland. Her publications include articles on the character of medical education in the United States and changes in status of the medical profession in the Nordic countries, as well as *Power, Politics and Health* (1985).

Katarina Wegar is a PhD candidate in sociology at Brandeis University, Massachusetts, USA. In addition to her work on women physicians in Finland, she has published articles on the fate of social science in American medical education and on sociological methodology. Her current work explores various sociological aspects of adoption in the United States, in particular the on-going controversy over adoptees' right to have access to genealogical information.

Acknowledgements

This collection of articles has its origin in a session on 'Gender and the division of labour in medicine: cross-cultural perspectives' organized by one of us for the World Congress of Sociology in Madrid in 1990 and arranged by the International Sociological Association (ISA). The suggestion for a session on this topic was originally made by Ray Elling, who at that time chaired the Research Committee on Health Sociology of the ISA. The considerable interest in the topic and the excellent papers presented at the session by leading authorities in the field made it natural to gather the papers in the form of a book available to a wider audience, in particular as there were few books available at the time in this subject area.

We are most grateful for the supportive attitude that the representatives of Sage have shown throughout the process of preparing the manuscript for publication. Special thanks are due to Robert Brym for his interest and assistance in the early process of compiling the manuscript. The commissioning editor at Sage, Karen Phillips, and the production editor, Rosemary Campbell, have shown admirable patience and kindness in assisting us with the final and tedious details of preparing the book for publication.

The assistance of a number of people in our everyday work context at Åbo Akademi University has also been invaluable. The list of these is long but we would especially like to mention Karin Kvideland and Gun Holmström, who assisted in typing and preparing the final version of the manuscript, and Katherine McCracken, who worked over our English.

As editors we feel our task to have been an easy and modest one: the contributors have prepared both interesting and original contributions to the sociological literature on health professions. We hope that readers will enjoy these contributions as much as we have done. They all provide new knowledge and essential theoretical insights on gender and the medical division of labour in various parts of the world.

Elianne Riska and Katarina Wegar

PART I
INTRODUCTION

Elianne Riska

The division of labour in society is a classical theme in sociology. Studies of the world of production and work have been and continue to be influenced by the traditions created by Durkheim, Marx and Weber. These traditions have shaped the studies of medical work as well. A majority of these studies have, however, focused on the work done by physicians and on the characteristics of the medical profession. Hence, concepts derived from classical sociology such as 'differentiation', 'rationalization' and more recently 'proletarianization' have primarily been used to signify structural changes taking place in physicians' work. Only a small fraction of the studies done on health and medical work have included other health-care occupations.

The dominance of the medical profession in research on the health labour force derives from the tradition set by Talcott Parsons. The norms guiding the behaviour of the medical practitioner was the focus of Talcott Parsons's (1951) seminal essay on the social institution of medicine. The physician described in Parsons's essay was a slightly more contemporary version of the old-time family doctor, whose medical technology fitted into his black bag. The physician portrayed by Parsons was an entrepreneur – a so-called solo fee-for-service practitioner – whose main professional relationship was with the clients and their family (Parsons, 1951: 447–9). Only once did Parsons (1951: 436) note in passing that the technological development of medicine requires that 'an increasing proportion of medical practice is now taking place in the context of organization' and that it 'often involves the complex cooperation of several different kinds of physicians as well as auxiliary personnel'. This larger social organization of health care and the medical division of labour were not further discussed or analysed in his essay.

The Parsonian approach, generally referred to as the functionalist perspective, mainly explored the professional role of the physician. The proponents of this approach tend to view medicine as the application of neutral and rational knowledge in the treatment of illness. Furthermore, they explain the social organization of medicine in terms of the functional requirements set by a given level of science and technology of medicine. Representatives of the functionalist approach have not raised the question of gender in their study of professions. The central argument of Parsonian role theory is that 'public' or 'market' roles are based around universalistic criteria in contrast to the domestic domain, where gender has an important place. As Stacey (1988: 154) has noted, an underlying assumption in much of the work on the medical profession has been that the gender of neither the doctor nor the patient influences the interaction between them. In fact, the principal argument of the Parsonian role theory is that roles present their incumbents with certain requirements and expectations and that other social criteria ought to be subservient to them.

Scholars using the functionalist framework have viewed socialization into the professional role as crucial and considered all other parameters of the profession and its practice as secondary. The Columbia School tradition and the study *The Student-Physician* were the outgrowth of the concern with the proper inculcation of the medical-norm system into the presumptive new members of the medical profession (Merton et al., 1957). At the same time another study on the socialization of medical students emerged, the so-called Chicago School study *Boys in White* (Becker et al., 1961), which applied a symbolic interactionist approach. In his critique of the limitations of the contributions to the sociology of professions of the 1960s, Saks (1983: 5) notes that the symbolic interactionist perspective recognized that professional status and work were products of social and political processes involving divergent interests and power struggles. But although the representatives of the symbolic interactionist perspective identified political and social conditions as crucial in the formation and legitimation of the power basis of professions, this topic was not pursued further at that time.

By contrast the neo-Weberian approach, which appeared in the sociology of professions in the 1970s, brought attention to the social and historical conditions under which occupational groups become professions and to the power struggle entailed in the establishment of the prevailing medical division of labour and its hierarchy. Proponents of the neo-Weberian perspective have emphasized the profession's practice of social closure based on credentialism as a strategy for regulating market conditions. This approach avoided the ahistorical accounts of the functionalist perspective. An interest in the professional project (Larson, 1977: 66; Witz, 1992) of allopathic practitioners in the nineteenth century has challenged the liberal–rational myth of modern science and revealed the power aspects behind the unification of the modern medical profession and the concomitant subservience of other health-care occupations (Berliner, 1975; Parry and Parry, 1976; Starr, 1982). This genre of research has also generated new insights into how biomedicine and its emphasis on certain skills and on scientific knowledge led to the devaluation of women's skills and previous position as lay healers and midwives (Ehrenreich and English, 1973; Morantz, 1977). The new medical division of labour established medical men at the top of the hierarchy and female-dominated occupations serving them (Stacey, 1988: 96; Witz, 1992: 68).

By the mid-1980s, a new debate on the power and work of the medical profession was, however, in full swing. At issue were the implications of the on-going changes in medicine, which were identified as the mounting 'corporatization' of medicine. In his overview of the social history of American medicine, Starr (1982) spotted the emerging features of a new social organization of medicine and coined the term 'corporate medicine'. Even within the ranks of medicine, this emerging structure was observed and named the 'new medical–industrial complex' (Relman, 1980). A more stringent sociological analysis of the phenomenon was later offered by McKinlay and his colleagues (McKinlay and Arches, 1985; McKinlay and Stoeckle, 1988). They identified the structural change in medicine as the gradual 'proletarianization' of physicians and later in more neutral terms as the 'social transformation of doctoring'. The argument was that medical technology and third-party payers channelled the practice of medicine into big bureaucratic settings and forced physicians to become salaried employees. For McKinlay and his colleagues this process in medicine was but a replication of the changes in the mode of production taking place under advanced capitalism. The argument of the proletarianization thesis is that directors of corporate medicine rather than physicians will control medicine.

This Marxist interpretation of the status of physicians under the terms of corporate medicine has been challenged by the restratification hypothesis. The latter is a revised version of Freidson's (1970) original theory of 'professional dominance'. The restratification thesis proposes that an internal stratification of the medical profession has evolved. The profession has come to be divided into an administrative elite, a knowledge elite and ordinary practitioners. This internal differentiation, it is argued, will enable the profession to maintain its control over and autonomy of its work despite recent threats to its professional dominance (Freidson, 1984). But although Freidson recognizes an internal stratification of the medical profession, he does not recognize the segregation of the profession by gender. Nevertheless, as the first four chapters in this volume on the medical profession, amply document, the structural changes in health care and the medical profession are intricately intertwined with the gender issue.

In summary, none of the mainstream sociological accounts of professions and professionalization address what Stacey (1988: 80) has called the genderized nature of the division of labour in health care (see also Atkinson and Delamont, 1990: 94). As indicated above, the Parsonian approach explains professional behaviour as the adherence to certain norms arising from the functional requirements of a given level of medical knowledge and technology. In Parsons's own account, all the actors – both the physician and the patient – are male although in essence his theory of human action is gender-neutral. The underlying assumption is that the role forms the behaviour of its incumbent.

In Weberian and Marxist accounts of professions the actors have been portrayed as social groups or classes engaged in struggles to ensure or expand their interests. They are not the altruistic servants of their clients as they are in the Parsonian accounts. Instead, they are portrayed as consciously or saliently defending their self-interest under the pretence of 'scientific expertise' and a 'service ethic'. However, although the power aspect of the profession's position is recognized, the gendered nature of this power structure is not. The primary movers of the history of medicine are not medical men but structural factors that shape the actions of social groups or classes depicted in gender-neutral terms.

This way of conceptualizing the structure of health care is most vividly exemplified in the current debate on the future of the medical profession. Proponents of the proletarianization and restratification theses have tended to ignore gender in their analyses. Nevertheless, the very structural processes and changes they have analysed have resulted in the growing entry of women into medical work and a new type of sex segregation in it.

Gender divisions in health care

As indicated above, a gender-neutral view has dominated mainstream accounts of professions and professionalization. Stacey (1988: 9–10) has characterized this as the 'problem of the two Adams' in social theory. While the division of labour in the sphere of production has been analysed in social theory (the heritage of Adam Smith), the sexual division of labour in the sphere of reproduction (the heritage of Adam and Eve) was for a long time not conceived as a problem. Stacey argues that until the 1950s the economy and its technology were viewed as major reasons for the social divisions in society whereas the gender divisions were not seen as a problem.

Nevertheless, American social historians and many others after them have shown that, at the rise of the industrial society, the division between the public and the domestic domain was even further accentuated as the ideology of domesticity or True Womanhood became a norm for most middle-class women (Gordon and Buhle, 1976: 284). As women began to work outside their own home, they first entered the world of paid work through other women's homes – they worked as midwives, domestics, governesses, piano teachers and household nurses. Midwifery and hospital nursing were the first female-dominated occupations to be integrated into the new organization of medicine as the paradigm of allopathic or biomedicine established and confirmed its position in most western countries in the latter part of the nineteenth century. Although women were allowed to study medicine by the turn of the century in most western countries, their practice was first restricted to children and other women. This early pattern of sex segregation of medical work is exemplified in the contribution by Chidambaram on Indian physicians in this volume.

A later pattern of sex segregation of medical work by gender is portrayed in the contributions in this book by Mary Ann Elston, by Judith Lorber, and by Elianne Riska and Katarina Wegar. These chapters in Part II show that women more often than their male colleagues tend to practise in primary-care specialties, in low-rank positions, and in bureaucratic settings as salaried employees. Male physicians have maintained dominance over high-status specialties and practice settings that involve higher independence and incomes than their female colleagues have been able to achieve. As Lorber's contribution on American physicians' career opportunities indicates, there is a gatekeeping system or a 'glass ceiling' that women have trouble getting through.

The areas of medicine from which women are excluded are at the same time those where the skills of the elite segments rest upon 'mastery of the indeterminate' (Atkinson and Delamont, 1990: 107). This mastery entails the possession of an exclusive professional knowledge that exceeds the technical knowledge acquired through standard professional socialization. The predecessor was the 'art of medicine', a legacy of William Osler who emphasized that the essential skills and the professional ethic of medicine could only be acquired at the bedside and through apprenticeship. This version of the 'art of medicine', embodying the profession's inherent characteristics, has been challenged as medicine has come to be practised in bureaucratic settings (Vinten-Johansen and Riska, 1991). The tendency of male practitioners to work in the high-technology and capital-intensive areas of medicine has enabled them to define the terms of the new knowledge requirements in the more prestigious areas of medicine.

The mastery of the indeterminate as the basic prerequisite for the power of the medical profession was already noted by Parsons (1951: 469) as he pondered the element of magic included in endeavours like medicine characterized by elements of uncertainty. Citing Malinowski's work, Parsons noted that the basic function of magic is to bolster self-confidence where skills do make a difference but where outcomes cannot be guaranteed because of large uncertainty factors. Noting this element in medical practice, Fox (1957) characterized the professional socialization of medical students in *The Student-Physician* as the 'training for uncertainty'. Light (1979) has shown that socialization for uncertainty and control of uncertainty are particularly important in the training of medical students.

It is, however, not only within the medical profession that such strategies are used to demarcate the boundaries of work; frequently they have been applied in other health-care occupations as well. For example, the medical 'risk' of pregnancy and delivery has bolstered the development of gynaecology and obstetrics as a medical specialty, as indicated in DeVries's chapter on midwifery in this book. The medicalization of birth has meant that gynaecologists and obstetricians have claimed the whole process of human reproduction as their exclusive domain. A medicalization of childbirth has meant a collective mobility – Larson's terminology (1977) – for gynaecologists and obstetricians but career immobility for subordinate health-care occupations – for example, that of midwife. More recently, advances in medical technology – both in the detection of risks related to pregnancy and in the treatment of infertility – have expanded the territory of detectable medical risks available to this group of physicians. Hence, physicians have a vested interest in future technological advances in reproduction technology and in legislation and financing to permit assisted conception.

A sociology of the division of labour in health and medical care

This volume is intended to fill a significant gap in the literature on health-care occupations, a literature in which the gender issue has largely been neglected. During the past ten years, three separate, almost ghettoized discussions have been waged about professional work. The areas are commonly referred to as the 'sociology of professions', the 'sociology of nursing' and 'labour market theories'. There has been little cross-fertilization among the three strands of research; and only the last one, exploring the character of sex segregation of the labour market, has explicitly raised gender as an issue. A central theme of this volume is that a sociological understanding of professional work in medicine and health care requires an exploration of the salient gender aspect of the division of labour in health and medical care. The contributors to this book not only address the neglected gender dimension in mainstream research on professions but integrate in their analysis broader concepts concerning the processes and structures that generate divisions in the labour market. This is essential in order to provide an adequate explanation of gender inequalities both between and within health-care occupations.

It is hard to think of any other sector of the economy that is still as labour-intensive and segregated by gender as health care. The basis of the divisions rests on the medical profession's claim that it possesses a special knowledge, which Freidson (1970) has called 'esoteric knowledge' and Larson (1977: 15) the 'cognitive exclusiveness' of the profession. However, as several chapters in this book demonstrate, this knowledge is not gender-neutral. Male physicians as well as female physicians and nurses themselves have assigned women the role of 'emotional experts' because of their presumed womanly perceptiveness in handling interpersonal relations. Medical educators have begun to foresee the problems that follow when a majority of medical practitioners are ignorant of or insensitive to such aspects of medicine. Since the 1970s, medical schools have begun to add sensitivity-training topics – behavioural science and medical ethics – to the medical school curricula to counter public criticism of the lack of altruism and empathy for the concerns of patients (Vinten-Johansen and Riska, 1991).

Feminist commentators have, however, been optimistic about the future breed of physicians and predicted marked changes in the practice of medicine as more women are entering the medical profession (Altekruse and McDermott, 1987: 85). These foresights are based on an essentialist viewpoint, which in this case involves two basic assumptions about women in health work: the superior social and emotional competence of women, and their homogeneity. Most empirical work that has attempted to verify these assumptions has contained methodological flaws in the research design: results indicating that women are more patient-oriented have not been controlled for specialty. Hence, a comparison of male and female physicians without controlling for practice setting or specialty will automatically show that women are more oriented toward primary care and patients since primary care and 'people work' constitute their special task in the medical division of labour.

But an empirical verification of women's superior empathic skills in medical work should not be the most important task for sociologists. A more crucial one is to identify how far gender has been used as a social category in order to establish and to maintain a division of labour that only advances the interest of a narrow group. A humane treatment of persons in the health-care system either as carers or as patients requires an analysis of how stereotypic and oppressive categories like gender, class or race interfere in medical work. Hence, the purpose of this book is to address how gender as a social category intervenes in the construction and reproduction of the medical division of labour.

The second theme that enables us to understand the gender aspect in health care is the role of the state. The state acts both as a licensing authority for health-care occupations and professions and as a source of funding. In this respect, the state can create or expand the territory of health-care occupations through publicly funded or subsidized sheltered markets and restrict the power and autonomy of professions by means of various regulations. Nevertheless, some have not seen the state merely as a benevolent subsidizer of services but as a representative of certain class interests (Navarro, 1976) or as a historical continuation of a patriarchal order (Ehrenreich and English, 1973; Daly, 1990). According to the latter views, the medical profession is but an extension of an organized class or patriarchal rule, and women as a social category are subservient both as patients and carers (see also Fee, 1977).

Recent neo-liberal policies aimed at curbing spending in the public sector have highlighted women's vulnerable and powerless positions as work for which women were previously paid is delegated to unpaid voluntary workers – the 'family' or the 'community' – or to the private market (Doyal, 1983). The effect of past welfare-state measures and recent neo-liberal policies on the position and power of female health-care workers will be addressed in most of the chapters in this book.

The impact of structural arrangements on health-care occupations is best exemplified by a comparative approach, which is the third theme of this volume. A cross-national review of the medical division of labour will show the universal features in the division of labour by gender but also document the existence of national variations.

The body of the book begins (Part II) with four chapters that examine the position of women in the medical profession in four societies representing different organizations of health care. Chidambaram, writing on women doctors' practice in India, describes how women are only allowed to practise in restricted fields of medicine. The gender-based division of labour in medicine is supported by the strict segregation by gender in Indian society at large. In Chidambaram's contribution a westerner can easily identify and relate the sexual division of labour in medicine to the larger economic and gender order of Indian society. The same reader might be blinded by her or his own cultural lenses in the endeavour to identify the matrix that links women's tasks in medicine in western societies.

The three other contributions in Part II suggest that the processes whereby women are assigned their tasks in medicine are not only subtle but also intertwined with various recent structural changes in health care. The development of the National Health Service in Britain has provided a market shelter for physicians fearing the consequences of a free market. The opening of new medical schools and state intervention outlawing sex discrimination facilitated women's entry into the medical profession. But Elston identifies a clear gender-based division of labour in British medicine and examines women's position within three practice settings – community medicine and community health, general practice and hospital medicine. Physicians practising in the latter two settings are dependent on professional networks for originally entering practice and later for receiving clients. Since women doctors are not well integrated into these networks, they tend to be marginalized. Lorber, writing on the American context, finds a similar, stratified structure of practice in the history of American medicine. The early stratification within the medical profession was upheld by a limited access to medical schools, to teaching hospitals, to lucrative practices. As American medicine is changing from a solo fee-for-service practice system to a bureaucracy, Lorber predicts that women will occupy low positions and have limited access to policy-making positions. She argues that there are invisible barriers – a glass ceiling – to the top positions and that women physicians will constitute 'a company of professional unequals'.

The picture portrayed by Elston and Lorber looks discouraging for women physicians. But several scholars have argued that as women physicians cease to be tokens and constitute a larger group in the future they will have a chance to change the content and character of medicine. This argument, reflecting a belief in a sociology of numbers and a notion also figuring in Kanter's (1977) views on women's position in large organizations, is the point of departure in the contribution by Wegar and Riska. They describe the position and work of women physicians in Finland, a Nordic country where 43 per cent of the physicians were women in 1992. In Finland, as is the case also in Sweden and Norway, a majority of the members of the modern medical profession have always practised in bureaucratic settings and been state or municipal employees, and the private practitioner has been more the exception than the rule. During the past twenty years, government health policies promoting primary care have provided a government-funded market for it. In the Finnish context this policy resulted in the creation of a new organizational setting where the so-called municipal health centre physician works. This new breed of physician is a municipal employee, and does not need to specialize in order to practise. This pattern of public primary care contrasts with the contractual arrangements with third-party payers created in Britain and Norway and set to be implemented even in Sweden (American Health Maintenance Organizations constitute a special version of this type of primary-care delivery). How much control primary practitioners have over their work in a contractual setting seems to depend on how far they have organized as a specialty, developed collegial networks and been able to control the amount of contractual arrangement allowed in the area. The chapters in Part II suggest that the more these parameters of practice are controlled by the medical profession rather than by external agencies, the fewer women doctors are found in primary care. But, as Wegar and Riska document, women doctors' own views about their segregated tasks in medicine make a complex picture. Women physicians are not simply objects of a male-dominated order of medicine but tend to have their own strategies for claiming some areas as their own.

Part III focuses on a number of health-care professionals in the health labour force. The contribution by Carpenter on nursing in Britain draws attention to the neglected gender, class and race dimension of this occupation in the medical division of labour. He suggests a social divisions approach as a tool for analysing both the gender dimension and the subordinated role of nursing.

The characteristics and status of midwifery in a number of societies are the focus of DeVries's review. In his presentation he looks at the influence that four factors – geography, technology, the structure of society, and culture – have had on the work of midwives in developing and developed countries. He argues that midwives have high status if they are the primary managers of risks, regardless of the technology involved, and that otherwise they have low status.

The division of labour in health care in British Columbia, Canada, is the topic of Kazanjian's contribution. She notes that human-resources planning in health care has traditionally focused solely on economic determinants of labour-force participation without con-sidering social aspects, in particular, gender. Kazanjian argues that state policies governing health-care systems and professions have a gender bias.

Part IV is a concluding discussion by Katarina Wegar of some of the major findings and overarching theoretical themes of the preceding articles.

References

Altekruse, Joan M. and McDermott, Susanne (1987) 'Contemporary concerns of women in medicine', in Sue V. Rosser (ed.), *Feminism within Science and Health Professions: Overcoming Resistance*. Oxford: Pergamon Press. pp. 65–88.

Atkinson, Paul and Delamont, Sara (1990) 'Professions and powerlessness', *Sociological Review*, 38: 90–110.

Becker, Howard, Geer, Blanche, Hughes, Everett C. and Strauss, Anselm L. (1961) *Boys in White: Student Culture in Medical School*. Chicago: University of Chicago Press.

Berliner, Howard (1975) 'A larger perspective on the Flexner report', *International Journal of Health Services*, 5: 573–92.

Daly, Mary (1990) *Gyn/Ecology: the Metaethics of Radical Feminism*. Boston: Beacon Press.

Doyal, Leslie (1983) 'Women, health and the sexual division of labour: a case study of the women's health movement in Britain', *International Journal of Health Services*, 13: 373–91.

Ehrenreich, Barbara and English, Deirdre (1973) *Witches, Midwives and Nurses: A History of Women Healers*. Old Westbury: The Feminist Press.

Fee, Elisabeth (1977) 'Women and health care: a comparison of theories', in V. Navarro (ed.), *Health and Medical Care in the US: a Critical Analysis*. Farmingdale, NY: Baywood Publishing Co. pp. 115–32.

Fox, Renee C. (1957) 'Training for uncertainty', in Robert Merton, George G. Reader and Patricia L. Kendall (eds), *The Student-Physician*. Cambridge, Mass.: Harvard University Press. pp. 207–41.

Freidson, Eliot (1970) *Profession of Medicine*. New York: Dodd, Mead & Company.

Freidson, Eliot (1984) 'The changing nature of professional control', *Annual Review of Sociology*, 10: 1–20.

Gordon, Ann D. and Buhle, Mari Jo (1976) 'Sex and Class in Colonial and Nineteenth-century America', in Bernice A. Carroll (ed.), *Liberating Women's History: Theoretical and Critical Essays*. Urbana, Ill.: University of Illinois Press. pp. 278–300.

Kanter, Rosabeth Moss (1977) *Men and Women of the Corporation*. New York: Basic Books.

Larson, Magali S. (1977) *The Rise of Professionalism*. Berkeley: University of California Press.

Light, Donald (1979) 'Uncertainty and control in professional training', *Journal of Health and Social Behavior*, 20: 310–22.

McKinlay, John B. and Arches, Joan (1985) 'Towards the proletarianization of physicians', *International Journal of Health Services*, 15: 161–95.

McKinlay, John B. and Stoeckle, John D. (1988) 'Corporatization and the social transformation of doctoring', *International Journal of Health Services*, 18: 191–205.

Merton, Robert K., Reader, George G. and Kendall, Patricia L. (eds) (1957) *The Student-Physician*. Cambridge, Mass.: Harvard University Press.

Morantz, Regina Markell (1977) 'Making women modern: middle-class women and health reform in 19th century America', *American Journal of Social History*, 4: 490–507.

Navarro, Vicente (1976) *Medicine under Capitalism*. New York: Prodist.

Parry, Noel and Parry, Jose (1976) *The Rise of the Medical Profession: A Study of Collective Social Mobility*. London: Croom Helm.

Parsons, Talcott (1951) 'Social structure and dynamic process: the case of modern medical practice', in *The Social System*. New York: Free Press. pp. 428–79.

Relman, A. S. (1980) 'The new medical industrial complex', *New England Journal of Medicine*, 303: 963–70.

Saks, Mike (1983) 'Removing the blinkers? A critique of recent contributions to the sociology of professions', *Sociological Review*, 31: 1–21.

Stacey, Margaret (1988) *The Sociology of Health and Healing*. London: Unwin Hyman.

Starr, Paul (1982) *The Social Transformation of American Medicine*. New York: Basic Books.

Vinten-Johansen, Peter and Riska, Elianne (1991) 'New Oslerians and real Flexnerians: the response to threatened professional autonomy', *International Journal of Health Services*, 21: 75–108.

Witz, Anne (1992) *Professions and Patriarchy*. London: Routledge.

PART II

THE MEDICAL PROFESSION

1

Sex stereotypes in women doctors' contribution to medicine: India

S. Muthu Chidambaram

While the percentage of doctors who are women has increased in India during the past decades, their number has remained low. Historically, Indian women doctors have worked mainly as gynae-cologists and obstetricians. In other specialties, despite the recent decrease in the sex segregation of tasks within the Indian medical profession, women doctors are still drastically underrepresented. Furthermore, Indian women physicians generally do not pursue higher studies in medicine, and they are more likely to be employees in governmental or private organizations than to be private prac-titioners (Abidi, 1988: 236–45). In short, the professional position of women physicians in India is similar to that of women physicians in the west, but the segregation of tasks by gender is more extreme. The institutional causes are the same mechanisms that have been noted to influence the careers of women physicians in the west. In addition, however, the position of Indian women doctors is affected by culturally specific social norms regulating not only the division of labour in medicine but also women's position in Indian society at large.

Studies of physicians in western countries have shown that collegial relationships form an integral part of professional life. Consultation and referral (the practice of referring the client to a colleague) are principal characteristics of professional work (Freidson, 1960). Moreover, only the peer group is considered to have the knowledge necessary to evaluate professional performance (Greenwood, 1957: 49; Freidson, 1970). The patient is not considered competent to evaluate the professional service he or she receives (Greenwood, 1957: 48) and is hence supposed to submit himself or herself to the 'affectively neutral' judgement of the professional. Collegial relationships thus constitute a precondition for successful medical practice, as well as a significant vehicle whereby occupational sex segregation is created and maintained.

The sex segregation of medical work is furthermore affected by the clients' preferences. In India, cliental relationships are particularly important, since social norms crucially restrict the relationship between female patients and male physicians and since male patients are more reluctant to be treated by women than by men (Abidi, 1988: 242). Moreover, in western countries the overrepresentation of women physicians in certain specialties and types of practice has been shown to reflect women's efforts to balance domestic and professional demands (Lorber, 1984: 80–98). For Indian women doctors, social norms of femininity, marriage and motherhood make it particularly hard to combine having a family with a professional career. A study found that over 70 per cent of Indian women doctors were single (Venkataratnam, 1979: 33).

This chapter explores the interplay between the specialty choices of women doctors and institutional causes of sex segregation in India. Focusing on the specialty choices of women physicians in the district of Madurai in Tamil Nadu, the chapter highlights the relationship between institutional processes of closure, women's preferences, and shared cultural notions of femininity, masculinity and medical expertise. First, I will briefly review the history of medical practice in India, and discuss the reasons for women's comparatively early entry into medical education. Second, I will on the basis of interviews with women doctors discuss various factors affecting their choice of specialty. Several different but interrelated causes for the sex segregation of medical practice are noted: collegial networks, social norms restricting patient–physician interaction, and women's own preferences based both on their difficulty in combining professional work with family demands and on the belief that women are better suited for certain types of tasks.

Medical practice in India

The ancient system of medicine practised in India is called Ayurveda. This system treats the body as a whole in relation to the cosmos. Medicine was taught in the ancient centres of learning at Texila in the sixth century BC and at Nalanda between the fifth and twelfth centuries AD. The Siddha system, another system of medicine associated with Ayurveda, was also practised, particularly in Tamil Nadu. This system was founded by holy men claiming divine power. Later, the Unani system practised in ancient Greece was brought to

India by Muslim conquerors. In addition, homeopathic medicine, which originated in Germany at the end of the eighteenth century, was introduced into India. Lastly, allopathic medicine was brought to India by the British (Lebra, 1984: 127–8; Jaggi, 1979: 12–27).

During the time of British rule, the need for medical personnel to serve the army led the British to start medical schools in India. In the beginning, only Europeans and Eurasians were admitted to these schools. Indians gained entry into medicine later, when medical schools were founded in Bombay in 1826 and in Madras in 1827. These schools conducted diploma courses in medicine. Gradually medical colleges were established in large Indian cities such as Calcutta, Madras and Bombay, and in a few other cities. Medical schools and colleges existed side by side, qualifying medical men to serve the army (Jaggi, 1979: 27–64).

Women's entry into medical education

The entry of women into medical education in the late nineteenth century was necessitated by the strict purdah system practised not only by Muslims but by Hindus. The purdah system prevented women from being attended by male doctors, a circumstance that led to a high rate of maternal and child mortality (YWCA, 1971: 98; Lebra, 1984: 128; Jaggi, 1979: 93). In addition, the low social status accorded to women in India resulted in the neglect of their health (Mamoria, 1981: 142; Mehta, 1982: 239–41; *India*, 1988: 34). Girls were looked upon as a burden, and their health was generally not attended to except at times of sickness and childbirth. Moreover, the custom of feeding all the menfolk and children of the house first, women eating last, often left women with little nutritious food. Consequently, malnutrition and anaemia were the most common causes of a high maternal and child mortality. Furthermore, the custom of child marriage often resulted in health problems among young mothers (Mamoria, 1981: 142). Births were usually attended by illiterate and untrained nurses who had learnt midwifery by experience and from their female elders. In addition, lack of knowledge about infection and sanitation caused high mortality among women who had given birth (Lebra, 1984: 127–8; Jaggi, 1979: 93). All these conditions created a need for qualified women doctors to provide health care to Indian women.

The first organized attempt to teach medicine to women was made in the late nineteenth century by one Mrs Scarlieb in the Madras Presidency, an Englishwoman who accompanied her barrister husband to India. Moved by the plight of Indian women who died during delivery, she underwent a one-year course in midwifery but found her training inadequate. The initiative of Mrs Scarlieb led in 1875 to her admittance and that of four other women to the three-year certificate course at Madras Medical College. While the universities and medical associations in Great Britain were debating whether women should be permitted to study medicine, this progressive step was taken in India (Jaggi, 1979: 93–7).

At the same time Christian missionaries made attempts to train Indian women in medicine. Prominent among such missionaries was Dr Clara Swain, who trained fourteen girls from an orphanage as health-care workers in 1873. Another pioneer was Dr Ida Scuder, who in 1900 started a dispensary that gained the status of a medical school and in 1942 became a University College. Gradually women gained admission to the medical colleges in Punjab (1882), in Bengal (1885) and in Bombay (1887). Their fellow students and teachers were mostly men. Some women had to follow the practice of seclusion, sitting behind a curtain even in their classes. This led to the realization of the need for separate medical schools for women. One such school was started in Ludiana in 1905, followed by another in Delhi in the same year. A third was started by Dr Ida Scuder in Vellore in 1918. In 1923 two more schools were founded exclusively for women, one in Madras and another in Agra. Women were also permitted to enrol in various coeducational medical colleges in India. Moreover, a separate fund, the Dufferin's Fund, was established in order to encourage and finance the training of women doctors. With money from this fund hospitals were built in Agra and Lahore (Jaggi, 1979: 108–9; Lebra, 1984: 130). As a result of these combined efforts, the number of women doctors gradually began to increase (Abidi, 1988: 235). Among the pioneers were Anandabai Joshi, Ms Annie J. Stid, Rukmabai and Dr Muthulakshmi Reddi (Mehta, 1982: 131; Sri Devi, 1965: 40–1; YWCA, 1971: 117–18; Jaggi, 1979: 106–7).

In sum, the entry of women into medical education was motivated by the need for women doctors to serve Indian women. Conscious efforts were made by the British government, western missionaries and social reformers in the midst of a social milieu that did not favour even basic education for women. The women and their families, who broke with tradition by entering into the profession, had to fight the social opposition of the day (Mehta, 1982: 164; Abidi, 1988: 237). But the status of women doctors gradually rose and is today well established. Medicine and teaching were the first professions women were accepted in. The ideal of service, the 'ideal of healing', the high social status and the monetary gains continue to attract women from high caste and class into the profession (YWCA, 1971: 95; Mehta, 1982: 132; Lebra, 1984: 133). As the history of medical education in India shows, women were admitted to medical schools before an all-male tradition had been established (Lebra, 1984: 133).

Specialty choices of women doctors

This section documents the sex-typing of specialties practised by women doctors living in the Madurai District. Madurai is the largest city after Madras, the capital of Tamil Nadu. The district consists of many towns and villages and has a population of almost three million. The history of Madurai as the capital of the early Pandya Dynasty dates back to the second century BC. Historically, it is famous for its scholarship and learning. At present it is one of the foremost Indian centres of learning, including medicine. Because of its long history and the impact of modernization and westernization, it is a place where traditional and modern value systems interact.

From the 306 women doctors working in the Madurai District in 1987, 74 with various post-graduate specializations were randomly selected. Information was collected by means of semi-structured interviews, covering the respondents' professional careers from 1948 to 1987. To allow analysis of changes over time, the period studied was divided into shorter, equal periods: Period I, from 1948 to 1960; Period II, from 1961 to 1974; Period III, from 1975 to 1987. Each respondent has been designated by a letter followed by two numbers. The letter is the initial letter of her name, the first number is a serial number, and the second number is her age. The findings are summarized in Table 1.1.

Table 1.1   *Distribution of the specialty choices of women doctors in the Madurai District, India, 1948–1987*

| | Period | | | | | | | |
| Specialty | I (1948–60) | | II (1961–74) | | III (1975–87) | | Total | |
	N	%	N	%	N	%	N	%
Obstetrics and gynaecology	1	25	15	60	28	62	44	59
Pediatrics	1	25	1	4	1	2	3	4
Maternity and child health	2	50	3	12	–	–	5	7
Anaesthetics	–	–	3	12	3	7	6	8
Ophthalmology	–	–	1	4	4	9	5	7
General medicine	–	–	–	–	1	2	1	1
Non-clinical	–	–	2	8	8	18	10	14
Total	4		25		45		74	

Period I

During Period I (1948–60), all the women doctors specialized in areas pertaining to the treatment of women and children. Describing the importance of choosing obstetrics and gynaecology during this period, one woman doctor (I-9-56) explained:

> Medicine in those days meant a clinical specialty which served women only. So I specialized in obstetrics and gynaecology. There was no other specialty we could think of.

The choice of specialty was also explained by women's special propensity for such tasks. Another woman (G-2-61), who had specialized in pediatrics, said:

> As a woman I had a natural inclination to deal with children and to treat their ailments.

Women's career roles in work outside their homes were thus extensions of their family roles as wives and mothers: tending the sick and caring for children, with an added service component (Nieva and Gutek, 1981: 41–2). Notably, the first profession Indian women entered was the one in which their entry had been necessitated by the gender segregation in society at large. Their entry into medicine thus reinforced the gender segregation already existing (Abidi, 1988: 242). According to one woman doctor (P-1-65),

> The demand for women doctors was so heavy in our time. Though we could do general practice, we were posted in medical wards to serve only women and children.

The norms that prohibited male doctors from treating women effectively during Period I created an atmosphere favourable to allowing women to enter specialties that provided services to women. Male physicians in fact welcomed women doctors, who could function better in such situations. All the women interviewed who worked along with male doctors in government hospitals praised how their senior male colleagues encouraged and taught them the intricacies of the profession. On the other hand, the absence of informal collegial networks between men and women made it difficult for women doctors to establish referral and consultancy in their private practice. This is demonstrated in the fact that all the women doctors who specialized during this period either had joint practice with their doctor-husbands or carried out private practice with the help of their husbands. Referral and consultancy during this period were mainly through their husbands.

Though the women doctors treated mostly women and children during this period, they were on certain occasions expected to treat both men and women. While it has been argued that the women doctors did not express inhibition in treating male patients because of their professional socialization (Annapoorani, 1986: 220), the present study found that the ideology of male dominance influenced the interaction between male patients and female doctors. Since the physician was an authority figure, it was against the cultural norm for a woman to be a physician. And because of sex segregation, patients preferred to be treated by doctors of the same sex so that they could talk about their complaints freely and avoid violating another cultural norm. As one woman doctor (M-5-58) observed:

> Though as doctors we do not differentiate between male and female patients, men prefer a male doctor. They think that it is not necessary to be treated by women unless it is an emergency situation.

The sex segregation in medical treatment thus reflects and reinforces the segregation in the wider society.

Period II

The specialties chosen during Period II (1961–74) reveal continued sex stereotyping and reinforcement of sex segregation. Out of 25 respondents who specialized during this period, a majority specialized in obstetrics and gynaecology; three in both maternity and child health; and one in pediatrics. A total of 76 per cent specialized in fields relating to women and children. Women's specialty choices during Period II thus continued largely to reflect women's domestic roles. Among those who specialized in the above specialties, a majority (84%) said that they chose them because of their own preference for these specialties, in part because of the advantages of restricting their service to women. Here are the words of a woman (B-56-38) who had chosen obstetrics and gynaecology out of her own interest:

> Delivering a baby is a thrilling experience. The happiness that I get after each successful delivery is incomparable. The specialty is such that in each delivery I save two lives.

Another woman (S-22-45), who had chosen pediatrics, said:

> As a woman I feel interested in treating children . . . I like them because they don't talk lies.

The interviews also revealed that some women doctors – 16 per cent – had been eager to depart from existing stereotypes, but that they had been pushed into traditional specialties because of institutional patterns of discrimination. Among those who specialized in obstetrics and gynaecology, three said that they had wanted to do surgery but that they were forced into obstetrics and gynaecology because they were women (Lebra, 1984: 130; Annapoorani, 1986: 238). According to one of them (N-18-46):

> I wanted to do surgery. But women were not admitted in surgery in those days.

Another respondent (B-13-48) said:

> I wanted to do surgery. But I was told that male doctors do not give women students enough chances to do surgery in the theatre. Moreover, when I started my practice, male patients would not come to a woman doctor for surgery.

Surgery is still considered a masculine specialty requiring a high level of confidence and assertion, and since women tend to be considered weak and emotional, they are thought to be unsuitable for the practice of surgery (see also Lorber, 1984: 32). Moreover, both senior colleagues and clients discriminated against women attempting to enter the specialty.

Two of the three women doctors who specialized in anaesthetics had initially wanted to specialize in obstetrics and gynaecology but were offered anaesthetics instead. One of them (P-35-42) reported:

> I wanted to do obstetrics and gynaecology. But there was heavy competition for that specialty. The selection committee offered me anaesthetics. They considered it a lighter work and suited to woman.

Even when traditional male-dominated specialties were offered to women, the offers were guided by the stereotypical assumption that women are weak and that this makes them suited for certain specialties only (see also Lorber, 1984: 32–4).

The trend noted among women who chose non-traditional specialties during this period was their sense of dependence on their husbands (see also Lorber, 1984: 88) or a larger health-care organization. For example, one woman who specialized in anaesthetics, chose the field with the intention of working as anaesthetist for her surgeon husband in the future. Still, all the three anaesthetists interviewed were at the time of the study working in government hospitals. Another woman doctor working in a government hospital specialized in ophthalmology with the intention of setting up a joint practice with her ophthalmologist husband.

The choice of non-clinical specialties tended to be guided by the advantages of fixed work hours, vacation and absence of night duty (Lebra, 1984: 88). These characteristics of non-clinical work enabled the women to adjust their career roles to their family roles (Abidi, 1988: 245). One (S-17-46) who chose non-clinical work observed:

> The fixed hours of work, vacation, and release from night duty save me from a lot of tension and enable me to accommodate my career roles and

family roles . . . I do not want to do injustice to my family and at the same time [I want to] utilize the knowledge I gained. So I chose this specialty.

Women doctors who specialized during Period II reported that they were invited by their male colleagues to provide consultancy service in cases pertaining to obstetrics and gynaecology. The indispensability of the service of women doctors in those specialties might have helped them in establishing referral and consultation between male and female doctors in private practice. On the other hand, the study also shows that the number of women doctors had been progressively increasing in Period II. As a result, their contact with male colleagues decreased and they received less support and encouragement from men (see also Lorber, 1984: 40). The period was seen as marked by both envy and competition between male and female practitioners. One woman (U-30-44) described the envy she faced from a male colleague:

> Male doctors are envious of women doctors because women specializing in obstetrics and gynaecology earn more money than any male doctor practising any specialty. A male doctor who was my colleague in a government hospital gave me a lot of trouble by not cooperating with me for no reason except envy.

Studies of women doctors in the west have revealed that, as women's confidence in their ability to succeed increases with their rise in numbers, men resist the competition in fear of losing their dominant status (Nieva and Gutek, 1981: 64–5; also Lorber, 1984: 112). All the women who specialized in non-traditional specialties like anaesthetics and ophthalmology were in joint practice with their husbands or served in governmental hospitals. This may show women doctors' fear of success in pursuing the specialties independently of male patronage, as well as show that women doctors were not well accepted in the male-dominated specialties. Regarding the lack of acceptance of women in surgery (Bock, 1967: 532; Lebra, 1984: 130; Lorber, 1984: 32), one of the women (T-20-46) said:

> Men were not able to succeed in gynaecology. Hence men want to keep surgery as their prerogative and discourage women from entering into it.

As the number of women doctors increased and as professional socialization changed their attitudes, they expressed a willingness to treat male patients. However, according to the women who specialized during this period, they started having trouble with male patients: sexual harassment and refusal to accept the women's professional status as doctors. Consequently, the women doctors treating both male and female patients in the organizations where they worked as salaried personnel, in their private practice restricted their treatment to women only. They adopted the strategy of 'pragmatic avoidance' in situations where they might encounter harassment (Nieva and Gutek, 1981: 63). One of the women doctors who worked independently in private practice (T-42-41) said:

> I restrict my treatment only to women patients. I treat only those male patients who come as escorts for female patients or the male relatives of my female patients.

Women doctors in joint practice with their husbands solved the problem by treating only females while their husband treated the males (U-47-40):

> I treat women patients and my husband treats male patients. This we rather do as a policy to avoid facing mischief from male patients.

Period III
In Period III (1975–87), sex stereotypes continued to guide the women doctors' choice of specialty. Among the 45 women doctors who specialized during this period, 28 specialized in obstetrics and gynaecology and one in pediatrics. Among those who chose obstetrics and gynaecology, a majority did so because of the convenience of treating patients of the same sex and the feeling of security they got in restricting their service to women only. Better income associated with the practice, they said, was an additional reason for choosing obstetrics and gynaecology (I-119-29):

> Obstetrics and gynaecology is a money-minting specialty. Apart from the fact that more women seek medical aid for deliveries, there is an increasing number of women who adopt family-planning measures. As a result more women come to the doctors for treatment.

The other three women interviewed wanted to do surgery but had been advised to go into obstetrics and gynaecology since surgery still was a man's prerogative. One woman (S-100-31) reported:

> I was eager to do surgery. But all my colleagues said I could not succeed in a male-dominated field.

The doctor who chose pediatrics attributed her choice to her natural inclination as a mother to treat children.

The other clinical specialties chosen by women during Period III were anaesthetics, ophthalmology and general medicine. Two of the women who chose anaesthetics did it with the intention of practising it with their surgeon husbands. One of the ophthalmologists chose the specialty because of family tradition (N-99-31):

> My husband's grandfather was a famous ophthalmologist. I was very much impressed by his service. I wanted to maintain that family tradition.

She had a joint practice with her husband, also an ophthalmologist. Another woman said she chose ophthalmology because it suited women (T-120-29):

> The eye is an intricate organ. The surgery has to be done patiently and carefully. Hence women are suited for it.

The doctor who was working in a government hospital specialized in general medicine with the hope of helping her doctor husband. Even women who choose non-traditional specialties depended on their husbands in practising their profession. Most of them still linked the choice of specialty to women's gender-specific qualities.

Non-clinical specialties were chosen by eight women doctors during this period. The choice was attributed to the convenience associated with these specialties, such as fixed work hours, vacations, and absence of night duty. These specialties, moreover, saved them from frequent relocation. It was considered an additional advantage not to be posted to a village (Lebra, 1984: 140; Venkataratnam, 1979: 36). One woman described the limited relocation associated with such specialties (D-41-41):

> Non-clinical specialties are attached to medical colleges. Since medical colleges are few, the posting will be within those places. Hence my transfer will be less frequent.

Another woman (A-33-42) reported:

> I chose [my] specialty mainly to avoid working in villages. Since the departments associated with my specialty exist only in towns, I will be posted there.

Like the women who specialized in the 1960s and early 1970s, the women doctors who specialized during Period III reported that they had cooperation but also competition from male doctors. Surgery was still kept as the prerogative of male doctors. Not only did male doctors keep some specialties as their prerogative, they also tried to go into specialties formerly dominated by women – gynaecology for example.

> For quite some period, female doctors could succeed in gynaecology without competition from males. Now men started entering into that field and tried to compete with women. (U-77-35)

As in the previous period, women doctors continued to practise jointly with their husbands, following the policy of sharing the treatment of patients according to their sex. Women who practised independently continued to treat only women patients. One woman (R-87-34) reported:

> After the opening of liquor shops, this area is full of drunkards. Some drunkards began to knock at the doors of my hospital during nights and gave me trouble.

In order to avoid trouble in future, she kept a sign outside her hospital stating that only women and children would be treated.

Earlier studies have found the association of women doctors only with the specialties of obstetrics and gynaecology to be very strong in the mind of the Indian public (Abidi, 1988: 242). This circumstance was reflected also in the specialty choices of the women interviewed for this study. As one (B-86-34) said:

> I and my husband have a joint practice in ophthalmology. Since I am a woman, people associate me with obstetrics and gynaecology. People came to me for deliveries and I am forced to attend to them.

Patients tended not to believe that female doctors had the same knowledge as male doctors in specialties other than obstetrics and gynaecology (Bock, 1967: 531). A woman who specialized in ophthalmology (A-140-27) reported:

> When we conduct eye camps in rural areas, I go with other male doctors. Not only the male patients want to be treated by male doctors – even women wait in longer queues to be examined by a male doctor, rather than come to me for check up. I feel this is really an insult to my knowledge since I am a woman. But in Muslim-dominated areas women come to me because they follow more the policy of seclusion.

Conclusions

Women's entry into medicine in India was necessitated by the need to provide health care for women. Initially, women doctors only practised in specialties associated with the treatment of women and children. While all women in this study who specialized before 1960 worked in specialties related to the treatment of women and children, some women who specialized in the 1960s and early 1970s chose non-traditional specialties. Yet, even in the 1970s and 1980s, the choice of specialty remained strongly associated with gender-specific predispositions. The sex-typing of tasks within the medical profession did not merely reflect the attitudes of male colleagues and educators; the women doctors themselves advanced the argument that women were best suited to caring for women and children. Another guiding principle in the choice of specialty was the perceived compatibility between occupational and family roles. Those women doctors who chose non-clinical specialties did so because of fixed work hours and the less frequent need to relocate associated with some specialties. Yet, the limited possibilities for women doctors to practise such non-traditional specialties led them either to have joint practice with their husbands or to work as employees in large health-care organizations.

Because of cultural norms restricting the relationship between the sexes, men and women patients chose doctors of the same sex for treatment. In dealing with men patients, women doctors followed the policy of pragmatic avoidance. Moreover, the association of women doctors with specialties such as obstetrics and gynaecology was strong in the minds of the patients. According to the women doctors interviewed, neither men nor women patients considered women doctors in non-traditional specialties as having knowledge equal to that of men doctors.

The case of women doctors in India is particularly interesting because of the purdah system that radically separates the life spheres of men and women. The Indian case also provides an extreme example of the dual nature of the gender structure. While sex stereotyping of medical practice in India has crucially circumscribed the work options of women doctors, this gender order has also enabled them to gain entrance into a male-dominated profession from which they otherwise would have been excluded. Since women doctors because of the strict purdah system were needed to provide health care for female patients, Indian women gained entrance to the medical profession at a time when, for example, British universities had not yet permitted women to enrol in medical schools. However, as gender segregation has over the past three decades become less marked in Indian society at large, women doctors' job opportunities have expanded (see Abidi, 1988). The partial breakdown of the purdah system has also enabled men to enter into areas of medical practice that earlier were occupied exclusively by women, while they at the same time have continued to limit women's possibilities of practising in male-dominated specialties.

References

Abidi, Nigar Fatima (1988) 'Women's participation in the medical profession: the Indian case', *International Sociology*, 3: 235–49.

Annapoorani, M. R. (1986) 'A study on professional socialization of women medical and nursing students in medical college'. Unpublished PhD dissertation, Madurai Kamaraj University.

Bock, E. Wilbur (1967) 'The female clergy: a case of professional marginality', *American Journal of Sociology*, 75: 531–639.

Freidson, Eliot (1960) 'Client control and medical practice', *American Journal of Sociology*, 65: 374–82.

Freidson, Eliot (1970) *Profession of Medicine*. New York: Dodd Mead.

Greenwood, Ernest (1957) 'Attributes of a profession', *Social Work*, 2: 45–55.

India, National Perspective Plan for Women 1988–2000 AD (1988): Report of the Core Group set up by the Department of Human Resources Development.

Jaggi, O. P. (1979) *Western Medicine in India: Medical Research, History of Science, Technology and Medicine in India*. New Delhi: Atma Ram and Sons.

Lebra, Joice (1984) 'Women in medicine', in Joice Lebra (ed.), *Women and Work in India: Continuity and Change*. New Delhi: Promilla and Co. pp. 126–56.

Lorber, Judith (1984) *Women Physicians: Careers, Status, and Power*. New York: Tavistock.

Mamoria, C. B. (1981) *India's Population Problems* (2nd edn.). Allahabad: Kitab Mahal.

Mehta, Sushila (1982) *Revolution and Status of Women in India*. Delhi: Metropolitan Book Co. P. Ltd.

Nieva, V. F. and Gutek, B. A. (1981) *Women and Work: a Psychological Perspective*. New York: Prager Publication.

Sri Devi, S. (1965) *A Century of Indian Womanhood*. Mysore: Rao and Raghavan.

Venkataratnam, R. (1979) *Medical Sociology in an Indian Setting*. Madras: Macmillan Company of India.

YWCA (1971) *The Educated Women in Indian Society Today*. Bombay: Tata McGraw-Hill Publishing Co. Ltd.

2
Women doctors in a changing profession: the case of Britain

Mary Ann Elston

For the medical profession in Britain, this last quarter of the twentieth century is a period of uncomfortable adjustment to internally and externally induced change.[1] Concern about doctors' status and power has been increasingly evident in the profession's own journals and the mass media since the mid-1970s. Over the last decade, particularly since 1987, there has been extensive political debate about the organization of health care and about the 'problem' of medical dominance in the face of escalating costs in Britain, as in many other western countries (Freddi and Bjorkman, 1989; McKinlay, 1988). A series of reforms to the National Health Service (NHS) (e.g. DH 1989a) have been seen as constituting an assault, in the name of managerial efficiency and accountability, on the medical profession's autonomy in the workplace (Davies, 1987; Strong and Robinson, 1990; Gabe et al., 1991; Beck and Adam, 1990; Hunter, 1991). At the same time, a 'consumerist' or ideological challenge to medicine's cultural authority and right to be entrusted with self-regulation has become increasingly evident (Rosenthal, 1987; Elston, 1991).

Alongside these developments there has been an increase in the numbers and proportion of women among new entrants to the profession, again a development found in other western countries. In 1970, 26 per cent of students entering medical schools in Great Britain were women. In 1980, the equivalent figure was 38 per cent and in 1989 49 per cent (UCCA Annual Reports). The proportion of women among active practitioners has risen from slightly under one-fifth in 1970 to over one-quarter in 1990 (DH, 1991).

These recent developments warrant a re-examination of hitherto orthodox sociological conceptualizations of the medical profession in Britain. For decades, the medical profession has occupied a prominent place in Anglo-American sociology, reflecting the strong moral overtones carried by the term 'profession' in English (see for example

Freidson, 1983; Rueschemeyer, 1986; Crompton, 1990). From the 1950s, medicine figured as the example *par excellence* of a publicly mandated and state-backed monopolistic supplier of a valued service, exercising autonomy in the workplace and collegiate control over recruitment, training and the regulation of members' conduct (e.g. Parsons, 1954; Freidson, 1970; T. Johnson, 1972). Although widely diverging theoretical explanations for the pre-eminent position of medicine were offered, medical authority and status were usually seen to be entrenched not only within modern systems of health care but also within society as a whole.

In the United States, increasing state and corporate involvement in medical care and education (bringing with it increased bureaucratization of work organization), decreasing public confidence in doctors and a weakening in doctors' market position are allegedly bringing about a gradual diminution of doctors' autonomy (Starr, 1982). This process has been variously described as 'deprofessionalization' (e.g. Haug, 1976, 1988), 'corporatization' or 'proletarianization' (McKinlay and Stoeckle, 1988; McKinlay and Arches, 1985). Even those who reject reports of the death of medical dominance do not dispute that major changes are occurring in the American health-care system and in medicine (Ginzberg, 1986; Stevens, 1986; Freidson, 1985, 1986; Rosenthal, 1987; Light and Levine, 1988).

Elsewhere I have reviewed the applicability of the 'deprofessionalization' and 'proletarianization' hypotheses to British medicine (Elston, 1991; see also Larkin, 1988; Hunter, 1991). In that paper, I argued that, while to consign 'medical dominance' to history would be premature, recent events have highlighted longstanding constraints on medical autonomy that were less apparent in a (now-ended) period of political consensus about welfare provision in Britain. They have also underlined the important but often overlooked differences between the American and British medical professions. For example, the United States has been characterized by an exceptionally low level of state funding or provision compared with most western countries during the second half of the twentieth century (see e.g. Dohler, 1989) and exceptionally high levels of economic autonomy for physicians (Harrison and Schulz, 1989). Recent increases in state intervention and salaried status have been seen as manifestations of the 'proletarianization' or 'corporatization' of medicine (McKinlay and Stoeckle, 1988). But, in Britain, the state has had a particularly strong role in funding and providing formal health care during this century, with a virtual monopoly over the purchase of doctors' services since the NHS began in 1948. The direction of change over the last decade has, if anything, been towards an increased role for the market in health care, although at the time of writing this still remains small (Gabe et al., 1991).

At the very least, the British experience suggests that medical dominance and autonomy are not necessarily inversely proportional to the extent of state intervention *per se*. Rather, as Larkin has argued, 'authority in [British] medicine has been both state-sustained and circumscribed' (Larkin, 1988: 121). In Britain, the coming of the NHS undoubtedly did set constraints over doctors' freedom of action on the wider political stage by making health care such a central part of public policy. Doctors have never been able to get all they want in a positive sense, particularly in financial matters (nor could they before the NIIS). But clinical autonomy, control over decision-making in the workplace, was enhanced for (senior) individual doctors under the market shelter of a state-funded health-care system. This has been combined with a 'monopoly of legitimacy among health service workers' as far as influencing more detailed aspects of NHS policy were concerned (Klein, 1983: 28, 56–7). It may be that British doctors are now having to adjust to challenges to these latter two dimensions of autonomy. In my earlier paper, I suggested that such adjustment may lead to new cleavages and segmentation within the British medical profession. But internal divisions and conflicts of interest within the profession are not new (Elston, 1977b; Honigsbaum, 1979; Klein, 1983). One longstanding division is by gender.

Before the 1970s, most of the literature on the medical profession ignored the question of gender. But in that decade, under the impetus of 'second wave feminism', many British and American sociologists came to see medicine as a paradigm of professions in a second sense: as a paradigm of male domination. Medicine has been held up as a particularly extreme case of patriarchal exclusionary closure, whereby overt and covert discrimination has kept out all but a handful of women. For many feminists, this exclusion was linked to the strategic importance of medicine in maintaining the social subordination of women by controlling women's bodies and reproductive capacities (e.g. Ehrenreich and English, 1974; Oakley, 1976; Blake, 1990). Increases in women's entry to medicine might, therefore, be thought to be of general sociological interest. Yet, as Riska (1988: 141) has pointed out, the recent debate about the changing character of the medical profession has largely ignored the question of gender, despite the growing numbers of women within the profession. My own recent paper on this topic (Elston, 1991) is vulnerable to Riska's charge (because of the constraints of space rather than lack of interest). So, in this chapter, I hope to redress that imbalance, as well as updating my earlier work on women doctors (Elston, 1977a, 1980).

This chapter investigates two questions in relation to the recent increase in women doctors in Britain. First, I consider whether there may be a causal connection between this development and weakening of professional autonomy. Then, I analyse trends in the distribution of women within the complex medical labour market that now exists in Britain. The aim here is to investigate how far the recent increase in women entrants has led to a reduction in gender segregation within the profession or to women's overrepresentation in those sectors of medical work particularly subject to bureaucratization, routinization or managerial control, as has been suggested for Nordic countries and the United States (Riska, 1988; Riska and Wegar, in this volume; Carter and Carter, 1981). The analysis is put forward tentatively both because of limitations in the data available and because it may be too soon to assess some of the recent developments.

Again, it is worth noting a significant difference between the British and American situation. The proportion of women among medical students and practising doctors is considerably higher in Britain than in the United States and has been for the past seventy years: a point that has been often ignored in the sociology of the British medical profession (Elston, 1977a, 1986). In 1970, just under 10 per cent of new American medical students were women and in 1987, 35 per cent. In Britain the equivalent figures were 26 and 46 per cent (see Lorber in this volume; UCCA Annual Reports). In any international league table showing the proportion of women in medicine since the Second World War, Britain would always appear closer to the Nordic countries than the United States, although well below the ex-Soviet bloc countries. This relatively high ranking has clearly not been incompatible with marked overt discrimination against women applicants for most of this period or with a particularly high degree of professional autonomy and status in the past. The question I now consider is whether the recent increase in absolute numbers and percentage of women entering the profession might be causally connected to changes in that high degree.

'Feminization' and medical autonomy examined

Control over selection and training of neophytes so as to ensure the reproduction of professional skills and values and the maintenance of adequate material rewards for all members has often been identified as a key characteristic of the ideal-type profession (e.g. Freidson, 1970). According to this theoretical model, loss of such control would represent a significant abrogation of professional power. This is the point drawn on by McKinlay when he argues that one manifestation of 'proletarianization' or 'corporatization' of American medicine is that medical schools have been '"forced" to recruit [a] proportion of minorities and women' as a result of equal opportunities legislation (McKinlay, 1988: 5). In Britain, the increase in women medical students has sometimes been attributed to the introduction in 1975 of the Sex Discrimination Act, which outlawed restrictive quotas and higher entrance requirements then imposed on women applying to medical schools (e.g. Hakim, 1979). Advocates of the 'proletarianization' thesis might regard this as an example of the state overriding medical privilege in a new way. A closer look, however, reveals that while the legal prohibition on overt discrimination has had some impact on women's entry it was by no means the sole factor. State intervention has certainly played a part in the increase in women's entry over the last forty years. But it has done so in ways that exemplify the general limits to medical autonomy in matters of general public policy, and not always in the face of entrenched medical opposition.

Two developments have conditioned the scale and the overall form of medical education since the Second World War. With the inception of the NHS, the supply of medical manpower (as it is conventionally termed) has been a matter of general public policy, rather than a matter for the profession or the market alone. However, as in most matters relating to the NHS, the medical profession has had a powerful influence in the details of manpower policy-making, with professional associations acting to safeguard the interests of members (Elston, 1977b). At the same time, medical education has become more fully incorporated into the university system in Britain, a system that has been mainly state-funded, at least since the end of the Second World War (through grants to both institutions and students). One outcome of the twin interests of the profession and the state Treasury is that there has been central determination of the number of medical school places for most of the period since the 1940s, in other words from before what many commentators now see as the 'golden age' of medical autonomy in the 1950s and 1960s. But it was in the 1940s that a crucial state-sponsored intervention in relation to women's access was made.

Trends in medical education
During the First World War, there was a very substantial increase in women medical students, taking the places left by men enlisting in the Armed Forces, including places in some medical schools which had

not previously admitted women. In 1920, women were more than one-fifth of all medical students. But many of the wartime concessions to women were withdrawn during the 1920s, as a reaction to an alleged 'glut' of females (Elston, 1977a, 1986). During the 1930s, women were, on average, 15 per cent of entrants to medical schools overall. But this overall figure disguises marked variations between medical schools, in particular between those which were relatively strongly integrated into their parent universities (that is, in Scotland, Wales and the English provinces) and those, in London, which were not.[2] In the former, women were on average about a fifth of students. But of the twelve main medical schools in London, responsible for training 40 per cent of the nation's medical students, nine admitted only men in the inter-war years. These London schools had developed around the great metropolitan voluntary hospitals and, although formally constituent colleges of the University of London, were very much independent bodies, to the extent that taking the University's degree was by no means the norm.[3] The three London schools that did admit women had a different history. Women were admitted in the inter-war period to preclinical studies in the two original multi-faculty colleges of the University, University College and King's College, but only very restricted numbers of women could proceed to their associated teaching hospitals. The twelfth school was another single-sex one: the London School of Medicine for Women (later renamed the Royal Free Hospital School of Medicine) which had been founded in 1874 when all other avenues to medical education appeared closed to women. During the 1930s, this one school was still training about a quarter of all women medical students in Great Britain (Elston, 1986).

Prior to the Second World War individual medical schools did act largely as autonomous professional institutions. But this was to change. Central planning of student numbers was introduced during the war, initially as an emergency measure, and has never been entirely lifted since. In 1944, a government-sponsored committee (the Goodenough Committee) with a majority of medical members, including one distinguished woman physician, was established to consider what kind of medical education was appropriate for a national health service, that is to determine what public policy should be in this matter. Among the committee's recommendations were that medical schools' receipt of public funds should be made conditional on their becoming coeducational, indeed on their admitting a 'reasonable' proportion of women, 'say about one-fifth' (Ministry of Health, 1944: 99). This recommendation was eventually accepted after much negotiation. And, as most medical schools were by then in receipt of substantial government grants, coeducation became universal in principle. What was to count as a 'reasonable' proportion was not specified precisely. The immediately pre-war average of 15 per cent (i.e. below the level already achieved in all schools except Oxford, Cambridge and eleven of the London schools) was recommended as a target by the University Grants Committee which distributed government funds to universities but it was not enforced (Elston, 1986).

The Goodenough Committee's recommendations were probably more important for their ending of absolute sex segregation in medical training than for their immediate impact on total numbers of women entrants. Indeed, its recommendations were, in many ways, the foundation of the subsequently notorious and well-documented 'quotas' for women that prevailed in most medical schools from the 1950s to the mid-1970s. Because of the pressure of women's applications, these 'quotas' did not operate as modes of positive discrimination fostering the opportunity of a disadvantaged group. Rather they became ceilings by which all but the very best-qualified women were kept out (Elston, 1977a, 1980). From the 1950s to the mid-1960s, the proportion of women medical students overall averaged 22 per cent, never falling below 20 per cent. But the pre-war differences between schools remained, with some of the English provincial and Scottish schools regularly admitting over 30 per cent of women and some of the ex-men's schools in London regularly admitting less than 15 per cent (Royal Commission on Medical Education, 1968: 274).

By the mid-1960s, there was growing public and professional concern about an overall shortage of doctors and undue reliance on overseas-trained doctors in Britain. A Royal Commission on Medical Education (1968) recommended a substantial expansion of home medical training in 1968, a recommendation which received substantial support from many of the medical professional associations. Expansion was not 'forced' on the profession. Once again, this was a development paralleled in many other western countries although the scale of expansion has been modest in Britain compared to many countries. Professional concern over unemployment and restrictions on public expenditure have meant that not even all the originally planned expansion has occurred. Britain remains a country with a relatively low doctor to population ratio (Freddi and Bjorkman, 1989). The number of medical school places available annually for home students has risen from just over 2,000 in 1960 and about 2,500 in the late 1960s to just under 4,000 today. Almost all the extra places provided after 1965 have been taken by women. Indeed, the number of male students entering medical school in 1989 was, at just over 2,000, almost exactly the same as in 1969, having fallen from a peak of almost 2,500 in 1979 (UCCA, 1970–90). The number of new women medical students has risen about two and a half times between 1969 and 1989, from almost 700 to almost 1,800. In fact, the rate of increase was greater in the five-year period immediately before the passage of the 1975 Sex Discrimination Act than in that immediately after. Several factors lay behind this rise of women besides the 1975 legislation.

In the late 1960s, increased numbers of places meant that more women could be admitted without encroaching on the existing number of men's places. The way the expansion was organized had the effect of increasing the proportion of medical students training in the English provincial schools, that is in the type of schools which were already admitting a significant proportion of women students. Three new provincial schools were opened which, by definition, had no sons of 'old boys' to seek places. These three schools accepted over 40 per cent of women from the start. By 1974, the average percentage of women in English provincial medical schools was 38 per cent while still less than 25 per cent in the London schools (excluding the former women's school) (UGC Annual Report, 1975). The ostensible reason given for 'quotas' was that women's professional contribution would be so much less than men's because of domestic commitments. During the 1970s, this kind of reasoning was losing its legitimacy in the face of calls for equal opportunities. But also the evidence was accumulating that medical women's participation rates were extremely high relative to other women's and rising (Elston, 1977a; Beaumont, 1978). The criteria for admission were also changing as, from the 1960s, medical schools placed increasing emphasis on formal credentials, specifically on the grades achieved at 'A'-level (the highest secondary school qualification). This was partly a pragmatic response to cope with the flood of applications, especially as medical schools gradually joined the Universities Central Council for Admissions (UCCA) scheme. But it also reflected a concern among some medical educators that the particularistic methods of selection traditionally adopted were inappropriate for a modern profession. Whatever the reasons, during the 1960s and early 1970s, medical education was moving more into line with the admissions procedures adopted in the rest of the university system, with its ostensibly meritocratic principles of access. In 1973, the Committee of Vice-Chancellors and Principals (a body composed of the heads of all British universities) recommended that restrictive quotas for women be abandoned throughout the university system two years before the Sex Discrimination Act was passed.

Other things being equal, a move to selection on the basis of

'A'-level would have favoured women, at least until the 1980s, as the qualifications of women applicants were better, on average, than men's, and at some schools the proportion of women among applicants was twice that among accepted students (e.g. *Journal of the Medical Women's Federation* 47: 42, 1965). Before 1974, 'other things' were apparently not equal as the entry qualifications of successful women applicants were also better on average than successful men's (Elston, 1977a). Subsequently, this consistent difference in achievement before entry has disappeared. There is much anecdotal evidence that a new phenomenon has been appearing in the London medical schools over the last decade: the 'less than academically outstanding woman'! It should be emphasized that, in arguing that universalistic and achieved criteria have become more important in the selection of medical students, I am not suggesting that they are the sole criterion or that covert discrimination in selection may not still exist (Collier and Burke, 1986). Nor does it follow that there has been a reduction in the barriers faced by women once within medical school. Medical education, particularly in the clinical years, still places great emphasis on the 'personal' qualities and behaviour of individuals, giving much scope for gender-related assessment by teachers (Atkinson, 1984; Atkinson and Delamont, 1990).

The discussion so far has shown that, by the time the Sex Discrimination Act of 1975 made differential selection criteria for men and women illegal, medical school intake had been a matter of public policy for thirty years. In this context, for sociologists to see medicine's lack of exemption from a major item of legislation affecting all walks of life as a significant loss of professional privilege would seem perverse. Exclusion of qualified individuals from occupations on the basis of gender was being eliminated (in principle) at the societal level. In any case, in medicine, the legislation was preceded by a significant rise in the number of women entrants. The majority of medical schools already admitted a substantial proportion of women, albeit on overtly discriminatory terms. Women's entry to medical education might have continued to rise in the absence of legislation to outlaw the imposition of these terms.

The 1975 Act and the preceding recommendation from the Committee of Vice-Chancellors and Principals did not have a dramatic and immediate impact on women's entry but they do appear to have had some effect over time. Just as the belief (well-founded or otherwise) in the existence of quotas will have suppressed women's applications to medical schools, so knowledge that quotas had been abolished would be expected to release some of this suppressed demand. Certainly the number of women's applications for medicine rose steadily from the late 1960s until the mid-1980s, whereas men's applications have not risen since the mid-1970s. As in the United States (Ginzberg, 1986), a recent small fall in the total number of applications to medical school (and in the proportion they constitute of all applications) has given rise to speculation about medicine's declining attractiveness as a career and a potential crisis in recruitment (e.g. *British Medical Journal* 298: 479, 25 February 1989). While it may well be that extensive media coverage about junior hospital doctors' grievances and the profession's disquiet at some of the proposed NHS reforms might be having a negative effect, other factors (including demographic ones) cannot be ruled out on the data currently available. What is clear is that there are still far more qualified applicants of either sex to medical school than there are places available.

The rise in women's applications and in admissions since 1975 has been particularly marked in the London schools where the 'quotas' for women were so small. The longstanding marked difference in women's entry between these schools and the rest has substantially diminished in the last decade. For the first time, all medical students are now training alongside almost equal numbers of the opposite sex. Contrast this with the mid-1960s when 60 per cent of all male medical students in England and Wales trained in schools where 80 per cent of the students were men, that is in the London schools (excluding the Royal Free) and at Oxford and Cambridge. Conventional wisdom (for which there is some supporting evidence) is that the professional elite, particularly in hospital medicine, has been disproportionately drawn from these schools. Certainly, in the recent past, their products have been more likely to enter specialist hospital practice than those from elsewhere (Johnson and Elston, 1980; Parkhouse, 1991). It seems that a natural experiment is now under way in which the relative importance of medical school and gender in shaping professional careers can be more rigorously investigated.

The effects on autonomy

This discussion of recent trends in medical school intake has shown that it would be misleading to regard the recent increase in women's entry as evidence of incipient 'proletarianization'. Any loss in professional autonomy over recruitment was sustained when the Goodenough Report's recommendations were implemented in the late 1940s, at the same time as the inception of the NHS underpinned other dimensions of professional autonomy more firmly than ever before. The gradual incorporation of medical education into the university system over this century has been actively sought by many sections of the profession (although opposed by some). If my analysis is correct, the increase in women's entry to medical school needs to be understood as being as much the (perhaps unintended) consequence of the profession's own actions as the result of externally imposed conditions (cf. Light and Levine, 1988).

If the partial 'feminization' of British medicine is not to be regarded as the outcome of general loss of power and status, there is another possibility: that the causal direction runs the other way. Is 'feminization' leading to deskilling, diminished professional prerogatives and the erosion of high social status and material rewards? One reasonable response to this question is that it is too soon to tell, 'feminization' of the profession not being extensive enough yet. But the idea that a high entry of women is a sufficient condition for the decline of a formerly powerful and prestigious male occupation is found often enough in the sociological literature to warrant some comment. For example, some discussions of the so-called semi-professions in health care appear to imply that this is the case (e.g. Hearn, 1982).

Taken at face value, a strong version of this 'feminization' thesis would seem to present a depressing prospect of biological determinism. Then there is the problem of a lack of British examples with which to test the hypothesis. In the highly gender-segregated occupational structure prevailing in Britain over the last century (Dex, 1985), it is hard to find examples of a high-status, skilled and strongly organized predominantly male occupation that has crossed to being predominantly female: an absence unlikely to be due to chance. Clerical work at the turn of the century, 'often cited as the major example of occupational "feminization"' (Crompton and Sanderson, 1990: 25) is hardly comparable to late-twentieth-century medicine in terms of status, authority, skill or degree of organization. It is only in the past decade that other 'male' established professions have begun to approach medicine in their proportion of women (Elston, 1986).

In the case of medicine, advocates of the 'feminization' thesis generally base their case on a putative analogy with either the penumbra of lower-status, less autonomous female-dominated occupations surrounding medicine or with medicine in the Soviet Union, where women comprise the majority of members of a relatively poorly paid occupation (Leeson and Gray, 1978). Both these analogies have obvious limitations. Those health-care occupations typed as women's work, such as nursing and physiotherapy, were so typed from their first crystallization as distinct occupations (Gamarnikow, 1978; Larkin, 1983). They did not undergo 'feminization' and men entering these occupations have shared the low material rewards accruing to such work (Crompton, 1987: 422). Although there were significant numbers of women training for medicine at home or abroad before the Russian Revolution, extensive 'feminization' occurred after it, following an ideologically motivated destruction of professional associations and self-regulation by the Soviet state. Since 1917, Soviet medicine has lacked the organized autonomy that has characterized British medicine notwithstanding its state funding (Field, 1988: 186).

To suggest that increased numbers of women will, in themselves, bring about deskilling and downgrading of British, or indeed American, medicine is to ignore the very features of professional ideology and organization in these societies that have attracted sociological interest. The conception of an egalitarian community of colleagues united by their common credentials and ethical code has no place for differential rewards for similarly qualified men and women doing the same work. To accept this would be to devalue the professionally validated licence to practise on which medicine bases its claims to skill (Larson, 1977). As Crompton has noted, a medical qualification is a powerful source of both social standing and identity, which may be sufficient to outweigh any negative impact of gender. She argues that increased access for women to the qualifications of established professions 'presents no threat – as long as "skill levels" are maintained' (Crompton, 1987: 422). The very syndicalist organization of British medicine that has been blamed for the exclusion of women in the past may also serve as a bulwark against any erosion of collective professional privileges as a result of women's entry, although it may be facing other challenges. But this ideology of professional unity is only part of the picture. Medicine is simultaneously a unified and organized occupation when it faces the outside world and, from the inside, a collection of different and sometimes competing interests and segments (Klein, 1983; Elston, 1977b; Atkinson and Delamont, 1990). A medical qualification today is both a passport into a professional community and only the first step into a complex internally segmented occupational structure offering very different career paths and opportunities. It is to these that I now turn.

Gender and the changing occupational structure of medicine

In the old sociological orthodoxy, the ideal-type medical practitioner was a 'solo' practitioner. In theory, doctors, once armed with their basic qualification, set themselves up in independent practice and waited for patients. And in practice, although collegial relationships and professional networks have long been important for professional success and some organization-based medical careers have a long history, beginning a medical career by 'putting up one's plate' was clearly widespread before the NHS. Women doctors were formally as free to do this as men, although gender might have affected access to capital or patient demand (Elston, 1986). But underlying the current debate about the transformation of the medical profession is a recognition that the organization of medical work and the associated labour market has been gradually but fundamentally changing over the twentieth century, particularly over the last thirty years. Increased specialization and associated extended training ladders (bringing in post-graduate credentialism) have created a complex technically based division of labour, with fields differing in prestige and in the indeterminacy involved in the application of their specialist knowledge. 'Solo' practice has been extensively replaced by 'doctoring together' with professional colleagues, generally in positions embedded in organizational contexts: the state health system or large corporations, complex hospitals, and the specialty organizations of medicine itself (Freidson, 1980; Derber, 1984). Two corollaries of this shift may have particular salience for women.

The first is that access to occupational positions in medicine has been increasingly mediated by formal and informal organizational factors: factors arising from the profession's own structures and culture and from third parties, the state in the British context. As this happens, so there is greater scope for covert and overt discrimination by professional 'gatekeepers', superiors and colleagues, employers and so on and for institutional barriers related to gender (Crompton and Sanderson, 1990: 69-71). The second possible outcome of these changes is the generation of increasing numbers of 'practitioner'-type work opportunities distinct from both traditional entrepreneurial self-employment and organization-based linear career tracks and typically involving relatively routinized work. If, as the 'proletarianization' and 'deprofessionalization' hypotheses imply, there is a trend for medical work to become routinized and bureaucratized, this is not happening evenly across the different fields of medicine and types of post. Rather, internal differentiation may be accelerating, placing new strains on the profession's solidaristic stance vis-à-vis the outside world (Elston, 1991; Freidson, 1986).

Crompton and Sanderson have hypothesized that as increased numbers of women enter the established professions they will be disproportionately found in 'practitioner' positions (Crompton and Sanderson, 1986, 1990; see also Carter and Carter, 1981). The point is that 'practitioner' positions may provide particularly flexible, part-time or office-hours-only work opportunities for qualified professionals seeking to combine practice and family responsibilities.

Doing this has become increasingly common among medically qualified women over the last twenty years as childbearing rates have increased at the same time as the practice of leaving or interrupting professional practice to raise a family has diminished still further. The need for emergency patient cover in much medical work may present particular difficulties for those with extensive domestic responsibilities, especially in a system, as in Britain, where, historically, great emphasis has been placed on the idea (if not always the practice) of continuity of care from the same doctor (Allen, 1988; Elston, 1980). Arguably, this is one example of the ways in which 'professional mystery' is invoked against pressures for routinization, when moves to the kind of formal hand-over arrangements that prevail in nursing are resisted. Given the strongly gender-based division of labour still prevailing in most British doctors' households, working part-time may provide solutions for individual women, while perpetuating sex segregation. It should be noted that working 'part-time' in British medicine often involves what passes for a normal working week in many other professional occupations.

The discussion so far suggests that the transformation of the occupational structure within medicine that is at the heart of the current sociological debate may be conducive to intensified sex segregation at the very time when more women were entering the profession. In earlier papers (Elston, 1977a, 1977b, 1980) I showed that, in the 1970s, there was indeed marked sex segregation within British medicine, broadly as predicted by the structural analysis outlined above. As in many other countries (see Riska and Wegar; Lorber, in this volume), women in Britain were unevenly distributed across the vertical (technically based) division of labour. They were overrepresented in certain fields of medicine, particularly those regarded as less prestigious within the profession, including those 'service' specialties which rapidly expanded in the 1960s and 1970s, such as anaesthetics and radiology and in primary care. In contrast, women were underrepresented in the major fields of acute adult medicine, especially surgical ones. There was also marked horizontal sex segregation. Women have been significantly underrepresented in the highest career grades even after controlling for changes in entry levels over time and for career breaks because of family responsibilities. Women were especially likely to be found in 'practitioner' positions off the main hierarchically ordered career 'tracks', positions which were often low in clinical autonomy.

My earlier analysis was carried out before the sharp increase of women entrants from the late 1960s could have had much impact on the patterns found. In the rest of this chapter, therefore, I update and extend the analysis, examining the trends in sex segregation in relation to recent structural changes within British medicine as these larger cohorts of young women have begun to enter professional practice. My emphasis is on the structural changes in medicine. In the space available, it is not possible also to consider in detail the career preferences and pathways of individual doctors. Two book-length reports of surveys of recent British medical graduates of both sexes have recently been published which contain much relevant evidence on the experiences of individual women (and men) (Allen, 1988; Parkhouse, 1991). In common with other recent writers on women in medicine, I would argue that it is not possible to explain fully the distribution of women in medicine in terms of their individual career preferences or competing role obligations alone (cf. Riska and Wegar, in this volume; Lorber, 1984; Davidson, 1979). These are important, but they need to be set in the context of the opportunity structure in which doctors make their more or less constrained choices, which, in turn, will influence that structure.

I consider in turn the three main branches of medical work within the NHS, for almost all doctors in Britain work in the NHS for most of their careers. These three branches differ significantly in the kind of work opportunities they provide and in the extent to which they have experienced change in or challenge to their control over their work or its organization in recent years.

Community medicine and community health: administrative and 'practitioner' doctors

The smallest of the three branches of NHS medicine is that concerned with planning and administering the state's population-based health care provision, including prevention. This sector employed just over 6,200 individual doctors (mostly part-time) in 1990 in England and Wales (DH *National Medical Staff Tables*). Doctors in this sector, who have been state employees since the last century, on the whole have long had limited professional autonomy and low esteem relative to their professional peers in clinical fields. The sector has suffered several extensive administrative reorganizations over the last half-century reflected in changes in designation. Before 1974, employment was with local government authorities, under the direction of Medical Officers of Health (MOH) rather than the NHS. The current upheavals in this sector of medicine are leading to a reversion to an older title, 'public health medicine', epitomizing its responsibility for safeguarding the population's health, largely through preventive measures. It is this sector that has been the main vehicle for state intervention to promote maternal and child health through screening and advisory clinics. Such work was, from its tentative beginnings, at the turn of the century, strongly typed as 'women's work', and it grew considerably in the inter-war years (Elston, 1986; Lewis, 1982).

Within the old Local Authority Medical Services there was a linear career structure leading, in theory, from the clinic staffing level to MOH. But biographical studies suggest that women faced many barriers in breaking out of the gender-typed work in maternal and child health in order to achieve senior administrative positions (Elston, 1986; Stacey and Davies, 1983). Thus the link between clinic work and administrative work was gradually attenuated, and finally formally ruptured when this sector was absorbed into the NHS in 1974. Community health clinics were staffed by clinical medical officers working on a truly part-time sessional basis under the direction of non-clinical community medicine specialists, now classed as equivalent to hospital consultants and with their own hierarchical career ladder. Clinic medicine thus has come to represent the clearest example of a 'practitioner' niche in British medicine with virtually no promotion prospects.[4] The work has, in many doctors' eyes, lost its pioneering edge in promoting maternal and child health, often being seen as 'pin-money' medicine, a highly routinized and gender-typed, 'soulless round' of contraceptive and 'well-baby' clinics (see Elston, 1977a).

It is against this background that trends in women's position in this sector must be assessed. Women have been over half the total numbers of doctors in public health medicine since before the 1970s. In 1990, they were 60 per cent of the total in England and Wales (DH/DHSS *National Medical Staff Tables*). But the extent of overrepresentation relative to their presence in the profession as a whole is different within the two branches. In 1979, women were 50 per cent of community health medical staff but only 27 per cent of community medicine staff in England and Wales. In 1990, the equivalent figures were 65 per cent and 42 per cent. But this relative increase in their presence in this 'practitioner' niche needs to be set against a fall in the total number of doctors employed in this sector and a virtual standstill in the numbers of women clinical medical officers under the age of 35 since the 1980s. The increased numbers of new women entrants to medicine are not going into 'clinic medicine', or not yet.

A combination of structural changes within the NHS over the last decade and the aspirations of younger women doctors are important here. The desire to reduce health service expenditure and the professional aspirations of general medical practitioners (primary-care doctors) are leading to the gradual transfer of many medical preventive health functions, including contraceptive provision and child health surveillance, away from community health clinics to general practice (Davies, 1984; Calnan and Gabe, 1991). At the same time, surveys of newly qualified women doctors have shown them as very reluctant to go into community health, wanting 'proper' jobs in medicine instead (Allen, 1989: 12). It may be that, as more of these young doctors face the full constraints of combining motherhood and professional practice, their aspirations may be modified in the direction of community health. But the opportunities in this field are likely to have reduced by then. Thus, developments in community health over the past decade do not clearly support the hypothesis that the increases in women entrants will be absorbed into routinized practitioner positions although women's relative overrepresentation within this field has increased.

It was noted above that women were also overrepresented, but not to the same degree, in the far smaller community medicine branch of public health. This has increased over the past decade and looks set to do so in the future. In 1990, women were one-third of the consultant-grade doctors (although only a quarter of the top positions) but over half of those on the training ladder (DH *National Medical Staff Tables*, 1991). Although organized around linear career structures, community medicine is unusual within medicine in providing opportunities for relatively regular hours from an early stage and it has also experienced a shortage of recruits, probably exacerbated by recent reforms which have produced low morale in the field (Harvey and Judge, 1988). Thus institutional and organizational barriers to women's advancement may be less than in many fields, that is, for those women who do not wish to practise clinical medicine. But it is notable that only a quarter of the top positions of district and regional medical officers are held by women.

In the 1974 reorganization of the NHS these positions were given quite extensive managerial responsibilities vis-à-vis their clinical colleagues to be exercised through engineering consensus rather than direct management. A perception that community physicians had not succeeded in this task has been one factor behind the promotion of stronger general management within the NHS (DHSS, 1983; Strong and Robinson, 1990). Community medicine's managerial role is being narrowed while the more traditional functions such as infectious disease control and service evaluation are being enhanced. One can speculate that while considerations of gender may have impeded women's promotion to the ostensibly managerial positions, these might, in the future, have less force in a more narrowly skill-based field (cf. Carpenter, 1977). If so, this would be one way in which women's career opportunities are being conditioned by structural changes in British medicine that are perhaps too complex to be subsumed under the single label 'bureaucratization'.

Women in general practice: unequal partners?

General practice (primary care medicine) is the largest single career destination for British medical graduates of either sex, with some 27,000 principals in England and Wales in 1990, of whom just over one-fifth are women (DH *National Medical Staff Tables*, 1991). British general practice still exhibits many of the features of the 'solo practice' model. General practitioners are not state employees but self-employed contractors with the NHS. Apart from weak state controls over entry to heavily overdoctored areas, qualified doctors can, in theory, set up in practice where they like. Until the early 1980s, the basic medical qualification was sufficient. Now a three-year vocational training is mandatory, a considerably shorter training than that expected in hospital medicine. But since 1948 general practice has changed from a 'cottage industry' based on single-handed practice to one based primarily on extensive group partnerships employing ancillary workers. Partners either share in the capital investment and rewards in privately negotiated proportions, or, less commonly, are employed by senior partners. Thus, over the past thirty years, access to positions in general practice has become increasingly mediated by professional colleagues and the state's contractual conditions. While this shift was fostered by government policy particularly through wide-ranging reforms in 1966 it was also being actively sought by the relevant professional associations (Jefferys and Sachs, 1983).

The implementation of the Family Doctors' Charter in 1966 followed a serious crisis in morale among general practitioners and led to a striking boost to the financial rewards obtainable comparatively early in a professional career. The late 1980s, however, have brought new controversy around the implementation of two reforms. These were, to some extent, imposed upon the members of the profession by a government defining health politics as part of the wider political arena. First a new contract was introduced in 1990 which had the explicit aim of improving the efficiency of general practitioners. Their contracts were made more financially sensitive to work performed and the regulatory powers of the bodies administering their contracts were increased. Secondly, the reforms to be implemented during 1991 placed increased emphasis on general practitioners' role as 'gatekeepers' to the more expensive hospital services (Day and Klein, 1986; Elston, 1991; Calnan and Gabe,

1991). At present, it would appear that general practitioners' power and autonomy are being simultaneously circumscribed and enhanced.

The last two decades have seen a marked upsurge in the popularity of general practice as the first-choice career destination of newly qualified doctors (Allen, 1988; Parkhouse, 1991). Surveys of new medical graduates since the 1960s have consistently shown general practice to attract a higher proportion of all women qualifiers than of men (e.g. Allen, 1988; Parkhouse, 1991). There is no indication of women's preference for and entry to general practice decreasing as their numbers have grown. What has changed in the last fifteen years or so is that more men are opting for general practice as first choice, citing their wish for more regular hours and time for family, greater security earlier and a dislike for the competitive and arduous conditions in hospital medicine (Allen, 1988; Parkhouse, 1991). As a result, the total number of general medical practitioners has grown by about 20 per cent over this time (DH, 1990) and there is now some concern about an oversupply of recruits to this field from within the profession. A substantial part of this increase has been drawn from the growing numbers of young women entrants. Between 1977 and 1990, the total number of women doctors working in general practice in England grew by 3,513, almost 100 per cent, while men increased by 1,683, a 10 per cent increase. Controlling for age shows the growth in women even more clearly. In 1990, women were 47 per cent of the principals and trainees under the age of 30, but only 18 per cent of those aged between 50 and 59 years.

The relatively flexible conditions, short training and the type of work involved in NHS general practice, combined with considerable financial rewards and security since the mid-1960s, have been repeatedly shown to be particularly attractive to women (e.g. Allen, 1988). But men and women do not necessarily work on equal terms in general practice. Although the contracts held by individual doctors with the NHS are gender-blind, the arrangements obtaining within group practices may not be. Matters such as maternity leave cover, duty hours, holidays and the like are all matters for privately negotiated contract between individuals (although there are standard professional guidelines). It has been a longstanding complaint of women general practitioners that they are, at best, dependent on the goodwill of (their usually male) partners or, at worst, vulnerable to exploitation by partners as far as any recognition of women's domestic responsibilities is concerned. One writer has suggested, based on findings in one locality, that there is a trend for women to set up as single-handed practitioners, against the general pattern, in order to escape problematic relationships with male partners (Lawrence,

1987). There are insufficient data available to establish whether this has been a widespread phenomenon. But there are signs that the most recent changes in general practice could produce greater potential for tension between partners, particularly where part-time partners are involved.

From 1966 until 1990, the growth of group practice and of sharing emergency cover, or delegating it to agencies, along with the particular terms of the NHS contract, have facilitated the growth of 'quasi-practitioner' niches within general practice, terms being negotiated on a practice-specific basis as described above. The number of so-called 'part-time' partners, often salaried or receiving a reduced share of profits, formally responsible for smaller lists of patients, has expanded considerably over this time. And such partners are, not surprisingly, mainly women. Some representative surveys have indicated that 40 per cent or more of women general practitioners may be working less than (medically defined) full-time (Allen, 1988; Bosanquet and Leese, 1990; Butler and Calnan, 1987; Ridsdale, 1990). Part-time general practice has provided the growing numbers of women doctors with young children the opportunity to maintain a substantial commitment to professional practice, often working mainly with mothers and young children. In more ways than one, general practice has been replacing community health 'clinic medicine'. And, although part-timers in general practice may be disadvantaged relative to their full-time colleagues, their terms of service, financial rewards and clinical autonomy have hitherto far exceeded those of clinical medical officers. However, these terms are changing under the new contract introduced in 1990.

One of the stated aims of the new contract for general practitioners introduced in 1990 was to encourage women to enter and remain in general practice, in order to give patients more opportunity to choose a woman practitioner if they wished. The promise of special provisions to promote part-time working or job-sharing was held out (DHSS, 1987a: 19–20). But during the negotiations the two organizations specifically for women doctors, the Medical Women's Federation and the strongly feminist Women in Medicine, argued strenuously that the general terms of the new contract would have the opposite effect (e.g. Women in Medicine Newsletter, Spring 1988). For example, the relative financial penalties for smaller than average list sizes and limited hours were greatly increased. A woman doctor seeking a reduced load has become a less attractive financial prospect to her partners. At the time of writing, after a few months of implementation, reports that 'many women are finding the changes difficult to comply with' and that 'some women GPs are being unfairly treated . . . by their partners' are beginning to appear (e.g. *British Medical Journal*, 1991, 302: 368).

It is far too soon to know what the outcome of the new general practice contract will be for women. But there is at least the possibility that this structural change will deepen divisions between full-timers (mainly male) and part-timers (mainly female), with the latter being significantly more restricted in their professional prospects and financially disadvantaged compared with their pre-1990 situation.

Hospital medicine: a persistent imbalance?

Consultants and junior doctors
At any one time, just under two-thirds of all active British doctors are working in NHS hospitals. But only about one-third of these enjoy full clinical autonomy in the workplace and long-term financial security: that is those who hold consultant posts. Since 1948, the NHS hospital service has been built around the principle of established posts for salaried specialists, each supported by a team of junior doctors in short-tenure training posts. Within the NHS (and, hence, effectively within British medicine) there is no clear way for becoming an accredited specialist other than by obtaining a consultant post. Far from becoming 'proletarianized' by accepting salaried status, consultants have enjoyed great power and authority under this system. NHS hospitals have been 'ruled, not by a single manager, but by the collective power of individual medical preference'. The individuals in question have been consultants, each of whom has been more or less free to use 'his or her individual judgement in whatever way was thought best' about patient care and all that has followed from it (Strong and Robinson, 1990: 16; cf. Ham, 1981). The apparent challenge to their position implicit in the most recent reforms to the NHS was a powerful source of consultant grievance although the extent of real change cannot yet be determined (Beck and Adam, 1990; Elston, 1991).

Although greatly increased since 1948, the number of consultant posts has always been strictly limited. Expansion, even when widely recognized as desirable, has always been limited by the combined interests of the state in economy and of consultants in post in maintaining standards and privileges. New consultant posts carry with them the expectation of a new team of juniors. Throughout the NHS's history there have been recurrent 'crises' arising from the inherent tension between a pyramidal hospital staffing structure based on a small number of consultants assisted by many juniors, the

demand of those juniors for career posts and the need for experienced and skilled staff to provide adequate medical care (Elston,
1977b). One such crisis is occurring at the present time as the
products of the enlarged intake to medical schools over the last two
decades are seeking career-grade posts in a cash-limited service
(Allen, 1988; Parkhouse, 1991).

The other side of consultant security and status is junior doctors'
relative insecurity and ambiguous position as simultaneously appren-
tices and 'extra pairs of hands' providing essential services. Unlike
the situation in many countries, there is no set period after which
'training' is regarded as complete. Post-graduate specialist qualifications are taken early in training and act as filters rather than as the
final seal of approved specialist status. It is, in the recent words of a
junior doctor, a system of 'dead man's [sic] shoes' (quoted in ·
Roberts, 1991: 226). And vacant shoes are rarely found in less than
ten years' full-time work after qualifying, with the actual time taken
varying considerably according to the competitiveness of the
specialty. In 1990, only 22 per cent of consultant appointments were
to doctors aged less than 35, but this was true for 37 per cent of new
consultant appointments in psychiatric specialties and 6 per cent of
those in surgical fields (DH *National Medical Staff Tables*). Although
coordinated training rotations have increased, in general British
junior doctors are still faced with frequent job searches in order to
keep moving up the ladder. They also carry the main responsibility
for routine 'on-call' cover, giving rise to very long hours in some
specialties, the subject of a major campaign at present. When
promotion prospects have been good and the rewards of consultant
status appear high, juniors have been relatively accepting of this
situation, dependent as they are on established consultants. When, as
now, promotion prospects and future rewards appear to many juniors
to be receding, they employ both voice and exit (Hirschman, 1970).
But the current crisis is particularly acute because the availability of
the traditional exit routes, emigration and general practice, is greatly
restricted in comparison with earlier episodes of junior dissatisfaction. And, as dependence on foreign graduates in junior posts has
greatly diminished over the last decade, the blocked doctors are,
overwhelmingly, indigenous products: unambiguously part of the .
professional community.

There have been periodic attempts to resolve these recurrent
problems in hospital staffing, the latest proposals agreed by government and professional associations being issued with the subtitle
Achieving a Balance in 1987 (DHSS, 1987b). These propose new
permutations of two much tried, or rather often proposed but rarely
fully implemented, methods for reconciling training and service

requirements while still more or less guaranteeing some kind of a permanent post for everyone. First, further manipulation of the numbers to make the specialist ladder more like a 'cylinder' than a 'pyramid' (Roberts, 1991: 227) is called for. The proposal is to increase consultant numbers and further restrict those entering specifically specialist rather than general post-graduate training, that is, the registrar grade normally entered three to four years after qualifying. Second, further separation of the training and service components of hospital medicine is to be brought about. On the one hand, consultants are being pressed to take on more of the routine on-call responsibilities traditionally delegated to their juniors. On the other hand, a new non-consultant career 'staff' grade is proposed for those who do not wish or are not suitable to carry the full clinical autonomy and managerial responsibilities of consultant work.

Some small provision for such posts has always existed within the NHS, combining as they do a way of gaining extra pairs of medical hands without immediate implications for the training ladder and a way of solving some individuals' personal career problems. Such posts have long been controversial within the profession because of concern that they become 'second-class' niches into which women or ethnic minority doctors might be pushed (Elston, 1977a, 1980; Allen, 1988). *Achieving a Balance* provides for the possible increase in such 'practitioner' posts as part of the established staffing structure rather than entry just being on a personal basis. It specifically identifies them as perhaps especially suitable for doctors with extensive domestic responsibilities (code for women). At the same time, the report gives very little general consideration to the implications for the medical career structure of the increase in women's entrants or of the implications for these women entrants of the greater rigidity of career structures that their proposals portend (cf. Allen, 1988; Beck and Adam, 1990).

Achieving a Balance does promise a more far-reaching reform of the hospital career structure than previous attempts but its implementation only began in 1988. Moreover, its proposals may well be cut across by the more general changes to the NHS being implemented in 1991. These might lead, in time, to increasing differentiation in the consultant grade, with an expansion of clinical directorates in which some clinicians have some formal managerial authority over consultant colleagues (Elston, 1991; Hunter, 1991). But more immediately, there is provision for those hospitals which elect to become 'self-governing trusts' within the NHS to be exempted from national guidelines for medical staffing and pay. The implications of this for the training ladder are not clear yet. But there is some concern that such hospitals may be more concerned with their own staffing requirements than producing future specialists, leading to either an exacerbation of blockages on the junior training ladder or an expansion in non-consultant career posts. Whatever the outcome of these developments, it is clear that within hospital medicine recent and likely future developments have created a more rigidly defined mainstream career structure and pressures for expanding the 'practitioner' role alongside this. This labour market contains many institutionalized barriers to progress for both men and women, with extensive opportunities for subtle and not so subtle gender discrimination. Access to post-graduate credentials, for example, depends in practice on obtaining an accredited training post where clinical experience will be recognized. Achieving a consultant post generally demands intense professional commitment in the face of insecure prospects during the optimum childbearing years. While there is a nationally sponsored scheme for part-time training in hospital, in practice opportunities for this have hitherto been few and very unevenly distributed between specialties (Allen, 1988).

'Shortage' specialties

The overall career structure imbalance just described is cut across by a second maldistribution: that between specialties within hospital medicine. The existence of 'shortage' specialties in which the number of career posts available exceeds the number of potential recruits in training has been a recognized feature of British medicine since the 1960s, to the extent that the government publishes an annual forecast to guide doctors' career choices (e.g. DH, 1989b). Over the last decade, the expansion in qualifiers and the exercise of manpower controls have considerably reduced the extent of shortage in most of such fields but there are still marked differences in competitiveness between specialties. In general, a shortage of recruits is a reflection of a specialty's low prestige or clinical interest rating. But there are specific structural factors as well which have produced three main categories of specialties where career competition is less intense than in the main acute fields.

The marked expansion of hospital medicine and technological developments since the 1960s have brought increased demand for service specialists, particularly in anaesthetics, radiology and pathology. To describe such fields as carrying reduced clinical responsibility is to belittle the importance of, for example, skilled anaesthesia or radiotherapy for patient wellbeing. But the exercise of such responsibility is mediated at least initially by the actions of clinical colleagues. Government policy of encouraging expansion of the 'Cinderella services' for the mentally ill and handicapped and the elderly has led to the expansion of psychiatry and geriatric medicine consultant posts over the last twenty years, an expansion that has been constrained by the lack of well-qualified candidates. The third category is only recently becoming apparent. The deliberately engineered fall in overseas doctors seeking training in Britain and the growing flight to general practice are creating concern about recruitment difficulties in some of the principal acute specialties, particularly those such as orthopaedics which do not form part of general practice training rotations. In all three cases, it is clear that these developments have involved state intervention in the workings of the market for medical skills, as has the relative lack of expansion of posts in general surgery or obstetrics and gynaecology in the last twenty years.

Women in hospital medicine
After this long preamble, let us turn to considering women's place in hospital medicine. In 1990, 15 per cent of all NHS consultants in England and Wales were women. In 1977, they were 10 per cent (DH *National Medical Staff Tables* 1978 and 1991). So there has clearly been an increase over the decade as the numbers of qualified women on the training ladder have increased. But given that women have been 20 per cent of qualifiers for forty years, they are still considerably below the proportion one would expect from an even distribution across the three main sectors of medicine. Looking at recent appointments in the Staff Tables shows a similar picture, a 50 per cent increase over the decade and continued underrepresentation. In 1976–7, 16 per cent of new consultant appointments went to women, in 1989–90 21 per cent did.

The increased output of women from medical schools and their attrition from the hospital ladder is starkly shown when the junior grades are considered. Regardless of their eventual career destinations, almost all doctors take 'house' and 'senior house officer' posts giving general post-graduate training for about three years after qualification. (This incorporates the hospital component of general practice training.) Between 1977 and 1990, the proportion of women in such posts rose from 25 per cent to 38 per cent, a 50 per cent increase, sustained over a period during which the total numbers of house officers rose by 30 per cent. But at the registrar level, the level of (now controlled) entry to the specifically specialist training ladder, the increase has only been from 18 to 24 per cent. Unless this changes, the proportion of women among new consultants in the foreseeable future may not continue to rise.

There is, as yet, insufficient information on appointments to the new non-consultant staff grade to establish how far women are entering this particular 'practitioner' position. As predicted earlier, the previous equivalent grades have long shown a strong over-representation of women. The figures for 'associate specialists' for 1977 and 1990 were 43 and 38 per cent respectively (DH *National Medical Staff Tables*). Appointments to this grade have been on a personal basis and have been closed in recent years with the implementation of *Achieving a Balance*'s recommendations, so the numbers in such posts have fallen slightly as doctors retire. An alternative non-training position is that of clinical assistant, mainly intended for general practitioners doing supplementary hospital work but also held by growing numbers of women as their sole post. In 1977, women were 24 per cent of all clinical assistants and in 1990, 30 per cent. But they were over half of those for whom this was their only or main medical post (DH *National Medical Staff Tables*).

The majority of the women hospital doctors from the cohort of 1981 qualifiers surveyed by Allen showed a marked lack of enthusiasm for non-consultant career grades, although recognizing that such posts might suit some individuals and provide some opportunity to do interesting clinical work (Allen, 1988). Thus, the evidence is that the majority of the young women who are seeking careers in hospital medicine aspire to the full clinical autonomy of a consultant position (see also Parkhouse, 1991). But it is also clear that even more young women than men today consider that hospital careers are not for them (Allen, 1988; Parkhouse, 1991).

Allen's survey confirmed the picture shown by earlier studies of medical careers (e.g. Johnson and Elston, 1980; Elston, 1980; Hutt et al., 1979) of a hospital ladder in which access to consultant posts was seen as heavily dependent on relationships with and expectations of seniors and colleagues and organizational factors such as the requirements for post-graduate credentials and the exigencies of national and local medical manpower planning. It is not necessarily that such factors impinge only on one sex, but rather that they may impinge differently on men and women. If women, perhaps because of the pull of small children, are unable to participate fully in the informal aspects of hospital medical life, so they may be excluded from key informal networks and advice. But Allen's survey also presents clear evidence of directly discriminatory treatment in appointment interviews, particularly for hospital jobs. She also found that the most recent graduates she surveyed were more critical about the extent of patronage and private influence in determining appointments than the older cohorts (Allen, 1988). I would suggest this is not necessarily because patronage has actually become more important in determining career outcomes. Rather the number of occasions when there is potential for patronage and 'gatekeeping' to be exercised has probably increased over two decades as the hospital

Table 2.1   *New NHS paid consultant appointments: England and Wales (selected specialties)*

Specialty	Appointments made					
	1 Oct 1977–30 Sept 1978			1 Oct 1989–30 Sept 1990		
	Total Appts.	Fem. Appts.	% Female	Total Appts.	Fem. Appts.	% Female
All specialties	634	120	19	956	202	21
Surgical group	117	3	3	176	8	51
Medical group	187	20	11	277	67	24
Obstetrics and						
gynaecology	28	4	14	62	13	20
Pathology group	51	11	22	83	24	29
Anaesthetics	80	28	35	125	32	26
Radiology/radiotherapy	59	16	27	89	20	22
Psychiatry group	97	35	36	30	38	29

Note: Some minor fields are omitted from the breakdown of all specialties.

Sources: DHSS *National Medical Staffing Statistics*, 1978; DH *National Medical Staffing Statistics*, 1991.

career structure has become more rigid and competitive. Younger doctors may feel more vulnerable as they are still on the receiving end (or not) of any such patronage. At the same time, the strengthening ethos of equal opportunities and selection on merit in society as a whole has made the exercise of informal influence appear less legitimate.

Allen's survey found that women were more likely than men to perceive sponsorship as more easily obtained by men and as more fateful in the highly competitive high-status specialties such as medicine and surgery (Allen, 1988: 166–8). Even if ill-founded, belief in differential sponsorship may condition women's aspirations and specialty choice. This may be one factor in the longstanding differences in the presence of women in different specialties. Table 2.1 shows new consultant appointments for 1977–8 and 1989–90 making clear how few annual vacancies there are in some fields. (The small numbers also mean that there is a degree of chance fluctuation between years.) The strong presence of women in the service specialties is shown, although anaesthetics, which is no longer a shortage field, shows some relative diminution in women's entry. In pathology however it has increased. The significant entry of women into the psychiatric specialties is also clear. These are the shortage specialties in which provision for part-time training and consultant grade posts are comparatively well-developed (Allen, 1988).

In general, at registrar level and above, there is a higher proportion of women in shortage specialties compared to competitive ones, in the service specialties compared to direct patient care ones, in medical specialties compared to surgical ones and in child medicine compared to adult medicine. This overall pattern has changed little over the past decade. There is no reason to think any one factor can explain the whole of this pattern. Rather it is the outcome of a constellation of factors relating to the different specialties and of factors relating to individual doctors who might work in them, the two sets often becoming conflated in practice. Thus women's specialty preferences on qualifying and subsequently do tend to show some differences from men's but these preferences may be partly conditioned by knowledge of the obstacles and opportunities. As indicated above, it is not just that some fields lend themselves particularly well to routinization into regular hours and specified commitments. They may do, although they all require degrees of emergency cover (and women have shown themselves willing to work these hours). Some fields may also be particularly attractive to women because of the nature of the work. But, in the context of state policy for expansion of some fields faster than normal recruitment would have permitted, there has been incentive to encourage women's access to these fields, perhaps reducing the pressure on others to change.

Two areas where women are poorly represented warrant particular comment: surgery, and obstetrics and gynaecology. As in many western countries, women in Britain have long been poorly represented in surgery.[5] In 1990, women were only 3 per cent of all consultants in surgical specialties, the eleven new appointments in the previous year representing 10 per cent of the total in post. Furthermore, half of the women surgeons were specialists in paediatric surgery, with only twelve women general surgeons and four women cardio-thoracic surgeons in the whole of England and Wales. Surveys such as Allen's have shown the many factors that combine to make surgery appear (and to a great extent be) 'a white male preserve' (Allen, 1988: 253): these include strong competition, long demanding training with very limited part-time provision, a 'macho' image of consultant style. Surgery has been very resistant to the routinization of its training requirements, in that great emphasis is placed on the 'total immersion' of the neophyte in the work. But there is a small sign of change. In 1991, concern about the low level of female recruits to surgery has led to the establishment of a government-funded support scheme for those few intrepid women considering a surgical career (DH, 1991), a low-key approach to overcoming some of the hurdles individual women face.

In Britain, unlike in many other western countries, obstetrics and gynaecology has not recently been a 'woman's field'. In 1988, women were 12 per cent of consultants in the field, a proportion that has risen slightly over the last decade. Many of the same obstacles that women face in surgery apply here, not least because obstetrics and gynae-cology training has been regarded as primarily surgical training for much of the last fifty years. It too has resisted routinization of training although more opportunities for part-time training have been created very recently (Allen, 1989). Interestingly, before the NHS, this was a field in which women were comparatively well represented, and this was carried over into the early years of the NHS. It appears that, as a pre-war trained generation of mainly single women who had often made their careers in the women's medical school and the few women's hospitals retired (or as these institutions closed or went mixed), they were replaced by men (Elston, 1986). In recent years there are small signs of a resurgence, perhaps as indicated in Table 2.1. Almost one-third of registrars in obstetrics and gynaecology were women in 1990 (DH *National Medical Staff Tables*). Here is one instance where the aspirations of the increased numbers of women entrants may be having some effect but reports of their experience show that it is a gruelling struggle for a woman to pursue a specialist career in caring for women in Britain today (e.g. Allen, 1988; Savage, 1989).

Conclusion

I have examined two issues relating to the recent increased numbers of women entering British medicine, the factors accounting for this increase and its impact to date on sex segregation within the profession (an impact that has yet to be fully felt). My discussion has attempted to relate these issues to the current sociological debate about a more general transformation of the medical profession in western countries in order to redress the gender-blindness of this debate. Britain's long history of an essentially state-funded medical profession that has enjoyed great clinical autonomy and political influence and comparatively high proportion of (largely invisible) women doctors makes it a particularly interesting case study in this debate. I have attempted to show that such concepts as 'proletarian-ization' or 'deprofessionalization' are too crude to capture the development within British medicine over the last forty years or even the last decade. Rather, I have pointed to the longstanding con-straints on some aspects of medical autonomy in Britain, particularly over medical school intake and the career structure arising from the state system of health care, particularly through control over the purse strings. In the past two decades there has been significant change, both internally and externally induced, which has resulted in more women being admitted and strengthened some of the forces conducive to sex segregation within medicine. My analysis of changes in the medical labour market constituted by the NHS has indicated that new cleavages and internal differentiation have been developing, some of which have different implications for women and for men. There is a real possibility of the widening of the gap between 'practitioner' and mainstream positions in both general practice and hospital medicine. As yet, such cleavages do not appear to be gravely threatening the organized collegial character of the profession in its dealings with the outside world but this remains a possibility.

My structural analysis of the medical career structure may be thought by some readers to have presented a rather depressing picture of the constraints to women's advancement within British medicine now that they are admitted in such large numbers. This is partly the inevitable result of the particular focus chosen. But it also reflects a strong current in the profession today, especially among its younger members. In the context of widespread concern among young doctors about their career prospects and current working conditions and with the current reforms to the NHS, 'the saddest' are the women (Roberts, 1991: 226). The publication of a large-scale government-funded survey which found significant discontent among younger men and especially younger women (Allen, 1988) clearly struck a chord among this section of the profession. It also attracted much official attention leading to the establishment of a working party which has just reported at the time of writing with various proposals to ease some of the difficulties women face (DH, 1991). It is important to keep a sense of proportion. I have indicated that there are areas where women have made inroads on sex segregation. Many of the women who entered medicine in the last twenty years have found rewarding careers in medicine and some have achieved great professional distinction. The full impact of the increased entry of women in the 1970s and 1980s is still to come. How much these young women may change the quality of medical care is another question, beyond the scope of this chapter. But both they and their male colleagues will face continued pressure for change in the ways their work and, consequently, their careers are organized as we move towards the twenty-first century.

Acknowledgements

I should have presented this chapter at the session on 'Gender and the division of labour in medicine: cross-national perspectives' at the International Sociological

Association's conference in Madrid, 1990. I was unable to do so because of one of the many contingencies that make combining motherhood and professional life so difficult at times. I am grateful to Elianne Riska for her understanding of this.

Notes

1 'Britain' is used throughout as a convenient, if occasionally imprecise, term. The small differences in health-care organization between England, Wales and Scotland are not pertinent to my arguments. Health services in Northern Ireland are somewhat differently organized and are not considered here, although I have no reason to think that my arguments would not apply in Northern Ireland.

2 Oxford and Cambridge did admit women in small numbers to study medicine (through their women's colleges) in the inter-war period but clinical studies for both men and women normally had to be pursued elsewhere, most commonly in London.

3 The alternative was the 'Conjoint' Diploma of the London Royal Colleges of Medicine and Surgery.

4 For a minority of clinical medical officers, this work is an extra commitment on top of full-time work. But for most, especially most women, it is their sole medical employment or is combined with other part-time practitioner opportunities (Elston, 1986; Allen, 1988).

5 Elsewhere I have shown how women's exclusion from major hospitals in the nineteenth century deprived them of the necessary clinical experience, unless they went to India (Elston, 1986).

References and further reading

Allen, I. (1988) *Doctors and Their Careers*. London: Policy Studies Institute.

Allen, I. (ed.) (1989) *Discussing Doctors' Careers*. London: Policy Studies Institute.

Atkinson, P. (1984) 'Training for certainty', *Social Science and Medicine*, 19: 949–56.

Atkinson, P. and Delamont, S. (1990) 'Professions and powerlessness', *The Sociological Review*, 38: 90–110.

Beaumont, B. (1978) 'Training and careers of women doctors in the Thames regions', *British Medical Journal*, 6106: 191–3.

Beck, E. J. and Adam, S. A. (eds) (1990) *The White Paper and Beyond*. Oxford: Oxford University Press.

Blake, C. (1990) *The Charge of the Parasols: Women's Entry to the Medical Profession*. London: The Women's Press.

Bosanquet, N. and Leese, B. (1990) *Family Doctors and Economic Incentives*. Aldershot: Gower.

Butler, J. R. and Calnan, M. W. (1987) *Too Many Patients? A Study of the Economy of Time and Standards of Care in General Practice*. Aldershot: Gower.

Calnan, M.W. and Gabe, J. (1991) 'Recent developments in general practice: a sociological analysis', in J. Gabe, M. Calnan and M.R. Bury (eds), *The Sociology of the Health Service*. London: Routledge.

Carpenter, M. (1977) 'The new managerialism and professionalism in nursing', in M. Stacey, M. Reid, C. Heath and R.C. Dingwall (eds), *Health and the Division of Labour*. London: Croom Helm. pp. 165–93.

Carter, M. J. and Carter, S. B. (1981) 'Women's recent progress in the professions or, women get a ticket to ride after the gravy train has left the station', *Feminist Studies*, 7: 477–504.

Collier, J. and Burke, A. (1986) 'Racial and sexual discrimination in the selection of students to London medical schools', *Medical Education*, 20: 86–9.

Crompton, R. (1987) 'Gender, status and professionalism', *Sociology*, 21: 413–28.

Crompton, R. (1990) 'Professions in the current context', *Work, Employment and Society*, Special Issue: 147–66.

Crompton, R. and Sanderson, K. (1986) 'Credentials and careers: some implications of the increase in professional qualifications amongst women', *Sociology*, 20: 25–42.

Crompton, R. and Sanderson, K. (1990) *Gendered Jobs and Social Change*. London: Unwin Hyman.

Davidson, L. R. (1979) 'Choice by constraint: the selection and function of specialties among women physicians-in-training', *Journal of Health Policy, Politics and Law*, 4: 200–20.

Davies, C. (1984) 'General practitioners and the pull of prevention', *Sociology of Health and Illness*, 6: 267–89.

Davies, C. (1987) 'Viewpoint: things to come; the NHS in the next decade', *Sociology of Health and Illness*, 9: 302–17.

Day, P. and Klein, R. (1986) 'Controlling the gatekeepers', *Journal of Royal College of General Practitioners*, 36: 129–30.

Derber, C. (1984) 'Physicians and their sponsors: the new medical relations of production', in J. McKinlay (ed.), *Issues in the Political Economy of Health Care*. New York: Tavistock. pp. 217–56.

Dex, S. (1985) *The Sexual Division of Work*. Brighton: Wheatsheaf.

DH [Department of Health] (1989a) *Working for Patients*. London: HMSO, Cm 555.

DH (1989b) 'Medical and dental staffing prospects in the NHS in England and Wales', *Health Trends*, 21: 99–106.

DH (1990) *Health and Personal Social Services Statistics for England*. London: HMSO.

DH (1991) 'Women doctors and their careers: Report of the Joint Working Party', London.

DH/DHSS *National Medical Staff Tables: England and Wales*. (Published annually) London.

DHSS [Department of Health and Social Security] (1983) *NHS Management Enquiry*. London: HMSO. (Griffiths Report.)

DHSS (1986) *Primary Health Care: an Agenda for Discussion*. London: HMSO, Cmnd 9771.

DHSS (1987a) *Promoting Better Health: the Government's Programme for Improving Primary Health Care*. London: HMSO, Cm 249.

DHSS (1987b) *Hospital Medical Staffing – Achieving a Balance-Plan for Action*. London.

Dohler, M. (1989) 'Physicians' professional autonomy in the welfare state', in G. Freddi and J.W. Bjorkman (eds), *Controlling Medical Professionals: the Comparative Politics of Health Governance*. London: Sage. pp. 178–97.

Ehrenreich, B. and English, D. (1974) *Complaints and Disorders: the Sexual Politics of Sickness*. Westbury, NY: Glass Mountain Pamphlet No. 2.

Elston, M. A. (1977a) 'Women in the medical profession: whose problem?', in M. Stacey, M. Reid, C. Heath and R. Dingwall (eds), *Health and the Division of Labour*. London: Croom Helm. pp. 115–38.

Elston, M. A. (1977b) 'Medical autonomy: challenge and response', in K. Barnard and K. Lee (eds), *Conflicts in the National Health Service*. London: Croom Helm. pp. 26–51.

Elston, M. A. (1980) 'Medicine: half our future doctors?', in R. Silverstone and A. Ward (eds), *Careers of Professional Women*. London: Croom Helm. pp. 99–139.

Elston, M. A. (1986) 'Women doctors in the British health services: a sociological study of their careers and opportunities'. Unpublished PhD thesis, University of Leeds.

Elston, M. A. (1991) 'The politics of professional power: medicine in a changing health service', in J. Gabe, M. Calnan and M. Bury (eds), *The Sociology of the Health Service*. London: Routledge. pp. 58–88.

Field, M. (1988) 'The position of the Soviet physician: the bureaucratic professional', *Milbank Quarterly*, 66, Suppl. 2: 182–202.

Freddi, G. and Bjorkman, J.W. (eds) (1989) *Controlling Medical Professionals: the Comparative Politics of Health Governance*. London: Sage.

Freidson, E. (1970) *Profession of Medicine*. New York: Dodd, Mead.

Freidson, E. (1980) *Doctoring Together*. Chicago: University of Chicago Press.

Freidson, E. (1983) 'The theory of professions: state of the art', in R. Dingwall and P. Lewis (eds), *The Sociology of the Professions*. London: Macmillan.

Freidson, E. (1985) 'The reorganization of the medical profession', *Medical Care Review*, 42: 11–35.

Freidson, E. (1986) 'The medical profession in transition', in L.H. Aiken and D. Mechanic (eds), *Applications of Social Science to Clinical Medicine and Health Policy*. New Brunswick: Rutgers University Press. pp. 63–79.

Gabe, J., Calnan, M.W. and Bury, M.R. (eds) (1991) *The Sociology of the Health Service*. London: Routledge.

Gamarnikow, E. (1978) 'Sexual division of labour: the case of nursing', in A. Kuhn and A-M. Wolpe (eds), *Feminism and Materialism*. London: Routledge. pp. 96–123.

Ginzberg, E. (ed.) (1986) *From Physician Shortage to Patient Shortage: the Uncertain Future of Medical Practice*. Boulder: Westview.

Hakim, C. (1979) 'Occupational segregation', Research Paper No. 9. London: Dept of Employment.

Ham, C. J. (1981) *Policy-making in the National Health Service*. London: Macmillan.

Harrison, S. and Schulz, R. (1989) 'Clinical autonomy in the United Kingdom and the United States: Contrasts and convergence', in G. Freddi and J.W. Bjorkman (eds), *Controlling Medical Professionals: the Comparative Politics of Health Governance*. London: Sage. pp. 198–209.

Harvey, S. and Judge, K. (1988) *Community Physicians and Community Medicine*. London: King's Fund Institute Research Report No. 1.

Haug, M. (1976) 'The erosion of professional authority: a crosscultural inquiry in the case of the physician', *Milbank Memorial Fund Quarterly*, 54: 83–106.

Haug, M. (1988) 'A re-examination of the hypothesis of deprofessionalization', *The Milbank Quarterly*, 66, Suppl. 2: 48–56.

Hearn, J. (1982) 'Notes on patriarchy, professionalization and the semi-professions', *Sociology*, 16: 184–201.

Hirschman, A. O. (1970) *Exit, Voice and Loyalty*. Cambridge, Mass.: Harvard University Press.

Honigsbaum, F. (1979) *The Division in British Medicine*. London: Kogan Page.

Hunter, D. (1991) 'Managing medicine: a response to the crisis', *Social Science and Medicine*, 32: 441–8.

Hutt, R., Parsons, D. and Pearson, R. (1979) *The Determinants of Doctors' Career Decisions*. Brighton: Institute of Manpower Studies.

Jefferys, M. and Sachs, H. (1983) *Rethinking General Practice: Dilemmas in Primary Health Care*. London: Tavistock.

Johnson, M. L. and Elston, M. A. (1980) 'Medical careers: an end of grant report prepared for the Social Science Research Council'.

Johnson, T. J. (1972) *Professions and Power*. London: Macmillan.

Klein, R. (1983) *The Politics of the National Health Service*. London: Longman.

Larkin, G. (1983) *Occupational Monopoly and Modern Medicine*. London: Tavistock.

Larkin, G. (1988) 'Medical dominance in Britain: image and historical reality', *The Milbank Quarterly*, 66, Suppl. 2: 117–31.

Larson, M. S. (1977) *The Rise of Professionalism*. Berkeley: University of California Press.

Lawrence, B. (1987) 'The fifth dimension: gender and general practice', in A. Spencer and D. Podmore (eds), *In a Man's World: Essays on Women in Male-Dominated Professions*. London: Tavistock.

Leeson, J. and Gray, J. (1978) *Women and Medicine*. London: Tavistock.

Lewis, J. (1982) *The Politics of Motherhood*. London: Croom Helm.

Lewis, J. (1987) *What Price Community Medicine?* Brighton: Harvester.

Light, D. and Levine, S. (1988) 'The changing character of the medical profession', *Milbank Quarterly*, 66, Suppl. 2: 10–33.

Lorber, J. (1984) *Women Physicians*. London: Tavistock.

McKinlay, J. (1988) 'Introduction to "The changing character of the medical profession"', *Milbank Quarterly*, 66, Suppl. 2: 1–9.

McKinlay, J. and Arches, J. (1985) 'Towards the proletarianization of physicians', *International Journal of Health Services*, 15: 161–95.

McKinlay, J. and Stoeckle, J. (1988) 'Corporatization and the social transformation of doctoring', *International Journal of Health Services*, 18: 191–205.

Ministry of Health (1944) *Report of an Interdepartmental Committee on Medical Schools*. London: HMSO. (Goodenough Report)

Oakley, A. (1976) 'Wisewoman and medicine man', in J.Mitchell and A. Oakley (eds), *The Rights and Wrongs of Women*. London: Penguin

Parkhouse, J. (1991) *Doctors' Careers*. London: Routledge.

Parsons, T. (1954) 'The professions and social structure', in *Essays in Sociological Theory*. New York: Free Press.

Ridsdale, L. (1990) 'General practitioners' workload', *British Medical Journal*, 301: 455–6.

Riska, E. (1988) 'The professional status of physicians in the Nordic countries', *Milbank Quarterly*, 66, Suppl. 2: 133–47.

Roberts, J. (1991) 'Junior doctors' years: training not education', *British Medical Journal*, 302: 225–8.

Rosenthal, M.M. (1987) *Dealing with Medical Malpractice: the British and Swedish Experience*. London: Tavistock.

Royal Commission on Medical Education (1968) *Report*. London: HMSO, Cmnd. 3569.

Rueschemeyer, D. (1986) *Power and the Division of Labour*. Cambridge: Polity Press.

Savage, W. (1989) *A Savage Enquiry*. London: Virago.

Stacey, M. and Davies, C. (1983) *Division of Labour in Child Health Care: Final Report for the SSRC* (mimeo). Coventry: University of Warwick.

Starr, P. (1982) *The Social Transformation of American Medicine*. New York: Basic Books.

Stevens, R. (1986) 'The future of the medical profession', in E. Ginzberg (ed.), *From Physician Shortage to Patient Shortage: the Uncertain Future of Medical Practice*. Boulder: Westview. pp. 75–93.

Strong, P. M. and Robinson, J. (1990) *The NHS Under New Management*. Milton Keynes: Open University Press.

UCCA [Universities Central Council for Admissions] (1970–) *Annual Reports*. Cheltenham.

UGC [University Grants Committee] (1975) *Annual Report*. London.

3

Why women physicians will never be true equals in the American medical profession

Judith Lorber

By virtue of their medical degree, all physicians are supposed to be equal in their authority over and responsibility for patients' treatment. In the 1940s, Oswald Hall (1946), in a study of the medical community in Providence, Rhode Island, found that a physician's policy-making power and access to medical resources depended on whether or not the physician was a member of the local medical elite. To become part of the inner elite, a physician had to have the sponsorship of an established member. A second circle, not quite as favoured with good hospital affiliations and referrals of patients, consisted of what he called 'friendly outsiders'. Most of the women physicians in the community were friendly outsiders – that is, not members of the inner circle.

Other groups of physicians in the United States, regardless of the quality of their work, have not been sponsored for membership in the inner circles of the medical profession by their colleagues (Starr, 1982). These have been the members of groups with disfavoured social characteristics – Jews, Catholics, blacks and those with foreign medical educations. David Solomon (1961), in his study of medical practices in Chicago, found, however, that Jews and Catholics were able to develop their own medical communities, with patient referrals and hospital affiliations. Through federal funding, blacks had Howard Medical School and tax-supported hospitals to work in (Moldow, 1987). Black women physicians had no medical community of their own, and white women physicians, after the 1930s, were never more than 'friendly colleagues' to the men of any group – WASP, Jewish, Catholic or black.

Today, women physicians in the United States are approaching a substantial minority – about 30 per cent of all practising physicians (Eisenberg, 1989; Relman, 1989). While they have an active association – the American Medical Women's Association – and caucuses in specialty associations, as well as conferences and a journal, they have not developed their own colleague networks or hospitals, despite advice to that effect from radical feminist physicians (Howell, 1975). All-women clinics were run by advocates of the women's self-help movement, which relegated the women physicians on their staff to minor, legally necessary roles (Ruzek, 1978). Women physicians, therefore, unlike men physicians with devalued social characteristics, have had few places to show their leadership capabilities.

American women physicians are, of course, no longer subject to the formal discrimination that discouraged application to medical school, denied them internships and residencies, and tracked them into specialties that tended to be less lucrative and prestigious. Nor are they openly barred from staff appointments in good hospitals, from membership in group medical practices, or from heading laboratories and services. However, as in other professions, there has been a 'glass ceiling' on their upward mobility. Women physicians who aspire to the very visible top tier of positions hit invisible barriers when they try to attain them. As a result, women physicians rarely direct large, prestigious services, are rarely heads of teaching hospitals, and are almost never heads of large medical centres. For example, when the University of California named Mary A. Piccone its first woman head of a teaching hospital and medical centre, it was unusual enough to warrant a newspaper story (*New York Times*, 1988).

This chapter will discuss the role of women physicians in American medicine in the 1980s and 1990s, and will argue that the bureaucratization of medical practice and the increasing control of medical decisions by the government and other third-party payers will not impact equally on all members of the medical profession. As in the past, while all physicians may have equal (albeit lesser) authority over and responsibility for their patients' treatment, physicians continue to be unequal in their control over medical resources and priorities.

My argument is that, as in other professions, there is a 'glass ceiling' on women physicians' upward mobility. They are kept from top-level positions, I will argue, through the subtle process of a kind of colleague boycott – not keeping them out entirely, but not including them in ways that allow them to replace the senior members of the medical community. This process is the 'Salieri phenomenon' – a combination of faint praise and subtle denigration of their abilities to lead which delegitimates women physicians' bids to compete for positions of great authority.[1] The reason men are so reluctant to allow women into the inner circles, I contend, is their fear that if too many women become leaders, the profession will 'tip' and become women's work – and men will lose prestige, income and authority.

Stratification within the medical profession allows all holders of certification to work; thus, their training is not wasted, nor can the profession be accused of open discrimination. The policy-making positions of great authority, however, are still held by members of the socially dominant group, and it is their values and priorities that prevail.

The 'glass ceiling'

The 'glass ceiling' has been reported for every male-dominated profession and occupation that American women have entered in increasing numbers in the last twenty years (e.g. Adelson, 1988; Berg, 1988; Blum and Smith, 1988; Goldstein, 1988). Women are kept out of the top positions by sexism that is ingrained in men's attitudes and built into the structure of career mobility (Reskin, 1988). If a woman becomes a mother, she is out of the running for top positions, even when she works twelve-hour days and weekends, because professions are structured on the concept of the professional's total devotion to the career (Hunt and Hunt, 1982; Lorber, 1984). But professions are happy to have hard-working professional employees who will not compete with dominant-group men for the power, privilege, authority – and income – that being at the top means.

The process of creating these companies of professional unequals was beautifully summed up by a front-page story in the *New York Times* entitled, 'Women in the Law Say Path is Limited by "Mommy Track"' (Kingson, 1988), which argued that in the prestigious law firms in the United States, women who took advantage of flexible working hours, child care and lenient maternity leave were out of the running for the competition for partnership. According to the article, women lawyers feel that '. . . the highest barriers . . . are the ones that cannot be legislated away. They are the traditional attitudes that reflect a double-edged sexism, attitudes that say a man must give everything to his career or be considered weak, and that a woman cannot give everything to her career and still be a good wife or mother.'

While it is true that women physicians with children spend more time with their families than men physicians with children (44.3 to 28.9 hours per week in a sample of 30 young women and 96 young men physicians), the difference in practice hours was not enormous (43.5 per week for women, 52.7 per week for men) (Grant et al., 1990). The *perception* of differential commitment resulted from the men physicians with children spending more time at work than with their families (by about 13 hours), and doing so deliberately. The mothers in this study satisfactorily adjusted their working hours; the fathers did not: 'Although fathers apparently desired more hours with families, they seemingly experienced and acquiesced more often to self-imposed demands to work more hours and forfeit family time' (Grant et al., 1990: 46).

This perception that married women physicians with children are less committed to their careers than childless women and all male physicians justifies keeping them out of positions of authority in the medical profession (cf. Constanza, 1989; Levinson et al., 1989). I would argue that the work is structured to keep them out. It is possible to integrate a variety of work schedules into even a primary-care faculty practice, as Wheeler and colleagues (1990) reported when describing their experiences in their urban community health centre that is also a major residency training site for a university hospital. In addition to family care, including obstetrics, practitioners working 30–40 hours per week taught and supervised residents, instructed medical students, shared responsibility for student and resident evaluations, participated in departmental activities, including committees, as well as in community and statewide organizations and task forces, and did research, published and presented papers at national meetings. The level of career participation was not accidental but the result of careful attention to professional advancement, regular communication within the organization, and participatory scheduling. In sum, all workers in this medical organization were considered highly committed professionals, and the work was structured to foster, not impede, that commitment.

However, as feasible as such part-time work structures are, it is unlikely that they will be widely implemented unless married women with children refuse to work without them. Structuring work in the usual way, as if all physicians worked 50–60 hour weeks, advantages those without childcare responsibilities – primarily male physicians – and it is unlikely that they would voluntarily give up their competitive edge, especially as they may increasingly become a minority in the profession.

Why are men physicians so reluctant to allow substantial numbers of women into the elite inner circles or to support the ambitions of more than a select safe few for leadership positions? Competition is one reason. Yet other men are competitors, too. Catholic and Jewish physicians, once also subject to discriminatory quotas in American medical schools, are more successfully integrated than women into the prestigious ranks of the profession. I argue that male physicians feel the profession will become feminized – will 'tip' – if too many women are heads of medical centres, chiefs of prestigious services and directors of policy-making bodies. Just as whites seem to fear neighbourhood tipping when too many blacks move in, male physicians in the United States may be afraid that if too many women become leaders of the profession, the profession will become women's work – and the men in it will lose prestige, income, their control over access and resources (cf. Carter and Carter, 1981) and their masculine differentness (Reskin, 1988).

Preserving gender difference

In an address to the 1987 Berkshire Conference on the History of Women, Alice Kessler-Harris (1988: 245) said of comparable worth that it '. . . challenges the legitimacy of gender lines. It purports to delegitimize one element of the market pattern – namely, sex. The end result would be to equate female and male workers; to threaten a male worker's sense of self, pride, and masculinity; and to challenge the authority of the basic institutions that touch all aspects of social and political life.' To pay women and men equivalently would, Kessler-Harris points out, raise the value of '. . . those presumed qualities of womanhood – nurturance, community and relational abilities'.

The same erosion of gender differences would occur if women and men were equally to be found at the top levels of the prestigious professions. To promote women and men physicians equivalently would mean that those presumed qualities of womanhood – nurturance, community and relational abilities – were as valuable to those in positions of authority as they are to those who give primary care (and, of course, bedside care). However, the American medical profession today is far from a true company of equals, and prevalent informal discriminatory practices against women indicate that it is never likely to be one.

The current climate in the medical profession

A study of the career development of 176 women and 106 men recent medical school graduates found that as medical students, in postgraduate training, and in practice, women perceived more career hindrances than men did (Cohen et al., 1988). According to the authors, 'The primary disadvantages perceived by women during both medical school and postgraduate training are sexist attitudes and behavior and being taken less seriously than men' (Cohen et al., 1988: 151). Of the 78 women reporting a gender disadvantage in practice, 31 per cent felt they were taken less seriously than men, and 21 per cent reported overt sexism. A 1985–6 survey of the women and men graduates of Howard University College of Medicine found that for the 168 women respondents, 94 per cent of whom were black, sexism was as much of a problem in their career advancement as racism (Titus-Dillon and Johnson, 1989).

A study done in the early 1980s (Grant, 1988), based on interviews with 173 men and 97 women medical school seniors from five successive graduating classes of a leading midwestern medical school, found that male doctors on the medical school faculty and on the staffs of teaching hospitals still feel free to be openly sexist towards women medical students. Some of the older men, especially those with physician daughters, were great supporters of their women students, so they seemed to exhibit both ends of spectrum. Since both the sexism and the support women physicians get from older male physicians early in their careers fades as they advance, it is more important to look at their future colleagues – their fellow students and the residents a few years ahead of them – to predict whether the medical profession will change substantially in the direction of real gender equality.

Here, the data were more disturbing. In many ways, the male residents were the source of the most sexism   teasing women students, subjecting them to endurance tests and sexual harassment. To quote Linda Grant of the study:

> Several [of the women students] suggested that it was the residents, only a few years ahead of the women students in their careers, who felt the most threatened by the women students. One student felt the problem was particularly acute in obstetrics/gynecology and pediatrics, areas where women are the primary consumers of medical services and where many patients now explicitly request treatment by women doctors. (Grant, 1988: 115)

Some men students said they were the victims of reverse discrimination because of patients' preferences for women physicians. They also expressed resentment at what they felt were the effects of affirmative action in allowing less qualified women to be accepted to medical school – in actuality, the admission credentials of the men and women students were virtually equal. Male classmates were likely to attribute blame to the women targets of gender discrimination, and, according to the women students, to sometimes join in the teasing, and to be generally oblivious of subtle sexism. However, the higher the class ranking of the man, the more likely he was to have been aware of gender discrimination toward women classmates.

So, unless this school is atypical, what researchers have found in other settings is true in medicine – as more women enter an occupation, and as they are increasingly successful as competitors, there is less support from their male peers and immediate superiors

(South et al., 1982a; Zimmer, 1988). That is, while established and very secure men can treat women colleagues as equals, those who see them as formidable competitors will use social weapons to keep them down.

Some of these weapons are described by Benokraitis and Feagin in *Modern Sexism* (1986): condescending chivalry, supportive discouragement, friendly harassment, subjective objectification, radiant devaluation, liberated sexism, benevolent exploitation, considerate domination and collegial exclusion. What is in actuality structured and institutionalized sexism is often transformed into women's seemingly free choices to limit their ambitions, not work too many hours, and put their families before their professions. Forgotten are the nasty remarks about women as assertive competitors, the hostility to women who become mothers, and the dismal marriage and divorce statistics for well-educated and successful women; ignored are the long hours and hard work women actually put into their jobs (Bielby and Bielby, 1988; Weisman and Teitelbaum, 1987).

Women physicians' future place

Where women physicians supposedly fit best into American medicine in the 1980s and 1990s is very clear if we heed some influential policy-makers. It is as salaried workers in third-party-payment group practices and HMOs (Bowman and Gross, 1986; Ehrensing, 1986; Kroser, 1987; Lanska et al., 1984; Lisoskie, 1986; Lorber, 1987a).

The more bureaucratized practice of medicine will not create a company of equals any more than did solo fee-for-service medicine. The bureaucratization of medical practice and the increasing control of medical decisions by the government and other third-party payers will not impact equally on all members of the medical profession. As in the past, while all physicians may have equal (albeit lesser) authority over and responsibility for their patients' treatment, physicians will continue to be unequal in their control over medical resources and priorities, and women physicians are likely to be more unequal than others. Even those who ascend to top positions of authority are likely to get positions of lesser power than those held by their male peers. The woman physician who was appointed to head the University of California Medical Center, for instance, was not given the additional position held by her male predecessor – that of vice chancellor for administrative and business services at the campus where the medical centre was located, a position which gave him greater control over allocation of resources.

A stratified structure of practice will continue. When American medicine was predominantly solo fee-for-service, the profession was stratified through limited access to elite medical schools and teaching hospitals and lucrative specialties. Now that it is more bureaucratized, the profession is stratified through limited access to policy-making positions in HMOs, hospitals, insurance agencies, and city, state, and national governments (Freidson, 1983). Instead of inner circles, friendly colleagues and boycotted loners, the profession is stratifying into powerful administrators, policy-makers and rank-and-file professional employees (Freidson, 1986: 134–57). As in the past, when their numbers were few, women will be heavily over-represented for the duration of their careers in positions where they have discretion and autonomy in their treatment of patients but where they do not control budgets, allocate resources, or determine the overall direction of the organizations for which they work. The need for reliable, hard-working, non-rebellious professionally satisfied rank-and-file professional employees will be neatly solved, as will the problem of what to do about the increasing numbers of women physicians.

If women physicians do not advance in significant numbers from rank-and-file professional employees to management positions, they will not be any more equal in the medical profession than in the past. For, as Freidson (1986: 154) says in *Professional Powers*, '. . . that power to allocate resources determines the particular kind of work that can be done and limits the way work can be done'.

What resources does management allocate that are so crucial to professional work? According to Freidson, these are: size of professional staff, caseload, and who is to be serviced – '. . . the critical variables are the number and type of tasks performed in a working day, the number and type of cases to be handled, and the supportive resources to be made available to aid performance – the rules of eligibility that determine, for example, task flow, equipment, space, and assisting personnel' (1986: 169). Physicians who cannot control how many patients they see and with what problems, and have little say in the allocation of supporting resources, are likely to end up doing routinized work. For example, an Israeli study found that primary-care women physicians in national health service clinics with heavy caseloads were least accepting of patients' initiatives and physician-challenging behaviour (Shuval et al., 1989). The most accepting were hospital-based specialists with lighter caseloads, who were most likely to be men.

While American women physicians who form their own group practices can shape them to be responsive to patients' needs and sensitive to feminist issues (Candib, 1987, 1988; Wheeler et al., 1990), those who work for larger third-party-payment HMOs as rank-and-file employees cannot. More important, women physicians without high-level administrative positions as chiefs of service in hospitals or deans of medical schools are unlikely to make any impact on the delivery of services or the production and dissemination of knowledge (cf. Freidson, 1986: 185–230).

The important questions in assessing whether or not all types of physicians (by race, religion, social class, gender and philosophy of practice) have equal opportunities to shape the profession are, according to Freidson:

> Who . . . creates, sustains, and alters the official framework of professional activities – the credential system that establishes staffing standards for employers and standards for the content of professional training? And who establishes the standards that define the substance of what is acceptable professional work? Who negotiates with the state to secure the official adoption of professional standards across work settings? (1986: 185–6)

Not numbers but strategic and central positions in the elite sector translate into the power to transform professional practice (Martin, 1985; Martin and Osmond, 1982; South et al., 1982b).

Will the future replicate the past?

In the nineteenth century, hospitals and clinics run by American women physicians used the extant technology, but structured the delivery of care 'with a heart' (Drachman, 1984; Morantz and Zschoche, 1980; Morantz-Sanchez, 1985). Women physicians were more alert to the potential for the spread of post-partum infection and to the social difficulties of unmarried mothers. Gloria Moldow's (1987) history of black and white women physicians in Washington, DC, at the end of the nineteenth century describes the female medical community there. Denied access to the dispensaries and clinics that gave novice doctors clinical experience and contacts, white women physicians set up four medical infirmaries. They were run for mostly women and children patients, and offered free and low-cost care. Only one, the Woman's Clinic, was completely staffed by women, and it was the only one that survived the rise of the scientifically oriented, better-equipped university hospitals, which became, in Moldow's words, 'no-woman's land'.

Moldow shows that the closing of the doors of the medical community to women happened before the findings of the Flexner Report were published in 1910. Both Flexner's recommendations that most of the American medical schools should be closed, and the escalating discrimination against women and blacks by established white medical men, were reactions to that era's 'oversupply' of physicians. The project of professionalization, high-minded as it may have seemed, was rooted in fear of competition. As Moldow says:

> Women appeared to be gaining ground in the medical profession just when their male colleagues were growing concerned about overcrowding in the field. Physicians in the nation's capital – as elsewhere – began to take action to limit the number of graduating doctors in order to sustain a fair income and a high level of status within the profession. Women were primary targets among those considered superfluous. (1987: 15)

After the First World War, when women got the vote in the United States, they helped to pass the Sheppard-Towner Act, which, in 1921, set up state and federally funded parental and child health centres throughout the country. These centres were staffed by women physicians and public health nurses, and they offered low-cost medical services and preventive care and education in maternal and child health. By 1929, in the face of the desperate need of its members for paying patients during the Depression, the American Medical Association, headed by men in solo fee-for-service practice, led the fight to deny further funding to the Sheppard-Towner clinics (Costin, 1983).

Today, in the late twentieth century, although women physicians are again a significant minority of obstetricians and gynaecologists and are sought out by clients as private practitioners and by administrators as valuable additions to group practices, they are in positions of authority only in their own solo or small group practices, where they are able to work differently from men physicians (Candib, 1987, 1988; Lorber, 1985). In training in hospitals, where few women physicians determine curriculum and where teaching physicians and senior residents tend to be men, they must suppress any criticism and work in standard, high-technology ways (Harrison, 1983; Scully, 1980). The high rates of routinized amniocentesis (Rothman, 1986) and hysterectomy (Fisher, 1986) and the use of *in vitro* fertilization in couples where the woman has a normal reproductive system but the man is infertile (Lorber, 1987b) are some examples of the effects of the continued domination of male doctors in American medicine. These procedures, not incidentally, can be quite profitable.

In sum, the structure of medical practice in the United States since the late nineteenth century has been stratified, and physicians have filled positions in that structure not randomly, but according to their race, religion, social class and gender. The lines of discrimination may shift somewhat, but the battle of the dominant white male majority to maintain control over access, resources and patients has not changed. Black, Catholic, Jewish and working-class male physicians have become more integrated into the medical profession, but women physicians are still vulnerable – and *not* because they limit their ambitions and practice hours and put their families first. If that were true, men physicians would have nothing about which to worry.

It is rather the opposite – American women physicians are formidable competitors for private patients and group-practice appointments because patients feel they offer a different practice style; they successfully compete for institutional and federal funding of clinical research; they do not turn down the chance to head services. But they are vulnerable because the current structure of American medicine will be used against them.

In the mid-nineteenth century, free-for-all medicine allowed women an equal chance to compete, and American men physicians fought bitterly (and unsuccessfully) to keep them out of medical schools, medical associations and hospitals. When the structure of medical practice changed, it was used against women, as a means of exclusion. The same is true today. In the 1960s, when American medicine was opening to greater access for patients and more varied practice styles, and money was freer, the doors of medical schools and hospitals opened to women. Now that eligibility for medical services is tightening and money is scarce, control over access, resources and paying patients is again a battleground (Hafferty, 1986; Lanska et al., 1984; Rushing, 1985). This time, because of anti-discrimination laws, American women physicians cannot be subject to 5 per cent quotas, but there will continue to be unacknow-ledged gender discrimination in men's efforts to hold on to their dominant position.

If the medical profession in the United States loses its dominance in the delivery of health-care services somewhere in the next 25 years, the profession *is* likely to tip into a women's profession. The tipping may be blamed on the influx of women, but the sequence goes in the other direction: as a profession becomes one of high demand for services which are moderately remunerated and increasingly govern-ment-regulated, it loses its attractiveness to high-status men, leaving an occupational niche that is filled by high-status women and lower-status men.

Current medical school enrolments already reflect this pattern. Over the past five years, the proportion of white male first-year students has declined by 13 per cent (Jonas and Etzel, 1988). However, the administrators and policy-makers are likely to con-tinue to be white men because the number of minority male physicians is small. Despite being a substantial proportion of the American medical profession, women physicians are unlikely to become a substantial proportion of the leadership because of a combination of institutionalized and informal sexist practices. The structure of work and family life still does not allow women with family responsibilities to add overtime administrative responsibilities or policy committee work to their allocated client contact hours (Ehrensing, 1986). Women who remain single or enter into childless dual-career marriages could be formidable competitors for men, but as I have argued, informal discriminatory practices are likely to present equally formidable barriers to their rise to the top.

In sum, as the medical profession in the United States comes to resemble the more bureaucratized systems of other countries (Elston, 1977, 1980; Lapidus, 1978; Shuval, 1983), the two-tier system will solidify – women physicians will do general practice, family medicine and primary care; white men physicians will allocate resources and make policy.

Acknowledgements

The editors would like to thank the author and JAI Press for permission to reprint this chapter which originally appeared as 'Can women physicians ever be equal in the American medical profession?' in Judith A. Levy (ed.), *Current Research in Occupations and Professions*, Vol. 6, JAI Press, 1991. pp. 25–37.

Note

1 In Peter Shaffer's play, *Amadeus* (1980), Mozart's lack of social graces gives Salieri, the court composer and gatekeeper of musical patronage, the opportunity to block the young musician's career advancement, not by direct opposition, but by lukewarm support. The effects of sponsorship and other processes of informal career advancement for women physicians are discussed at length in Lorber (1984).

References

Adelson, Andrea (1988) 'Women still find bias in engineering', *New York Times*, 8 March.
Benokraitis, Nijole V. and Feagin, Joe R. (1986) *Modern Sexism: Blatant, Subtle, and Covert Discrimination*. Englewood Cliffs, NJ: Prentice-Hall.
Berg, Eric N. (1988) 'The big eight: still a male bastion', *New York Times*, 14 July.
Bielby, Denise and Bielby, William T. (1988) 'She works hard for the money: household responsibilities and the allocation of work effort', *American Journal of Sociology*, 93: 1031–59.
Blum, Linda and Smith, Vicki (1988) 'Women's mobility in the corporation: a critique of the politics of optimism', *Signs: Journal of Women in Culture and Society*, 13: 528–45.
Bowman, Marjorie and Gross, Marcy Lynn (1986) 'Overview of research on women in medicine – issues for public policymakers', *Public Health Report*, 101: 513–20.
Candib, Lucy M. (1987) 'What doctors tell about themselves to patients: implications for intimacy and reciprocity in the relationship', *Family Medicine*, 19: 23–30.

Candib, Lucy M. (1988) 'Ways of knowing in family medicine: contributions from a feminist perspective', *Family Medicine,* 20: 133–6.

Carter, Michael J. and Carter, Susan Boslego (1981) 'Women's recent progress in the professions or, women get a ticket to ride after the gravy train has left the station', *Feminist Studies,* 7: 477–504.

Cohen, May, Woodward, Christel A. and Ferrier, Barbara M. (1988) 'Factors influencing career development: do men and women differ?', *Journal of the American Women's Medical Association,* 43: 142–54.

Constanza, Mary E. (1989) 'Women in medical leadership', *Journal of the American Medical Association,* 44: 185–6.

Costin, Lela B. (1983) 'Women and physicians: the 1930 White House conference on children', *Social Work,* March–April: 108–14.

Drachman, Virginia (1984) *Hospital with a Heart.* Ithaca, NY: Cornell University Press.

Ehrensing, R.H. (1986) 'Attitudes towards women physicians: a multi-specialty group practice perspective', *The Internist,* 27 (March): 17–18.

Eisenberg, Carola (1989) 'Medicine is no longer a man's profession', *New England Journal of Medicine,* 321 (November 30): 1542–4.

Elston, Mary Ann (1977) 'Women in the medical profession: whose problem?' in M. Stacey, M. Reid, C. Heath and R. Dingwall (eds), *Health and the Division of Labour.* London: Croom Helm. pp. 115–38.

Elston, Mary Ann (1980) 'Medicine: half our future doctors?', in R. Silverstone and A. Ward (eds), *The Careers of Professional Women.* London: Croom Helm. pp. 99–139.

Fisher, Sue (1986) *In the Patient's Best Interest.* New Brunswick, NJ: Rutgers University Press.

Freidson, Eliot (1983) 'The reorganization of the profession by regulation', *Law and Human Behavior,* 7: 279–90.

Freidson, Eliot (1986) *Professional Powers.* Chicago: University of Chicago Press.

Goldstein, Tom (1988) 'Women in the law aren't yet equal partners', *New York Times,* 12 February.

Grant, Linda (1988) 'The gender climate in medical school: perspectives of women and men students', *Journal of the American Medical Women's Association,* 43: 109–10, 115.

Grant, Linda, Simpson, Layne A. and Rong, Xue Lan (1990) 'Gender, parenthood, and work hours of physicians', *Journal of Marriage and the Family,* 52: 39–49.

Hafferty, Fred W. (1986) 'Physician oversupply as a socially constructed reality', *Journal of Health and Social Behavior,* 27: 358–69.

Hall, Oswald (1946) 'The informal organization of the medical profession', *Canadian Journal of Economics and Political Science,* 12: 30–41.

Harrison, Michelle (1983) *A Woman in Residence.* New York: Penguin.

Howell, Mary C. (1975) 'A woman's health school?', *Social Policy,* 6 (Sept./Oct.): 340–7.

Hunt, Janet G. and Hunt, Larry L. (1982) 'The dualities of careers and families: new integrations or new polarizations?', *Social Problems,* 29: 499–510.

Jonas, Harry S. and Etzel, Sylvia I. (1988) 'Undergraduate medical education', *Journal of the American Medical Association,* 260: 1063–71.

Kessler–Harris, Alice (1988) 'The just price, the free market, and the value of women', *Feminist Studies,* 14: 235–50.

Kingson, Jennifer A. (1988) 'Women in the law say path is limited by "Mommy track"', *New York Times,* 8 August.

Kroser, Lila Stein (1987) 'The growing influence of women in medicine', in David B. Nash (ed.), *Future Practice Alternative in Medicine*. New York and Tokyo: Igaku-Shoin. pp. 103–37.

Lanska, Mary Jo, Lanska, Douglas J. and Rimm, Alfred A. (1984) 'Effect of rising percentage of female physicians on projections of physician supply', *Journal of Medical Education*, 59: 849–55.

Lapidus, Gail (1978) *Women in Soviet Society*. Berkeley, CA: University of California Press.

Levinson, Wendy, Tolle, Susan W. and Lewis, Charles (1989) 'Women in academic medicine: Combining career and family', *New England Journal of Medicine*, 321 (30 November): 1511–17.

Lisoskie, Shelly (1986) 'Why work fewer hours?' *Journal of the American Medical Women's Association*, 41: 73, 90.

Lorber, Judith (1984) *Women Physicians: Careers, Status, and Power*. New York and London: Tavistock.

Lorber, Judith (1985) 'More women physicians: will it mean more humane health care?', *Social Policy*, 16 (Summer): 50–4.

Lorber, Judith (1987a) 'A welcome to a crowded field: where will the new women physicians fit in?', *Journal of the American Medical Women's Association*, 42: 149–52.

Lorber, Judith (1987b) '*In vitro* fertilization and gender politics', *Women and Health*, 13: 117–33.

Martin, Patricia Yanccy (1985) 'Group sex compositions in work organizations: a structural-normative model', in S. Bacharach and S. Mitchell (eds), *Research in the Sociology of Organizations*. Greenwich, CT: JAI Press. pp. 311–49.

Martin, Patricia Yancey and Osmond, Marie Withers (1982) 'Gender and exploitation: Resources, structure, and rewards in cross-sex social exchange', *Sociological Focus*, 15: 403–16.

Moldow, Gloria (1987) *Women Doctors in Gilded-Age Washington: Race, Gender, and Professionalization*. Urbana and Chicago: University of Illinois Press.

Morantz, Regina M. and Zschoche, Sue (1980) 'Professionalism, feminism, and gender roles: a comparative study of nineteenth century medical therapeutics', *Journal of American History*, 68: 568–88.

Morantz-Sanchez, Regina M. (1985) *Sympathy and Science: Women Physicians in American Medicine*. New York: Oxford University Press.

New York Times (1988) 'SUNY aide gets California post', 3 August.

Relman, Arnold S. (1989) 'The changing demography of the medical profession', *New England Journal of Medicine*, 321 (30 November): 1540–1.

Reskin, Barbara F. (1988) 'Bringing the men back in: sex differentiation and the devaluation of women's work', *Gender and Society*, 2: 58–81.

Rothman, Barbara Katz (1986) *The Tentative Pregnancy*. New York: Viking.

Rushing, William A. (1985) 'The supply of physicians and expenditures for health services with implications for the coming physician surplus', *Journal of Health and Social Behavior*, 26: 297–311.

Ruzek, Sheryl B. (1978) *The Women's Health Movement*. New York: Praeger.

Scully, Diana (1980) *Men Who Control Women's Health*. Boston: Houghton Mifflin.

Shaffer, Peter (1980) *Amadeus*. New York: Harper & Row.

Shuval, Judith T. (1983) *Newcomers and Colleagues: Soviet Immigrant Physicians in Israel*. Houston, TX: Cap and Gown Press.

Shuval, Judith T., Javetz, Rachel and Shye, Diana (1989) 'Self-care in Israel: physicians' views and perspectives', *Social Science and Medicine*, 29: 233–44.

Solomon, David (1961) 'Ethnic and class differences among hospitals as contingencies in medical careers', *American Journal of Sociology*, 61: 463–71.

South, Scott J., Bonjean, Charles M., Markham, William T. and Corder, Judy (1982a) 'Social structure and intergroup interaction: men and women of the federal bureaucracy', *American Sociological Review*, 47: 587–99.

South, Scott J., Bonjean, Charles M., Markham, William T. and Corder, Judy (1982b) 'Sex and power in the federal bureaucracy: a comparative analysis of male and female supervisors', *Work and Occupations*, 2: 233–54.

Starr, Paul (1982) *The Social Transformation of American Medicine*. New York: Basic Books.

Titus-Dillon, Pauline Y. and Johnson, Davis G. (1989) 'Female graduates of a predominantly black college of medicine: their characteristics and challenges', *Journal of the American Medical Women's Association*, 44: 175–82.

Weisman, Carol S. and Teitelbaum, Martha A. (1987) 'The work–family role system and physician productivity', *Journal of Health and Social Behavior*, 28: 247–57.

Wheeler, Rachel, Candib, Lucy and Martin, Meredith (1990) 'Part-time doctors: reduced working hours for primary care physicians', *Journal of the American Medical Women's Association*, 45: 47–54.

Zimmer, Lynn (1988) 'Tokenism and women in the workplace: the limits of gender-neutral theory', *Social Problems*, 35: 64–77.

4

Women physicians: a new force in medicine?

Elianne Riska and Katarina Wegar

Today women form a growing proportion of the members of the medical profession, a trend expected to continue in most western countries. This development has raised both critical and optimistic reactions among its observers. The critics have argued that women physicians are unwilling and unable to work as hard as doctors who are men. Support for this contention has been found in studies showing that women physicians work fewer hours per week and tend to take parental leaves (Elston, 1980; Kletke et al., 1990; Uhlenberg and Cooney, 1990). Some have even argued that, because of the lower productivity of women doctors, there is no need to be concerned about an oversupply of doctors in the future (Lanska et al., 1984: 855).

Several feminist scholars have, on the other hand, suggested that the increase of women in the medical profession will gradually eliminate the sexist bias in medical practice and medical science (Ehrenreich and English, 1973; Fee, 1977). It has been assumed that women physicians will guard the rights and interests of female patients by increasing the attention to women's health issues. Furthermore, the increase of women physicians and medical students has also been expected to change the prevalent norms of professional behaviour towards a more holistic and emphatic way of treating patients (Altekruse and McDermott, 1987: 85; Miles, 1991: 157). Only few studies have so far been able to show women physicians as more receptive than their male colleagues to psychosocial aspects of complaints or illnesses. There is some evidence that men and women doctors tend to differ in their style of communicating with patients (Martin et al., 1988) and that women's more patient-oriented style is conducive to allowing psychosocial complaints to surface (Meeuwesen et al., 1991: 1144).

The optimistic view that the mere number of women would radically change professional practice has, however, been challenged by a number of sociologists. Some have pointed to structural factors that tend to influence professional behaviour regardless of the gender of the professional (Kanter, 1977). Others have challenged this structural position and argued that it neglects the extent to which organizational structures are shaped by a male-dominated gender order. The impact and the reproduction of organizational structures, it has been suggested, cannot therefore be analysed in gender-neutral terms (Reskin, 1988; Blum and Smith, 1988; Zimmer, 1988; Stacey, 1988; Acker, 1989; Wharton, 1991).

The future impact of women doctors has been debated mainly in countries where the proportion of women in the medical profession is relatively small. The proportion in Finland has been higher than in any other Nordic or Anglo-American country during the past fifty years. In 1992, women constituted 43 per cent of all practising physicians there, and by the year 2000 they are expected to form the majority (SNAPS, 1986). Both the historical development and the present trend make Finland a suitable case for the examination of the status and impact of women physicians in health care.

The gendered division of labour in medicine: theoretical approaches

During the past ten years, occupational sex segregation has become a central area of interest among feminist scholars. Research on women's position in traditionally male-dominated professions has documented a marked segregation of tasks by gender (Fox and Hesse-Biber, 1984; Acker, 1989; Reskin and Roos, 1990; Crompton and Sanderson, 1990). The growing interest in occupational sex segregation has resulted in a number of studies on women's entry and current position in the medical profession. Research on women physicians in the United States (Carpenter, 1977; Walsh, 1977; Farrell et al., 1979; Rinke, 1981; Morantz et al., 1982; Lorber, 1984; Graves and Thomas, 1985; Drachman, 1986) and Britain (Elston, 1977, 1980; Allen, 1990) has documented a clear sex segregation of tasks within the medical profession. In general, women are over-represented in those areas of medicine that sociologists have characterized as having low professional status, such as general medicine, family medicine, anaesthetics and pediatrics. Further-more, women are more likely to be salaried employees than their male colleagues, who are more likely to be private practitioners. In addition, women physicians are underrepresented as medical educa-tors, researchers, and administrators or policy-makers in the organiz-ation of health care.

For the sex segregation of the labour market in general two types of explanations have been presented: individual and institutional. These explanations can also be applied to illuminate the factors shaping the sex segregation of medical work.

The individual-oriented approach has explained occupational sex segregation in terms of individual but gender-related preferences in occupational and career choices. It is common, for example, in research on medical education to explain the division of labour in medicine by reference to self-selection – that is, to gender-specific preferences and personality traits. Two kinds of explanations for the gender differences in occupational orientation can be identified in this literature. One is the socialization theory suggesting that the socially acquired gender identity will result in an occupational choice that fits and supports the gender stereotype. As observers of women's work have noted, women tend to be assigned 'people work' (Stacey, 1988) or 'emotion work' (Hochschild, 1979; James, 1989) because of their assumed 'natural skills' for this kind of work. The high proportion of women physicians in pediatrics, psychiatry and general practice has, for example, been related to specific gender-related interests and attitudes of female medical students and physicians. Female medical students and physicians have been shown to be more patient-oriented than their male fellows, who tend to be more technically and scientifically oriented (Haavio-Mannila, 1968; Heins et al., 1979; Frey, 1980; Leserman, 1981; Zimny and Shelton, 1982; Bergqvist et al., 1985). Although gender differences in the concern for the patient and in the perceptiveness to social and psychological influences on health and illness have been noted during medical training, research has, however, shown that professional values and behaviour tend to converge among men and women later in medical practice (Martin et al., 1988).

The other type of individual-oriented explanations derive from neo-classical economic theories, foremost among which is the human-capital theory (Marini and Brinton, 1984; Crompton and Sanderson, 1990: 28). In line with this theory, women and men make long-term 'investment' decisions about their human capital on the labour market. Hence, the division of labour in medicine has also been explained by women's conflicting role expectations. Like other women workers, women physicians tend to make their career choices by balancing their domestic and occupational roles. In comparison, men, in choosing a medical specialty, have been shown to take their parental role into consideration to a lesser degree (Davidson, 1979; Bergquist et al., 1985; Martin et al., 1988). More women physicians live alone than men physicians – another indication that women may find it hard to combine a family and a career (Uhlenberg and Cooney, 1990).

Yet the assumed negative impact of parenting on women's professional career has found scant empirical verification. Having children has not been shown to have a negative impact on the publishing activity of women in science (Cole and Zuckerman, 1987; Luukkonen-Gronow and Stolte-Heiskanen, 1983). Furthermore, studies have shown that women physicians with families are in fact more likely than those without families to hold leading positions in the organization of health care (Graves and Thomas, 1985; Äärimaa et al., 1988). However, this type of research is potentially misleading because it does not provide any information about those women who have decided to give up careers because they anticipate difficulties in combining roles.

The individual-oriented approach entails several shortcomings. Critics have noted that socialization theory is a theory of the acquisition of gender rather than of its construction (Walby, 1990: 91–3; Crompton and Sanderson, 1990: 28). It has also been noted that the human-capital theory assumes that women's career choices are a product of consensual and rational decision-making by equal partners within the family (Crompton and Sanderson, 1990: 28). Both theories fail, however, to recognize the aspect of power that is part of the existing gender order.

Recent research has tended to emphasize the importance of institutional factors in generating and reproducing occupational sex segregation (Reskin and Roos, 1990). Instead of focusing on individual preferences, the institutional approach points to structural barriers that restrict the entry of new recruits to the profession. The underlying criteria in this selection process, it has been argued, are gender-biased. These informal barriers – gatekeeping mechanisms – to the inner circles of the profession have been observed to hamper women's advancement in professions (Epstein, 1973, 1987; Kanter, 1977). Lorber's (1984) study of women doctors in the United States indicated that the recruitment of medical students to research and high-status specialties, as well as the physicians' referral system, was based on informal collegial networks that tended to exclude women. As the medical profession is characterized by a much more complex internal differentiation and hierarchically organized power structure than other professions (Butter et al., 1987: 140), the impact of informal networks is particularly important for understanding the gender-based structure of work in medicine. For example, in her historical account of women's entry into medicine in the United States, Walsh (1990) argues that the professionalization of medicine entailed a standardization of medical education that enabled women to enter the profession, while the highly personalized all-male apprenticeship system had hampered women's entry.

Despite the existence of barriers to women's early entry into and later to their advancement within the medical profession, the proportion of women in medicine has continued to increase in the

Anglo-American and Nordic countries during the past fifty years. At the same time, the structure of the medical profession and the organization of health care have undergone marked changes, most notably a trend towards capital-intensive health care and an increasing bureaucratization and routinization of medical practice. The expansion of the medical market has been fuelled by growing third-party financing of health care and in some countries by the creation of a public sector of health-care delivery. Sociologists, in particular in the United States, have debated the consequences of these changes for the professional autonomy and authority of physicians. The social transformation of doctoring has been interpreted by Marxist observers as an on-going process of 'proletarianization' of physicians (McKinlay and Arches, 1985). Others have argued that the changes will lead to an increased internal differentiation of the medical profession, which will guarantee that the profession maintains control over its work (Freidson, 1984).

However, both camps of scholars have neglected to associate the bureaucratization and routinization of medical practice with the growing number of women physicians working in certain areas of medicine and health care. Furthermore, the scholars involved in the debate on the social transformation of the medical profession have failed to consider the rich empirical data on women doctors that have been collected largely by women scholars (reviewed above). The ghettoization of the two on-going debates – on the future of professions and on the future of occupational sex segregation – is not fruitful for a future clearer understanding of gender and medical work.

We argue that the sex segregation of the work of doctors cannot be understood only as a product of self-selection or social selection during the course of medical training and later practice. Instead, the occupational choices of women physicians are to a large extent responses to institutional barriers that restrict their options. Moreover, the internal differentiation of medical work by gender must be analysed in the light of broader structural changes in contemporary health care.

Women physicians in Finland: towards integration, ghettoization or resegregation?

In their discussion of possible routes that occupational desegregation by gender can take, Reskin and Roos (1990: 71) propose three forms: genuine integration, ghettoization and resegregation. Genuine integration they see as the achievement of occupational equality between the sexes. Ghettoization is women doing different tasks from men

Table 4.1   *Women physicians in Finland 1860–1992*

Year	Total number of physicians	Women as % of total
1860	92	–
1890	236	0.4
1900	373	0.8
1910	523	2.6
1920	657	6.0
1930	1,000	9.0
1940	1,373	12.9
1950	1,997	21.3
1960	2,827	22.5
1970	4,797	26.5
1980	9,016	32.8
1985	11,582	38.0
1990	13,894	42.0
1992	14,810	43.0

Sources: Official Statistics of Finland XI: 56, 63, 72–3, 77; Finnish Medical Association, 1992

in the occupation. Resegregation is the occupation's changing from a male to a predominantly female one. The purpose of the following sections is to illuminate the forms of desegregation by gender that have evolved within the Finnish medical profession. To do this we will first document the increase of women physicians and their position in the medical division of labour. We will then describe their views about the structure of medical work. Finally, we will outline possible future trends in the gender composition of the medical profession.

In 1878, Finland became the first Nordic country to allow women to practise medicine, although their practice was first restricted to children and women. At the turn of the century women constituted less than 1 per cent of all practising physicians in Finland. The number of women physicians remained relatively low until the Second World War (Table 4.1). During the Second World War, women physicians became responsible for the health care of the civilian population while most of the men doctors served at the front. By the time the men resumed their positions at the end of the war, a generation of women physicians had obtained valuable work experiences. After the war, the number of female medical students began to grow, and women constituted a fifth of all practising physicians as early as 1950.

Table 4.2 *The proportion of women among medical specialists under 63 years (Finland, 1992)*

Specialty	Women as % of specialists
Anaesthetics	35
Child neurology	73
Child psychiatry	82
Clinical chemistry	10
Clinical microbiology	33
Clinical neurophysiology	26
Clinical pharmacology	9
Clinical physiology	7
Community health	21
Dermatology and venereology	62
Diagnostic radiology	30
Forensic medicine	24
General practice	34
Geriatrics	44
Internal medicine	25
Maxillofacial surgery	14
Medical genetics	47
Neurology	32
Neurosurgery	6
Obstetrics and gynaecology	39
Occupational health	23
Oncology and radiotherapy	35
Ophthalmology	43
Otorhinolaryngology	18
Pediatrics	56
Pathology	21
Phoniatrics	71
Physiatrics	32
Psychiatry	39
Pulmonary diseases	39
Sports medicine	0
Surgery	7
Total	32

Source: Finnish Medical Association, 1992

In 1985, 38 per cent of the physicians in Finland were women. In Sweden, a third of the doctors were women; in Denmark, a quarter; in Norway, a fifth (SNAPS, 1986). Despite the comparatively large proportion in Finland, statistical data on specialty choices and practice settings indicate a sex segregation similar to that within the medical profession in the other Nordic countries, Britain and the United States (Lindahl and Killi, 1984; Haavio-Mannila, 1982;

Haavio-Mannila and Sinkkonen, 1988; Rosenthal, 1979; Elston, 1980, and her contribution in this volume; Lorber, 1984; Altekruse and McDermott, 1987; Riska, 1989). Women physicians constitute, for example, a majority in pediatrics (56%) and in some other specialties catering to children such as child psychiatry (82%) and child neurology (73%) (Table 4.2). In some traditionally male specialties women are fairly well represented – for example, in obstetrics and gynaecology (39%). By contrast, in some of the newest specialties, women are less well represented – they constitute only a fifth of the specialists in occupational health, for example, and not a single woman has yet specialized in sports medicine. By contrast, women's proportion of the specialists in geriatrics, a new specialty, increased from 27 to 44 per cent between 1991 and 1992.

While the overall tendency to specialize has increased among medical practitioners in Finland, the proportion of female specialists has in fact decreased during the past thirty years. In 1960, 38 per cent of the women doctors were specialists compared to 42 per cent of the men. In 1992, 36 per cent of the women physicians worked as specialists, compared to 57 per cent of the men (Official Statistics for Finland, 1962; Finnish Medical Association, 1992). This gender difference can, however, partly be explained by the age structure of the present physician population: 39 per cent of the women were under 35 in 1992 in comparison to 20 per cent of the men. Hence, a large proportion of the women are new entrants to the profession and have not yet specialized. Nevertheless, another circumstance influences women's tendency to specialize as well. Physicians working at municipal health centres are not required to be specialized, and women constitute a majority of this group (Table 4.3). The Public Health Act of 1972 resulted in an expansion of public primary care through the establishment of municipal health centres, which offer their services free to local residents. Physicians at these centres are municipal employees, while specialists are generally employed by a hospital or work in a private group practice. Only 7 per cent of all physicians were in private practice in 1992 (Table 4.3), and most of these were specialists.

In short, women doctors are clustered in primary care and hence they tend to practise medicine in different organizational settings from their male colleagues. These settings generally lack the characteristics sociologists have associated with the independence of the medical profession. This type of bureaucratic medical practice has a low degree of occupational autonomy, a high degree of routinization, a low salary and low professional status in general.

Evidence for the devaluation of physicians' work is found in Finnish studies of the work situation of physicians that have

Table 4.3   *The distribution of physicians by main activity and gender (Finland, 1992)*

	Physicians		
Main activity	Number	% of total	% women
Hospital	6,150	42	38
Municipal health centres	3,150	21	54
Other public medical centres	380	3	58
Occupational health	590	4	40
Private practice	1,020	7	48
Teaching, research	1,030	7	26
Administration, military forces	350	2	27
Not practising (retired, abroad, maternity leave)	2,140	14	14
Total	14,810	100	43

Source: Finnish Medical Association, 1992

documented an increase of occupational dissatisfaction and work-related stress. A recent study, conducted by the Finnish Medical Association on working conditions and the experience of stress at work, showed that physicians working at municipal health centres generally were more dissatisfied with their working conditions and career development than those working in hospitals. Non-specialists, furthermore, had a higher stress index than specialists (Strid et al., 1988). Since women more often than men work at municipal health centres and as non-specialists, they are also more affected by the negative working conditions. A recent study of the public's perception of the work done by the municipal health centre physician in Finland showed, however, that 58 per cent regarded the work of the municipal physician as prestigious. Furthermore, 45 per cent thought that the health centre physicians tell the patients in detail about their illness, but only 36 per cent thought that the health centre physicians spent enough time with their patients (Finnish Medical Association, 1990: 769).

While women constitute a majority of the physicians in primary care, only about a quarter of the physicians working in teaching and research or administration are women (Table 4.3). The figures suggest that Finnish women physicians tend to work in routinized and bureaucratized medical practice and that they are largely excluded from decision-making in medical research, education and the administration of health care.

In this regard, a genuine integration has not been achieved and a partial ghettoization can be documented. A tentative answer to whether the future pattern will imply a further ghettoization or a resegregation is provided in the following section by the women physicians' own views about their role in medicine.

Three generations of women physicians: choices and concerns

In an effort to gain information about the processes that create and reproduce the internal differentiation by gender of the Finnish medical profession, 31 women medical practitioners, ages ranging between 28 and 80, were interviewed in the spring of 1987. The respondents were selected from the register of the Finnish Medical Association of 1987. Two of those selected declined to participate in the study. An effort was made to select representatives from three age groups: young (28–35 years old, n = 8), middle-aged (36–55 years old, n = 15), and elderly (56–80 years old, n = 8), and various specialties and work settings (municipal health centres, hospital-based practice, surgery, anaesthetics, pediatrics and medical research). The participants were selected from southern Finland, where a majority of the population is concentrated. The interviews were semi-structured, and the physicians were asked about their present work and choice of specialty.

The respondents related their position and task in medicine both to personal preferences and to institutional structures. Both the young and the middle-aged were more often inclined than the elderly to refer to structural factors and gender socialization that they perceived had influenced their career. The two younger groups perceived the opportunities of men and women doctors to be predominantly shaped by external factors while the elderly saw the sexual division of labour in medicine as primarily biologically based. The middle-aged in particular tended to emphasize the similarity between men's and women's professional behaviour. They saw professional behaviour and opportunities as shaped by the larger structure of medicine. As one psychiatrist in her forties remarked:

> I believe that some women physicians treat their patients differently. But just as Margaret Thatcher is no woman [*sic*] . . . if you get into this and get caught in the professional jargon you [and a man] are just alike. It has not always got to do with gender, but whom you identify with. . . .. Equally male nurses will be unlikely to have an impact [on health care] because the system swallows them as well. Unfortunately not . . . I must say that just in my own life, I think very seldom about this gender thing actually . . . I really think of myself primarily as a physician and as a woman physician secondarily.

The underrepresentation of women in medical research, administration and prestigious specialties such as surgery reveals that there are institutional features hampering women physicians' advancement within the organization of health care. In our study, the youngest women especially complained about the lack of opportunities for women students to gain surgical experience. One specialist in internal medicine characterized the male surgeons in her hospital as a 'football team' that women physicians did not fit into easily. According to a female gynaecologist in her early thirties:

> When it came to practical work, it was obviously more difficult . . . to gain admittance to the surgery room. . . . The requirements were clearly higher for female candidates. . . . In most of the places where I have been . . . female physicians have had a difficult time trying to gain surgical expertise. Specialists, even women who have gained specialist rights, say that they really don't know how to do surgery since they aren't allowed in the surgery department. . . . Actually you immediately notice that women often are better at small surgical operations and leave a neater scar. . . .

Although they lacked any experience of surgery, most of the middle-aged and elderly women physicians thought of the surgical specialties as physically too strenuous for a woman to cope with. As expected, the two female surgeons interviewed did not consider physical strain an obstacle, but emphasized technical expertise before physical strength. Another common explanation for the small number of women surgeons was the late and demanding working hours required in surgical practice. Although the working hours in anaesthetics and pediatrics were considered as tiring as those in surgical practice, the former specialties were not thought of as incompatible with women's domestic role. Anaesthetics is a branch of medicine characterized by high technology and low interaction with patients, a feature that has generally been associated with men's niches in medicine. Anaesthetics did, however, emerge as a medical specialty in the 1960s when the number of women in medicine already was high. But as other studies have indicated, the male surgeon is interested in keeping his authority and control over the operating room and a subservient female anaesthetist maintains the professional dominance of the surgeon (Miles, 1991: 146; Halpern, 1992: 1014).

Women physicians in Finland are furthermore largely excluded from influential positions in the administration of and policy-making in health care. As the figures above indicate, women are sparsely represented in medical academia and in the administration of health care. Respondents attributed this to conflicting role demands, but also to institutionalized informal and collegial mechanisms excluding women. For example, women were not offered the opportunity to take part in medical research as often as men. One woman in her late fifties, who has a faculty position at a medical school, noted:

First of all it has to do with having children and a family. If one had remained unmarried, it would have been possible to do it as well as a man. But here comes a 'but'. A woman is never offered research opportunities . . . I offer, of course, half of my students are women. But women are not asked to join research, while men are.

Yet the women physicians were not only well aware of the existence of institutional barriers within the medical profession but emphasized that they could best use their womanly skills in certain areas of medicine. Most interviewed referred to their gender-specific skills, and they did not see them merely as obstacles but as assets in their career. These respondents considered themselves to be more empathic and patient-oriented, and to have a more holistic perspective on health and illness. The youngest women in particular believed that their gender-specific skills and experiences would lead to more humane and holistic approaches in health care in the future when women physicians were the majority. This notion was also found common among women physicians in Norway: a nationwide study showed that two-thirds of all practising Norwegian women physicians regarded their gender-specific interests and experience as an asset to the future development of health care (Lindahl and Killi, 1984).

In line with this essentialist viewpoint, some women considered their work at municipal health centres as a contemporary equivalent to the physician employed by the municipality in the pre-industrial society. These women presented themselves as the bearers of the humanistic tradition of medicine that was about to wither away in a more and more technologically oriented medical practice. They perceived their skills as closely linked to women's life-experiences and traditional role in society. As one put it:

Men tend to think about these things in a more narrow fashion. They want to believe that if we have a problem, we deal with it and get it out of the way once and for all. Without taking the background [of the patient] and the totality into account, for example, regarding such practical issues as the patient's living conditions and life circumstances and how his or her continued care is to be organized.

These women preferred a practice in general medicine although they were fully aware of the relatively low professional prestige and low income in this field. The overrepresentation of men in surgery, by contrast, they explained by the male physicians' greater need for social recognition. One woman in her early thirties thought that women had a different notion about their task in medicine than the stereotypic male view of 'being a doctor':

Something that I also believe has an impact is that women don't experience a similar pressure to practise heroic medicine like surgery. . . . The reason why women don't choose a career in surgery I believe has to do with that they don't have such a need to be recognized or to hold the healer's knife in their hand. In some way men have different reasons for studying medicine. I believe that they are more success-oriented and have a clear sense of what a successful physician is like.

The women physicians identified barriers to entering the male-dominated areas of medicine. As a counter-strategy they emphasized their gender- specific skills in order to claim some areas as their own. Hence, by appealing to women's 'natural' propensity for 'emotional work' (Hochschild, 1979; James, 1989), and for understanding the social and cultural aspects of medicine, women physicians can secure their rights to the primary-care areas of medicine. In this sense, they are not merely passive objects of economic or technological processes shaping health care nor of the male-dominated order of medicine. Women are also social actors capturing certain domains where they can claim they possess the necessary knowledge, their female skills, for successful practice of medicine. But the strategy of emphasizing intrinsic gender differences has a double edge. It has given women access to the lower positions in medicine but also confronted them with lack of access to those areas where the crucial decisions about the future directions in medicine are made. In this sense, the current internal differentiation of medicine shows few convincing signs of progress towards a genuine integration. The pattern of ghettoization will prevail as long as men continue to control the mainstream knowledge of biomedicine, the administrative and the policy-making elite.

Women physicians and the social transformation of doctoring

Until the early 1970s, sociologists largely neglected the existence of women doctors in their study of the medical profession. In standard sociological works medical students and doctors were mostly referred to as male (Lorber, 1975). The current debate on the changing character of the medical profession is waged in gender-neutral terms although over the past twenty years women have entered the profession in growing numbers. Today, gender is one of the central characteristics that stratifies the profession.

Data on the status of women physicians in the Nordic and Anglo-American countries show a surprisingly similar gender-based division of labour. The case of Finland demonstrates that women physicians have failed to gain access to prestigious specialties or positions in the organization of health care. Segregation by gender prevails despite the fact that women have constituted a considerably higher proportion of the medical profession in Finland than in most western countries for the past fifty years. The slow advancement of women within the ranks of medicine is somewhat surprising also since women's participation in the labour market has been high in Finland since the Second World War. There has been a comparatively broad cultural approval of women's participation in the labour force and family policies supporting their working role.

Any assessment of the future impact of women in medicine must take into account recent changes in the structure of health care produced by economic and political forces external to the profession. Sociologists have envisioned an increased bureaucratic and corporative structure of health care. Whether the administration of health care is handled by administrators outside the medical profession (McKinlay and Stoeckle, 1988) or by an administrative elite of physicians (Freidson, 1984), women doctors' possibilities of determining the parameters of their work will not markedly improve. Women doctors have so far been excluded from administration. An increasing corporatization and privatization of health care might thus hamper even further women doctors' chances of advancing in or influencing the profession.

In the Nordic context an issue more pertinent than bureaucratization is the effect on the medical profession of deregulation of health care (Riska, 1993). Efforts to introduce market elements in the formerly mainly public and regulated health-care sector might influence the medical profession in two ways. First, the previous sheltered markets created by state and local governments will partly be challenged by physicians establishing themselves on a contractual basis with third-party payers. This will result in intensified competition and defensive mechanisms of collegial networks to maintain control of the medical market. Secondly, an emphasis on free-market elements in health care has been based on the assumption that this will make the use of resources and the delivery of services more efficient. An emphasis on efficiency will support the more technological elements of the medical profession that promise efficient solutions. In both cases women physicians are not very likely to be part of the profession's inner circle.

References

Äärimaa, Markku, Asp, Sisko, Juntunen, Juhani, Kanttu, Kyllikki, Olkinuora, Martti and Strid, Leo (1988) 'Mies- ja naislääkärien työ, ura, perhe ja stressi', *Suomen Lääkärilehti*, 43: 1282–8.

Acker, Joan (1989) *Doing Comparable Worth: Gender, Class and Pay Equity.* Philadelphia: Temple University Press.

Allen, Isobel (1990) 'Women doctors', in Susan McRae (ed.), *Keeping Women In.* Worcester: Billing & Sons Ltd. pp. 33–45.

Altekruse, Joan M. and McDermott, Susanne W. (1987) 'Contemporary concerns of women in medicine', in Sue V. Rossner (ed.), *Feminism within the Science and Health Professions: Overcoming Resistance*. Oxford: Pergamon Press. pp. 65–88.

Bergquist, Steven R., Duchac, Betsy, Schalin, Van A., Zastraw, Joseph F., Barr, Varonica L. and Borwiecki, Thomas (1985) 'Perceptions of freshmen medical students of gender differences in medical specialty choice', *Journal of Medical Education*, 60: 379–83.

Blum, Linda and Smith, Vicki (1988) 'Women's mobility in the corporation: a critique of the politics of optimism', *Signs*, 13: 528–45.

Butter, Irene, Carpenter, Eugenia S., Kay, Bonnie J. and Simmons, Ruth (1987) 'Gender hierarchies in the health labor force', *International Journal of Health Services*, 17: 133–49.

Carpenter, Eugenia S. (1977) 'Women in male dominated professions', *International Journal of Health Services*, 7: 191–207.

Carter, Michael J. and Carter, Susan Boslego (1981) 'Women's recent progress in the professions or, women get a ticket to ride after the gravy train has left the station', *Feminist Studies*, 7: 477–504.

Cole, Jonathan R. and Zuckerman, Harriet (1987) 'Marriage, motherhood and research performance in science', *Scientific American*, (February): 83–9.

Crompton, Rosemary and Sanderson, Kay (1990) *Gendered Jobs and Social Change*. London: Unwin Hyman.

Davidson, L. R. (1979) 'Choice by constraint: the selection and function of specialties among women physicians-in-training', *Journal of Health Politics, Policy and Law*, 4: 200–20.

Drachman, Virginia G. (1986) 'The limits of progress: the professional lives of women doctors 1881–1926', *Bulletin of the History of Medicine*, 60: 58–72.

Ehrenreich, Barbara and English, Deirdre (1973) *Witches, Midwives and Nurses: a History of Women Healers*. Old Westbury: The Feminist Press.

Elston, Mary Ann (1977) 'Women in the medical profession: whose problem?', in M. Stacey, M. Reid, C. Heath and R. Dingwall (eds), *Health and the Division of Labour*. London: Croom Helm. pp. 115–38.

Elston, Mary Ann (1980) 'Medicine: half our future doctors?', in R. Silverstone and A. Ward (eds), *Careers of Professional Women*. London: Croom Helm. pp. 99–139.

Epstein, Cynthia Fuchs (1973) *Woman's Place*. Berkeley: University of California.

Epstein, Cynthia Fuchs (1987) *Deceptive Distinctions: Sex, Gender and the Social Order*. New York: Sage.

Farrell, Kathleen, Witte, Marlys Hearst, Holguin, Miguel and Lopez, Sue (1979) 'Women physicians in medical academia', *Journal of the American Medical Association*, 241: 2808–12.

Fee, Elisabeth (1977) 'Women and health care: a comparison of theories', in Vicente Navarro (ed.), *Health and Medical Care in the US: a Critical Analysis*. Farmingdale, NY: Baywood Publishing Co. pp. 115–32.

Finnish Medical Association (1990) 'Mielikuvat terveyskeskuslääkäreistä myönteisiä kokemukset vielä parempia', *Suomen Lääkäriliitto*, 45: 769–70.

Finnish Medical Association (1992) *Physicians in Finland 1992: Abstract*. Helsinki.

Fox, Mary Frank and Hesse-Biber, Sharlene (1984) *Women at Work*. Palo Alto: Mayfield.

Freidson, Eliot (1984) 'The changing nature of professional control', *Annual Review of Sociology*, 10: 1–20.

Frey, Helen (1980) 'Swedish men and women doctors compared: comparison between Swedish-trained men and women doctors for background, demographic characteristics, professional activity and motives leading to choice of medical career', *Medical Education*, 14: 143–53.

Graves, P. L. and Thomas, C. B. (1985) 'Correlates of midlife career achievement among women physicians', *Journal of the American Medical Association*, 254: 781–7.

Haavio-Mannila, Elina (1968) 'The occupational value structure of the Finnish medical profession', *Social Science and Medicine*, 1: 425–40.

Haavio-Mannila, Elina (1982) 'Sukupuoliroolit Pohjoismaiden lääkärien ja hammas lääkärien keskuudessa', in *Nainen ja lääketiede*. Valtioneuvoston kanslian monisteita. 1: Helsinki. pp. 26–39.

Haavio-Mannila, Elina and Sinkkonen, Sirkka (1988) 'Nordiska kvinnor i vårdyrken ur ett historiskt perspektiv', in *Kvinnor och hälsa*. Socialnoch hälsovårdsministeriet. Serie D/1. Helsinki. pp. 85–97.

Halpern, Sidney A. (1992) 'Dynamics of professional control: Internal coalitions and crossprofessional boundaries', *American Journal of Sociology*, 97: 994–1021.

Heins, M., Hendricks, J. and Martindale, L. (1979) 'Attitudes of women and men physicians', *American Journal of Public Health*, 11: 1132–9.

Hochschild, Arlie Russell (1979) 'Emotion work, feeling rules and social structure', *American Journal of Sociology*, 85: 551–75.

James, Nicky (1989) 'Emotional labour: skill and work in the social regulation of feelings', *Sociological Review*, 37: 15–41.

Kanter, Rosabeth Moss (1977) *Men and Women of the Corporation*. New York: Basic Books.

Kletke, Phillip R., Marder, William D. and Silberger, Anne B. (1990) 'The growing proportion of female physicians: implications for U.S. physician supply', *American Journal of Public Health*, 80: 300–304.

Lanska, Mary Jo, Lanska, Douglas J. and Rimm, Alfred A. (1984) 'The effect of the rising percentage of female physicians on projections of physician supply', *Journal of Medical Education*, 59: 849–55.

Leserman, Jane (1981) *Men and Women in Medical School*. New York: Praeger.

Lindahl, Anne Karin and Killi, Marianne (1984) 'Familien eller yrket? En undersøkelse av kvinnelige legers livs- och arbeidssituation'. Statens institutt for folkehelse (SIEE): Gruppe for helsetjensteforskning, rapport nr. 6/84. Oslo.

Lorber, Judith (1975) 'Women and medical sociology: invisible professionals and ubiquitous patients', in Marcia Millman and Rosabeth Moss Kanter (eds), *Another Voice: Feminist Perspectives on Social Life and Social Science*. New York: Anchor Books. pp. 75–105.

Lorber, Judith (1984) *Women Physicians*. London: Tavistock.

Luukkonen-Gronow, Terttu and Stolte-Heiskanen, Veronica (1983) 'Myths and realities of role incompability of women scientists', *Acta Sociologica*, 26: 268–80.

Marini, Margaret Mooney and Brinton, Mary C. (1984) 'Sex typing in occupational socialization', in Barbara F. Reskin (ed.), *Sex Segregation in the Workplace*. Washington, DC: National Academy Press. pp. 192–232.

Martin, Steven C., Arnold, R.M. and Parker, Ruth (1988) 'Gender and medical socialization', *Journal of Health and Social Behaviour*, 29: 191–205.

McKinlay, John B. and Arches, J. (1985) 'Towards the proletarianization of physicians', *International Journal of Health Services*, 15: 161–95.

McKinlay, John B. and Stoeckle, J.D. (1988) 'Corporatization and social transformation of doctoring', *International Journal of Health Services*, 18: 191–205.

Meeuwesen, Ludwien, Schaap, Cas and van der Staak, Cees (1991) 'Verbal analysis of doctor–patient communication', *Social Science and Medicine* 32: 1143–50.

Miles, Agnes (1991) *Women, Health and Medicine*. Milton Keynes: Open University Press.

Morantz, R. M., Pomerlau, C. S. and Fenichel, C. H. (1982) *In Her Own Words: Oral Histories of Women Physicians*. New Haven: Yale University Press.

Official Statistics of Finland (1962) *Allmän hälso- och sjukvård 1960*: XI: 63: Helsinki.

Reskin, Barbara F. (1988) 'Bringing the men back in: sex differentiation and the devaluation of women's work', *Gender and Society*, 2: 58–81.

Reskin, Barbara F. and Roos, Patricia A. (1990) *Job Queues, Gender Queues*. Philadelphia: Temple University Press.

Rinke, Charlotta (1981) 'The economic and academic status of women physicians', *Journal of the American Medical Association*, 245: 2305–306.

Riska, Elianne (1989) 'Women's careers in medicine: the development in the United States and Finland', *Scandinavian Studies*, 61: 185–98.

Riska, Elianne (1993) 'The medical profession in the Nordic countries', in Frederic Hafferty and John McKinlay (eds), *The Changing Character of the Medical Profession: an International Perspective*. Oxford University Press.

Rosenthal, Marilynn (1979) 'Perspectives on women physicians in the USA through cross-cultural comparison: England, Sweden, USSR', *International Journal of Women's Studies*, 2: 528–40.

SNAPS (Samnordisk Arbetsgrupp för prognos- och specialistutbildningsfrågor) (1986) 'Den framtida läkararbetsmarknaden i Norden', N.p.

Stacey, Margaret (1988) *The Sociology of Health and Healing*. London: Unwin Hyman.

Strid, Leo, Asp, Sisko, Juntunen, Juhani, Kanttu, Kyllikki, Olkinrora, Martti and Äärimaa, Markku (1988) 'Lääkärien työlot ja stressi', *Suomen Lääkärilehti*, 43: 1277–81.

Uhlenberg, Peter and Cooney, Teresa M. (1990) 'Male and female physicians: family and career comparisons', *Social Science and Medicine*, 30: 373–8.

Walby, Sylvia (1990) *Theorizing Patriarchy*. Oxford: Basil Blackwell.

Walsh, Mary Roth (1977) *Doctors Wanted: No Women Need Apply: Sexual Barriers in the Medical Profession, 1835–1975*. New Haven: Yale University Press.

Walsh, Mary Roth (1990) 'Women in medicine since Flexner', *New York State Journal of Medicine*, 90: 302–308.

Wharton, Amy S. (1991) 'Structure and agency in socialist–feminist theory', *Gender and Society*, 5: 373–89.

Zimmer, Lynn (1988) 'Tokenism and women in the workplace: the limits of gender neutral theory', *Social Problems*, 35: 64–77.

Zimny, G. H. and Shelton, B. R. (1982) 'Sex differences in medical specialty preferences', *Journal of Medical Education*, 57: 403–5.

PART III

OTHER HEALTH PROFESSIONALS

5

The subordination of nurses in health care: towards a social divisions approach

Mick Carpenter

In fairy tales, donning the cloak of invisibility confers formidable powers on the hero, but for nurses invisibility underlines their subordination. A good nurse traditionally is one who is not noticed, but quietly and in a self-effacing way goes about her allotted tasks. Yet not only has this determined her position in the division of labour, it also appears to have shaped the attitude of sociologists, often replicating the gender oppression of nurses in health care within 'medical sociology'. Many sociologists still seem to believe that by dealing with doctors they have covered the main occupational actors in health care, and they can then get on with considering relations with users and state or corporate agencies. Others give significant coverage to nurses and other subordinated health workers (for example, Twaddle and Hessler, 1977; Turner, 1987; Stacey, 1988), but do not place them at the centre of their analysis.

Given that nurses constitute the largest element of female paid care, and form a significant proportion of national labour forces, it is particularly surprising that feminist analyses of nursing are so thin on the ground. Socialist feminist analysis of women's work has primarily focused on its role in capitalist production. While the analysis of housework and caring in the 'private' sphere has also been a prominent issue, women's contribution to nursing and other forms of 'caring' work in the public sphere has been a relatively neglected topic. In the analysis of health care itself, nursing has received very little attention compared with the burgeoning literature on the relation between women patients and male doctors. As one of the contributors to this literature, Ann Oakley, has acknowledged:

> In a fifteen year career as a sociologist studying medical services, I confess I have been particularly blind to the contribution made by nurses to health

care. Indeed, over a period of some months spent observing in a large London hospital, I hardly noticed nurses at all. (Oakley, 1984:26)

It is true that there have recently been signs that a critical sociological analysis of nursing is in the process of emergence (e.g. Davies, 1980; Salvage, 1985; Savage, 1987), influenced by a variety of perspectives. There remains the danger however that this could easily become ghettoized into a separate sociology of nursing which, in establishing a niche for itself might not, like nursing in the health care system, be able to alter its lower status and marginality in relation to the main discipline.

Not only is this neglect of nurses and nursing an injustice, it also limits the explanatory power and policy relevance of sociological analysis. Health care is currently undergoing a rapid restructuring in all industrialized countries,[1] reordering the relationships between all the 'actors' in the health care system. Whether coincidental or connected to this, social movements have arisen among nurses in recent years which have presented a radical challenge to traditional patterns of subordination. This chapter explores the possible links between these two sets of processes and the reasons why such a challenge may be occurring. It examines the prospects for changing nurse subordination, and how the powers and interests of others may be affected. It therefore makes a case for seeing nurse subordination as a central issue for the analysis of health care, and tries to begin developing appropriate means for analysing it.

I argue first that, though necessary, it is not sufficient to chart and explain the changing forms of gender oppression of nurses within the formal structures of health care. Instead I advocate a 'social divisions' approach which seeks to link gender with other forms of oppression such as 'race' and class, in a framework which also brings relations with users and lay carers into view. I then tentatively try to reconstruct sociological analysis of health care in ways which might make nurses visible within a social divisions approach. For example, I try to see how nurses might fit into Talcott Parsons's account of the 'sick role' or Michel Foucault's dissection of the medical 'gaze'. I conclude with an outline attempt to develop a social divisions approach to the history of nurse subordination in health care in Britain.

A social divisions approach to nursing and health care

One of the key features of a 'social divisions' approach is the insistence that developments in nursing and its general position in the health-care system are not autonomous, but crucially affected by balances of power in the wider society, which become represented in the health system. This is not to suggest that every aspect of nursing development has been determined from outside, or that 'technical' forces play no part in positioning nurses within the health-care system. And even if external forces do largely shape the room for manoeuvre available at any point in time to occupationally based social movements, this still leaves many choices open about what strategies such movements could realistically pursue.

Such a proposition is not of course entirely novel. Social scientists have long recognized that nursing, as a historically subordinated occupation, has been constrained by outside pressure from the medical profession (e.g. Devereux and Weiner, 1950; Davis, 1966; Katz, 1969; Freidson, 1970a). In Britain, emphasis has additionally been placed on the power of the state, as the main employer of nursing labour, to constrain the impact of professionalizing movements (Abel-Smith, 1960; Dingwall et al., 1988). Yet not always are these constraining features themselves fully situated in their wider socio-economic context. This chapter will suggest that the social divisions of gender, 'race' and class in the wider society (in no intended order of significance) are key external determinants.[2] The more these inequalities are generally challenged, the more likely it is that they are capable of being modified or even transformed within the health system. The more heightened they become, the greater the tendency of the health system to follow suit. I would emphasize that these are only tendencies, not least because the health system itself helps to shape and does not simply 'mirror' wider balances of social power.

Identifying the significant social divisions affecting nursing is one thing, handling them appropriately, by showing how they might both interlink and impact more generally on health care, is another. The relations between class and gender oppression have of course been the subject of much debate within different feminist traditions, and more recently the relation between these and race has been highlighted by anti-racist campaigners, who claimed that their concerns were being sidelined. This chapter follows Williams (1989) in seeking to develop an integrated approach to such divisions, but in ways which allow for the specificity of each to be acknowledged.

We need also to be aware that developing a social divisions approach to nursing and health care is fraught with additional complications. For one thing, not only do social divisions affect nursing's relation with doctors and others in the health service hierarchy, but nursing has itself been divided internally along class, gender and 'race' lines. We therefore should not assume the existence of a common occupational nursing 'interest' in relation to outside agencies like the medical profession or the state, but must take account of potential internal divisions of interest. Additionally, though it has not been as extensively documented as for doctors, nurses themselves exercise power over health service users, patients and unpaid carers, whose relation with the health system can also be shown to be affected by their 'race', gender and class positions in the wider society (for example, on class see Townsend et al., 1988; on gender see Doyal, 1979: Ch 6; Lewin and Olesen, 1985; on race see Brent Community Health Council, 1981; McNaught, 1988). Nurses are thus involved in complex ways in reproducing social divisions in their daily work within the health system. Because of this, we need to retain a two-fold focus: on the one hand, on social divisions as they impact upon nurses; on the other, the impact of nursing and nurses upon social divisions among users of health services.

This defines a very wide agenda of potential issues for a social divisions analysis of nursing. This chapter primarily deals with the impact of social divisions upon nurses and nursing, but hopefully in ways that are also sensitive to the possible impact of nursing and nurses themselves upon social divisions among users and lay carers. It thus tries to keep the whole labour process in view rather than just assuming it is restricted to the paid workforce.

Making nurses visible within sociological debates

The purpose of this section of the chapter is to begin making the contribution of nurses visible within the key sociological debates in health care. First of all I seek to show how they might fit into more 'traditional' sociological perspectives associated with Parsons and 'structural functionalism', and then in the critiques of more 'critical' writers such as Freidson and Navarro. To the extent that nurse subordination was noticed, I suggest that traditional approaches tend to see it as technically and even biologically determined, while critical sociologists more satisfactorily view it as socially and politically constructed through the weight of wider structures of social power. I want also to suggest that both traditional and critical theoretical traditions tend to place too much emphasis on the structures of power, to the neglect of processes. I argue therefore that there is a need to pay more attention to the findings of social interactionist research on nursing, and reconsider some 'taken-for-granted' assumptions about the subordination of nurses in health care. These show that hierarchies can be challenged, even if the continuance of structural power will ensure that they are not easily overturned.

Nurses and the sick role
One essential way of connecting nurse subordination to broader social issues within a 'traditional' approach would be to place it within Parsons's (1951) renowned structural–functionalist analysis of

the sick role. Unfortunately Parsons himself did not render nurses' role within it visible, and we will therefore have to paint them into the picture. First, though, let us briefly analyse Parsons's central assumptions.

It is true that the sick role concept is in a sense social constructivist. Sickness is seen as a threat to social cohesion, because it is disruptive of people's ability to fulfil their allotted roles. The temporary exemption of the individual from their normal obligations is conditional on their seeking professional help, and actively cooperating with physicians' efforts to make them better. Yet Parsons does not himself present a fully socially constructed view of illness subversive of the medical model of health and illness. Although his work represents a significant step in that direction which others have built on, it tends itself to reinforce rather than relativize the writ of biomedicine. Among other things, by defining sickness as a form of deviance it reinforces the crucial medical model notion of health as normality and illness/disease as abnormality, and hence the associated stigma of long-term illness. Although Parsons recognises some uncertainties in medical treatment, the sick-role concept is also generally supportive of biomedicine's claims to technical efficacy, in particular its ability to ensure that the sick role is only of temporary duration. It is thus highly supportive of physicians' authority, as well as their assumed altruistic intentions, and by implication their strategic position of power within the division of labour in health care.

Looked at in this way, the sick-role concept provides us with a clear statement of the dominant ideology that underpins medical power within the health-care system and in society as a whole. It clarifies how things 'ought' to work, as well as providing a useful starting point for analysing the causes and consequences of the system failing to do so: for one thing, the fact that in some instances entry into the role is not voluntary but forced, as in some areas of psychiatry; for another, that prolonged rather than temporary occupation of the sick role is becoming increasingly common, especially due to the growth in the numbers of those suffering from long-term illness.

These issues have been extensively examined, initially with the intention of developing a better taxonomy than to raise fundamental criticisms of the basic model itself. Yet as the exceptions and qualifications have multiplied, it has been increasingly suggested that the paradigm (see Kuhn, 1962) of the sick role itself, and the expectations surrounding it, were in some kind of 'crisis', not unconnected to that of the health-care system itself. We will return to this issue later and consider its implications for nurses. First, though, let us try to paint nurses into the traditional sick role.

In trying to do so, we immediately run into the problem that the sick-role construct is based on a triad between patient, doctor and lay associates. It needs substantial modification to take into account the organization of health care as a complex labour process, increasingly focused on hospitals and involving armies of other health workers, of which nurses are the largest group. Within the biomedical model the increasing application of technology in a hospital setting would be seen as beneficial, a reflection of medicine's increasing power to cure or at least contain sickness. However, it might still be acknowledged that not only does this create additional problems of organization and delivery, it also magnifies problems of patient motivation and compliance. Heroic technological interventions require a greater degree of patient subordination and generate considerable anxiety, both of which require active management. Since doctors have an increasingly narrow 'medical' focus, this task typically falls to the nurse (see also Strauss et al., 1982).

Thus according to one functionalist account, the nurse's role is to complement the male curative and 'instrumental' interventions, with a female caring and 'expressive' one, defining her primary task as one of engaging in 'emotional' labour. While mechanistic medicine necessarily depersonalizes and 'objectifies' the patient, the nurse reconstitutes him/her as a human being. As M. Johnson and Martin put it:

> Compared to the activities of the doctor, the nurse's activities are not directly related to the external problem of getting the patient well, but are designed . . . to establish a therapeutic environment. This may include a variety of specific behaviours from creating a comfortable, pleasant physical setting to the more directly nurturant activities of explaining, reassuring, understanding, supporting, and accepting the patient. (1965: 31)

Thus linked to this duality and hierarchy between cure and care are others, for example, between rationality and emotionality, body and mind, and male and female, all of which serve to reinforce the nurse's secondary and thus compliant, 'handmaiden' role.

Of course these supposed differences connect to wider hierarchies associated with male and female differences in society. There are parallels here worth pursuing, for example, with Parsons's (1951) separately developed view of the family. This suggests that the loss of productive and educative 'instrumental' functions to the economy and the state that was said to occur with industrialization reinforced the 'natural' if more specialized 'expressive' role of the family. It subsequently became an institution catering primarily for the social-ization of the young, and the provision of emotional and other forms of support for other family members, particularly those focused on the paramount needs of the male breadwinner. Implied here are notions of both evolution, the growing specialization of social institutions leading to social differentiation, and associated progress, though in the context of a persistent duality still indicative of an underlying biological determinism of social roles. As with the sick role, we can criticize this theory both on the grounds of its conservative ideological assumptions and as a depiction of reality (e.g. Gittins, 1985: Ch 3; Abercrombie and Warde, 1988: Ch 6). However, within its terms hospitals and other health-care institutions could be regarded as formal institutions in the public sphere which, because they are involved in 'people work', need to give some attention to the expressive effects of instrumental activities. And who are better fitted to provide it by their nature and socialization, than compliant women?

Thus the increasing application of technological, curative medicine, especially in the context of the development of hospital-based health care, transforms the sick role into a complex labour process. All kinds of caring responsibilities which traditionally were carried out within the family are in the process transferred to an institutional setting. The carrying out or supervision of these activities is one crucial element which defines the occupational space occupied by nurses, and the organization of nursing as a distinct division of labour. The other is of course her role as trusted physician's assistant, which grows as the technology becomes more complex, involving observation of the patient while the physician is not present and the carrying out of specifically delegated 'medical' tasks. In becoming embroiled in these two sets of responsibilities, the nurse inevitably gets drawn into the process of social control associated with the sick role. Her role, in theory at least, is to maintain the integrity of the patient as a human being within the increasingly fragmented and depersonalized environment of the hospital, at the same time securing the patient's and their lay associates' compliance with doctors' orders. She may also take over where the medical model fails, as with the long-term or terminally ill, on the assumption that this is the exception rather than the rule (Katz, 1969).

At this point we could also briefly build nurses into Foucault's analysis of the medical 'gaze'. Though it might seem inappropriate to bracket such a critic of medicine with a functionalist analysis, there is a sense in which he echoes Parsons's preoccupation with disease and deviance, and the relation between medical knowledge and control. Within Foucault's analysis professional power is embodied in the objectification of the patient involved in defining the body as a separated sphere, whose interior mysteries are deciphered by the medical gaze, with 'the clinic' as the means by which the associated surveillance and control are organized (Foucault, 1973; see also discussion in Turner, 1987: 9–14). The analysis in this chapter would suggest the need to expand the account to include an understanding of the process by which the nurse was incorporated as part of the surveillance system of the clinic, relegated to being a functionary of the 'gaze', an agent of the patient's objectification, herself subordinated on the grounds of the doctor's more privileged 'vision'.

Criticizing functionalism

One criticism that can be made against this account is that often levelled against functionalism, that it tends to serve as an ideology justifying the status quo, rather than spelling out how social relations have been socially constructed, and are hence in principle capable of being changed. However, my purpose was first to make nurses' crucial role within the sick role visible, before subjecting it to criticisms. These could seek to revise our understanding of nurse subordination, without radically challenging the sick-role paradigm as such, the implication being that aspects of it might be in need of reform. More fundamentally, the two basic assumptions of Parsons's analysis, those of medicine's general technical efficacy and the necessity to control the sick as a potential threat to 'society', might be challenged, and this would open up a much more radical agenda for change, which might also include the supposed immutability of the division between nursing and doctoring. At the very minimum, for example, it could be argued that though nursing and doctoring were still separate primary and secondary activities, the idea that men are more fitted to one and women to another sphere is unacceptably sexist. More substantially, it could also be suggested that as nurses come to carry out more delegated 'medical' activities of either a technical or caring kind, the 'functional' basis increasingly exists for a realignment of power within the division of labour, attenuating the strict hierarchical divisions of power between the two occupational groups.

Certainly the relatively few sociological studies of nursing work have shown that the reality does not always fit with the stereotype of a subordinated, completely compliant and nurturing nurse. Thus Mauksch (1965) drew attention to the fact that, in contrast to their traditional expressive image, nurses were increasingly playing the role of 'coordinator of patient care' in an ever more complex division of labour, as much a ward and institutional manager as 'mother figure'. They thus exercised considerable informal managerial power. He could have added that this also led to the development of a managerial role which some nurses exercised over their colleagues, a point we will return to later. Other studies have shown how this informal power was also exercised more directly in the 'clinical' domain. Sometimes this was transacted 'behind the throne', through the subtle conventions of what Stein calls 'the nurse–doctor game', in which:

> the nurse is to be bold, have initiative and be responsible for making significant recommendations while at the same time she must appear passive. This must be done in such a manner as to make her recommendations appear to be initiated by the physician. (1978: 109)

Other studies have suggested that more direct challenges to medical authority have been mounted by nurses. Thus Scheff (1970) outlined the power that attendants in a state mental hospital exercised when they refused to carry out their normal role as a buffer or 'gatekeeper' between patients and physicians, in order to frustrate attempts to 'reform' custodial regimes. The institution broke down when the physicians were overwhelmed with work. The possibility that such processes may operate more generally, and not only in health-care institutions, has become a commonplace of organizational analysis. Studies of hospital under-life have in fact formed the basis for more generalized theories which posit the existence of a 'negotiated order' in organizations, while they may on the surface appear to be governed by rigid bureaucratic and hierarchical rules. Rules cannot cover every eventuality and informal sources of power can be mobilized (e.g. Strauss et al., 1963). A more recent investigation within this tradition is that undertaken by Hughes (1988) of nurse–doctor relationships in a British walk-in casualty department. Hughes shows that in practice nurses take on many more decision-making responsibilities than their formal position in the structure would allow, including diagnostic and treatment responsibilities, and at times 'telling' doctors what to do. An interesting aspect of this power, from a social divisions perspective, is the fact that Hughes argues that it may have been reinforced by the fact that the casualty nurses were often white and experienced while the doctors were junior, of Asian origin and recently arrived from overseas. They were thus dependent on nurses for the more culturally specific transactions of the sick role, and deference was diminished by 'dilemmas of status' between nurse and doctor (in other words, racism).

Observational studies therefore indicate that nurse subordination may not be as predominant as is often assumed by structural theories of medical power. It is quite another thing, however, to suggest on the basis of these and similar findings that medical dominance is crumbling, or that a 'negotiated order' of power exists, from which a more formal assault on nurse subordination and the power of doctors

could be launched. For one thing, a one-sided emphasis on negotiated power has generally been criticized for giving a misleading
sense of a pluralistic process in which all structural power has been
negotiated away (Watson, 1989: Ch 2). Similar arguments could be
made regarding its application to health locales (Bond and Bond,
1986: Ch 7). Undoubtedly the kinds of developments that we have
identified do create the possibility for a more concerted formal
challenge to features of nurse subordination, but how far is another
matter. While some authors see the long-run possibility of an end to
'medical hegemony' in the division of labour, for example Armstrong
(1976), others such as Stacey (1988: Ch 13) believe that it is too soon
to sound the death-knell of medical dominance. Team work may be
the order of the day, but the doctor is still the 'leader of the team' as
one British Medical Association (BMA) report put it. As the BMA's
evidence to the Royal Commission on the NHS in 1977 also made
clear:

> No doctor fails to recognise the necessity of cooperation with the nursing
> profession and with other medical workers. But this does not mean that
> the doctor should in any way hand over his control of the clinical decisions
> concerning the treatment of his patient to anyone else or to a group or
> team. (quoted in Bond and Bond, 1986: 177)

In the absence of such a shift in power, the exercise of informal power
may in fact help to shore up the formal structure of power, by
ensuring its deficiencies and contradictions are addressed in practice,
and such processes may be a general characteristic of work organizations (Gorz, 1976). It may be of significance that both of the studies
cited examine settings where the writ of biomedicine has been often
questioned, and which are also at the 'low status' end of medical
practice. Unless more basic criticisms are to be made of the central
role of biomedicine within the health-care division of labour, it is
therefore unlikely that such developments would lead to more than a
renegotiation of the terms of subordination for some nurses,
particularly those who could claim some managerial authority or
significant role in technological medicine. This would, of course,
leave the basic model intact and thus underwrite the ultimate power
of doctors, at most leading to a more 'pluralistic' hierarchy.

There is, however, another issue which is raised by interactionist
studies, and that is the existence of controlling relationships between
nurses and users of services. Scheff's study in particular highlights the
way that nurse power can be deployed against patients, who seem to
be used as pawns in their battle with doctors (see also Goffman, 1961
for a further analysis of some of the processes involved). Casualty
work is also a locale where aspects of the work are particularly likely

to be concerned with social control (Jeffrey, 1979). Care can therefore easily become a form of custodialism, as Evers (1981) argued in her study of the long-term institutional care of older people. She argues that oppression was not just exercised against them as 'patients' within a dependent sick role, but also involved the gender oppression of women over women based upon sexist stereotyping. Ultimately, therefore, we can only satisfactorily deal with the policy implications of such studies by reaching some kind of assessment about the wider social purpose and validity of such institutions within a social divisions perspective.

As we shall see, in the final section of the chapter, since the 1970s new forms of nursing knowledge have emerged involving at least a partial critique of biomedicine's knowledge base, which as a result may raise more fundamental questions about the role of nurses and indeed patients and lay carers within the health-care division of labour. It is not possible to make sense of this challenge, without also testing it against the validity of radical critiques of medicine and health care that emerged at around the same time from the social movements of the late 1960s. Critiques of medical professional power were part of a more general dissatisfaction with the effects of professionalism and technical expertise within a managed capitalist society, made not long after conservative social philosophers like Daniel Bell (1961) had confidently proclaimed the 'end of ideology'. However, the radical critiques of the late 1960s onwards were not just a swing back towards ideology. They represented a growing and genuine concern at the failure of advanced capitalist societies to fulfil their avowed promise to realize, at one and the same time, both social justice and social efficiency.

Critiques of medicine and health care need therefore to be understood against this wider backcloth of concern and challenge to the status quo. The argument, made in various ways by a diverse set of critics, was that medicine was increasingly failing to deliver the goods. Its claims to technical efficiency were increasingly disputed, particularly the ability to deal, by increasingly technological interventions, with the 'degenerative' diseases characteristic of modern industrial societies. This led both to a neglect of prevention and the marginalization of the care that so many now needed. At the same time medicine's claims to serve social justice were turned on their head. Parsons's bland assurance that social control of the sick was in the interests of everyone became transformed into the doctrine of sickness as a form of oppression. Sometimes this was seen as exercised by doctors purely on their own behalf as part of a professional 'imperialism' against those defined as sick (e.g. Illich, 1976). More satisfactorily, in my view, it was also seen as serving interests of social control in a society divided by class, gender and 'race'. Either way, the idea of medicine as a socially benevolent occupation was increasingly challenged. All in all medical knowledge and medical intentions were viewed as increasingly suspect (Navarro, 1976; J. Ehrenreich, 1978).

My purpose here is not to assess in full the validity of this critique, though I would argue that there is a substantial case to answer. It is rather to work through some of the implications for nurses, since (as usual) they have been left out of these debates. To the extent that the critiques may be justified, they suggest a number of things. First, medical power is not as sacrosanct as once thought. If curative knowledge is often dubious, then perhaps caring knowledge has as much claim to authority. And if doctors are acting to promote their own interests, then this only serves to erode the foundations of the legitimacy of the power they exercise over nurses as heroic commanders in the 'battle' against disease. Second, however, not all features of this critique are necessarily comfortable for nurses, for it calls into question their participation in a high-technology, curative system which may be of dubious benefit, and their own role as agents of control within the health-care system. Nurses themselves also follow the biomedical model in according higher status and prestige to high-technology work (Oakley, 1984) and, as we have seen, caring is often linked to custodial forms of control. Radical critiques therefore invite them not just to protest against their own subordination, but also to fight against other injustices that may be present in the system, which in the past they may have been party to, including a reappraisal of their own relations of power with users. Because of these and other ambiguities, it is likely that many nurses will have divided feelings about the critique of medicine and the movements, such as for increased patients' rights, that may be associated with it.

These problems are perhaps likely to be magnified by the fact that so few radical critics have directly addressed the role of nurses within 'scientific' medicine. Indeed, by seeing them simply as subordinated, they have often missed the more contradictory and ambiguous reality which, in the context of a growing crisis in the biomedical model, creates more possibilities for it to be challenged. I now wish to turn to the question of how Weberian, Marxist and feminist critics of medicine have dealt with the 'nurse question'.

Radical critiques of professional power
One of the most significant departures from Parsons, and one still highly influential, was that of Freidson (1970a, 1970b, 1977). Freidson argued that professionals 'socially constructed' illness as a form of deviance with the support of the dominant elite and the

'public' as a whole, securing in the process a monopoly which ensured autonomy over its own affairs and dominance within the health-care system. Freidson drew his analysis from the Weberian tradition that viewed occupational strategies as at least partly motivated by self-interest and politically mobilized to expand the number of social activities monopolized through a process of 'professionalization'. Thus there was a tendency to inflate or mystify the skills required to sanction the 'social closure' of the occupation (Parkin, 1979). This approach contrasted with the less critical approach to professions as bearers of unique, unquestionable skills and altruistic intentions, which can be traced back through Parsons to late nineteenth century classical sociology (what T. Johnson (1972) calls the 'traits' approach to professions). However, as Freidson made clear (1970a: 277), there was no intention entirely to 'deprecate' medicine's technical accomplishments. It was thus a partial critique of the functionalist tradition, which tended to raise criticisms of aspects of medical power, within a reformist approach.

Freidson has something at least to say about nurses, who are seen as subordinated within the system of 'professional dominance' thus created. Attempts by nurses to professionalize will flounder because for nursing

> to escape subordination to medical authority, it must find some area of work over which it can claim and maintain a monopoly, but it must do so in a setting in which the central task *is* healing and controlled by medicine. (Freidson, 1970a: 66, original emphasis)

In a subsequent essay Freidson rightly added that professionalization of nurses and other 'technical' workers could also be thwarted by 'managerial agents of either the state . . . or corporate capital' (1977:25). Yet though he is substantially correct, the effects may be more contradictory than he suggests, as indicated by the counter-claim of Armstrong (1976) that state power over nursing through the National Health Service (NHS) enhances professionalization. Freidson's analysis may be compared with the claim of Etzioni (1969) that nurses (and allied occupations like social work and teaching) are 'semi-professions', differentiated from full professions by virtue of their shorter training, lower status, less 'privileged' communication with clients, less developed body of specialized knowledge, and less autonomy from supervision and societal supervision. The difference is that while Etzioni seems to regard these differences as largely technically determined, Freidson allows for the possibility that they may be partly constructed by the weight of social and political power.

The alternative Marxist analysis of professionalization is diverse, but two prominent themes or preoccupations can be identified which tend to differentiate it from Weberian approaches, and lead to a much more conditional view of professional power. Whereas Weberians tend to see professions as indicative of a class structure in which occupations have become the determining factor, through 'knowledge'-based systems of power, Marxists insist that this has not eroded or fundamentally fragmented the power of the ruling class. First, though professionals may come to exercise a degree of 'relatively autonomous' power, this is conditional in the last resort on it being perceived to be in the interests of the dominant groups in society. Although in theory dedicated to satisfying human needs regardless of clients' social position, professional power rests ultimately on the ability either to contribute in some way, directly or indirectly, to capitalist efficiency (accumulation), or alternatively to frustrate democratic control of society through the mystification of technocratic power (legitimation). Power is exercised, but within defined limits.

Second, however, this achievement of a degree of relatively autonomous power is insecure. It is likely to be eroded, leading to a long-run tendency towards proletarianization. Again this is in marked contrast to the traditional Weberian emphasis on the expansion of knowledge-based forms of power. Marx's account of the downfall of the independent artisan is by analogy applied to professionals, who are seen as becoming subjected to similar processes of 'deskilling' which might one day propel them into the working class. For example, Larson (1977) argues that the power that established professions secured belongs to an earlier 'liberal' period of industrialization, which is now threatened by a growing concentration of economic and political power and bureaucratized work environments under advanced capitalism. As a result professionalism becomes increasingly less a form of real power, and more a means of ideological control exercised from above over intermediate groups of workers, to convince them that their interests are different from other workers or their subordinated clients.

These are tendencies, and the emphasis varies within and between the Weberian and Marxist traditions. It can be argued that the 'professional dominance' thesis is not necessarily incompatible with a Marxist approach to professions (e.g. Turner, 1987). When Freidson (1977) himself argued that the prospects for a future advance in professional power beyond the established professions were limited, he specifically acknowledged the strengths of Marxist analysis. However, as Navarro (1988) has recently pointed out, within the 'professional dominance' thesis, it is not expected that the power of established professions themselves will be substantially eroded. When it does, it is a problem which needs explaining, rather than the more predictable event that it is in Marxist analysis.

Navarro himself focuses primarily on medicine and medical professionalization, though like Freidson he does have something to say about the role of nurses and other health workers. This is really an extension of his argument about 'professional dominance' which he argues, in a 'strong version' of the Marxist case, cannot be eroded because it never existed. He comes close to arguing that medical power was consciously orchestrated by the bourgeoisie,[3] in which

> professional power was and is submerged in other forms of power such as class, race, gender, and other forces that shape the production of the knowledge, practice, and institutions of medicine. (Navarro, 1988: 64)

However, Navarro also draws attention to the way health care and health knowledge are also shaped by pressures from below, by the struggle between capital and labour, and other subordinated groups, the outcome of which may vary between societies. For example, he attributes the earlier 'discovery' of black lung disease among miners in Britain than the USA to the greater social weight of the labour movement in Britain.

Within this model, it is the constitution of the medical profession as a 'fraction' of the ruling class that establishes its power over the health-care division of labour. Thus the social hierarchy in health care mirrors the class, gender and 'race' divisions of the wider society – both are ultimately socially rather than technically determined as forms of ownership and control. For example, the relation between doctor and nurse are seen as constructed as much on familial as technical lines, traceable back to Florence Nightingale's explicit intentions in this regard (Navarro, 1976: Part 3). Thus we can see that, as far as it goes, Navarro's analysis raises gender relations as a determinant of nurses' position, in a much more direct way than Freidson, who largely omits any reference to gender. He also suggests that broader challenges to women's subordination, including but not exclusive to nursing, are factors which are leading to a redefinition of relationships within the health team (Navarro, 1988).

It could also be argued that changes in the labour process have also been significant in providing a technical basis from which to challenge aspects of nurse subordination. For example Bellaby and Oribabor (1980) argue within a Marxist approach that the Nightingale model with its emphasis on basic care, hygiene and housekeeping, under the rigid control of the matron as head of the household, became an 'obstacle' with the development of the curative medical model, in which the hospital increasingly resembled the capitalist factory, and required a new kind of nurse who was more of a physician's assistant or technician, alongside other emergent 'paramedical' helpers. It was this, they argue, that led to the growth of an internal division of labour in nursing, which they call the 'grade system', in which 'basic', especially housekeeping and basic caring, tasks were handed on to untrained nurses or even domestics, while 'technical' nursing itself become a more specialized occupation, but one increasingly fragmented along the lines dictated by medical specialization. As a result the original unity and cohesion of the 'nursing structure' under the matron or head nurse was eroded. However, the creation of the 'grade system' could not itself prevent further fragmentation caused by the extension of medical specialization and high-technology care. As a result managerial hierarchies began to develop at a higher level, partly in order to coordinate this fragmented labour process, partly to control accelerating costs as labour-intensive curative medicine failed to fulfil its promise to 'work itself out of business'. Bellaby and Oribabor (1977) linked these developments to a supposed loss of control by ward-level nurses in the 1970s, associated with deskilling, proletarianization and increased trade-union militancy (see also Carpenter, 1977).

Their analysis is very persuasive, but perhaps too unilinear. It is interesting to compare it to the 'negotiated order' approach of Strauss et al. (1963), which suggests that fragmentation into a variety of work sites creates a *decentralized* authority structure. The tendencies they describe are real, but there are others running in counter directions. First, there is no doubt that the technical skills of some nurses are expanding as a result of these developments, but that these are underrecognized and undervalued within a system of professional dominance. Second, within the grade system the caring responsibilities of other nurses are also underrecognized and undervalued, not just by doctors and the health system as a whole, but also within nursing. The reasons are clear enough, for in the context of a capitalist model of health care curative medicine is more likely to be seen as 'productive' labour (making an indirect contribution to capitalist accumulation), while caring is largely 'unproductive'. Such distinctions are also eagerly reproduced by occupational elites seeking to monopolize the extrinsic and intrinsic rewards of 'interesting' work, and load off the rest to others.

Yet we do also need, as Navarro indicates, to look at the impact of external social movements upon nursing. During the period analysed by Bellaby and Oribabor, the trade-union movement in Britain was generally in a high state of mobilization, and many groups which had not formerly been very active were now taking part in militant activities, including nurses. Feminism can also be shown to be influential, though its impact may not be simple. Some more 'liberal' currents encouraged nurses to seek greater access to and recognition for technical and managerial skills, on the grounds of 'equal opportunities', and be supportive of professionalizing moves. More radical approaches questioned the division of cure and care itself in ways that described professionalism not only as a means of oppression and exploitation of nurses by doctors, but also an elitist and divisive force within nursing, and between nurses and patients.

The most influential account of the origins of nurse subordination which integrates class and gender within a radical perspective on cure and care is that of B. Ehrenreich and D. English (1973). Although its polemics have perhaps rightly been criticized (e.g. Versluysen, 1980), its attempt to locate nurses within the development of technological health care does have many strengths. The authors show that in the USA the emergence of the subordinated nurse fitted into a wider pattern, which they see as part of the reordering of patriarchy within the emerging industrial capitalist society. This involved the displacement of the traditional 'wisewomen' healers by 'scientific' doctors, the increasing exclusion of women and black people from medical schools, and the outlawing of potential rival practitioners like midwives (a process which went much further in the USA than Britain). Initially the new training scheme for nurses 'emphasised character not skills'. They argue that the nineteenth-century feminist movement went along with this in order to gain a foothold for women in the public sphere on the strength of displaying essential 'feminine' qualities, patterns also repeated in teaching and social work. However they also point out that the rationalization of medicine and the 'reform' of training associated with the rise of curative medicine in the early twentieth century, and symbolized in the USA by the Flexner Report, brought nurses more directly into an increasingly 'commoditized' system of medicine:

> The new, post-Flexner physician was even less likely than his predecessor to stand around and watch the progress of his 'cures'. He diagnosed, he prescribed, he moved on. He could not waste his talents or his expensive academic training in the tedious details of bedside care. For this he needed a patient obedient helper, someone who was not above the most menial tasks, in short a nurse. Healing in its fullest sense consists of both curing and caring, doctoring and nursing. . . . But with the development of scientific medicine, and the modern medical profession, the two functions split irrevocably. Curing became the exclusive province of the doctor; caring was relegated to the nurse. All credit for the patient's recovery went to the doctor and his 'quick fix', for only the doctor participated in the mystique of science. The nurse's activities, on the other hand, were barely distinguishable from those of a servant. She had no power, and no claim to the credit. (B. Ehrenreich and D. English, 1973: 58)

Another advantage of the Ehrenreich and English approach is that it connects the treatment of women within the health-care system as both producers and users. This does not mean that the female nurse will automatically ally herself with the female patient. In fact, the more she falls in behind the medical model, with its support for male medical control, the less this is likely to occur.

From our point of view, however, the main deficiency with this account is its failure to recognize that some nurses increasingly took on administrative and technical curative skills. The work of Davies and Rosser (1986) is relevant here. They showed that clerical workers in the health service, though in theory menial and low-skilled, often carried a large number of significant responsibilities, while the power or economic rewards went instead to male seniors. They suggest that this undervaluing occurred because such skills had been acquired as a result of women's life experiences, rather than through formal educational qualifications or occupational training. The danger as a result is that if work done by women lacks these formal trappings, it may by definition be assumed to be deskilled or of little value. Relevant here is the suggestion of Graham (1983) that to define work as 'caring' in either the public or private sphere may be to impose a label which subsumes a wide variety of disparate activities, the only common denominator being the low economic value associated with them. Yet caring involves both 'emotional' and physical labour, with at one and the same time expressive and instrumental outcomes.

Though class and gender are generally well represented in available sociological studies of nursing, 'race' has received hardly any attention. So if nurses have at least sometimes cast a faint shadow on the discipline of medical sociology, black nurses have been virtually invisible within the sociology of nursing. Yet it is clear that in many industrialized societies the kinds of developments in health care which have been described above have led to a significant degree of 'racialization' around the care–cure divide which has been particularly pronounced in an occupation like nursing. The employment of black nurses and other health workers has served three sets of purposes, whether in market or social systems of health care. First, their use as a disadvantaged labour reserve has served to cheapen the costs of health care in a labour-intensive service, in particular where low wages and/or the nature of the work itself would serve to deter recruits. In Britain the racialization of nursing became particularly pronounced in high-wage, high-employment areas like London and the South-East, and unpopular specialties like mental hospitals and the care of older people which employed fewer qualified or registered nurses (Doyal et al., 1981–82; McNaught, 1988). Second, the process of social closure, reinforced by discrimination, serves to promote individual and collective mobility for white men and women within nursing, heightening divisions in, and management control over, the workforce. This too is of course part of a more general process of discrimination in which white aspirations for occupational mobility are more likely to be satisfied by drafting in black people to carry out low-status work, particularly in the service sector. Thirdly, as with women, such treatment of black workers within the health-care system is also matched by discrimination against them as users, with a heightened emphasis on exclusion and control (Williams, 1987).

Of course in practice we cannot separate out different social divisions of class, 'race' and gender in the way that we have analysed them here. Social interests given by class, 'race' and gender run in complex directions, particularly when also considered across the producer–user divide. However, the general historical and sociological analysis that has been developed here shows that the traditional picture of nursing as a subordinated and low-skilled occupation can to an extent be questioned. I have also suggested the low value and power accorded to both technical and caring skills is now more of an issue because curative medicine is itself in crisis.

Nursing and the crisis in health care

I have placed most emphasis on understanding this crisis within a radical perspective, which would imply the need for a breakdown of divisions between cure and care and the hierarchies associated with them, within a system that also gave much greater priority to addressing the social causes of ill health. Though one possibility, it is of course not one that is likely to be implemented without an intense struggle, because it is not in the interests of the entrenched white male class structure which dominates the health system and society at large.

As a result, we are seeing attempts to impose 'solutions' to the health-care crisis of industrialized societies which involve attempts to shift to more 'explicit rationing' of health care (Turner, 1987: Ch 10) and which are likely to heighten rather than diminish social divisions in health care. However, in the process, tensions are emerging within the professional groups which dominate health care, and the more powerful dominant groups in the wider society. Already this is leading to inter- and intra-occupational splits which run along complex rather than single fault lines. As part of this, some nurses, particularly those with marketable skills, may stand to enhance their position in the scramble for power, partly because a degree of nurse substitution for doctors makes some sense from the viewpoint of a managerial rationalization. Others, particularly those involved in more caring forms of nursing, stand to lose as these are devalued further and even removed from the health-care system. In other words moves toward a more explicit rationing of health care are more likely to favour the development of a more streamlined, efficient curative system, involving attempts to work the biomedical model harder within more closely defined limits, within the same 'mechanistic' and capitalistic model of health, rather than to transform it. Thus, though this is likely to involve a degree of attenuation of medical power, subjected increasingly to greater managerial and/or market discipline (with high rewards for some doctors to entice them to break ranks), it will fall short of full-scale medical proletarianization.

The competitive struggle for power within and between health-care occupations is likely to be matched by a similar competitiveness among users of health care. An increased emphasis on 'consumerism' will ensure that those with more social and/or economic power will be able to gain most out of a system in which health care will be increasingly rationed rather than freely available to all. And of course occupational power within the health-care system will depend on what individuals and groups can contribute to the emerging 'streamlined' curative system.

This kind of solution is not inevitable, especially since it is hopelessly flawed, but the ability to exploit its contradictions will depend in part on the strength of social forces in a particular society. I have suggested that nurses, according to ideology and position, are likely to be pulled in different directions by such developments, and towards different sets of alliances within the health-care structure and outside it. I now wish to consider such issues specifically in the context of a historical analysis of the development of social divisions in British nursing. Before I do, it might help to present the basic theoretical argument about social divisions and nursing in the form of a diagram (Figure 5.1).

The diagram (5.1) suggests that the hierarchal division of labour in health care should be understood in an overlapping and dual sense as both a socially made capitalist (class) and patriarchal (familial) labour process. The position of nurses within the dual system of subordination is constituted by ambiguities in both the capitalist 'disease' and the patriarchal 'illness' models. In the capitalist labour process there are ambiguities about whether the nurse is a technician or manual labourer, and in the patriarchal labour process about whether she is a servant or a complementary partner. Professionalizing movements have traditionally organized around these contradictions by seeking to reform patterns of subordination, initially by reshaping the definition of the nurse as a whole in more universally favourable terms. However as this proves difficult due to cost and the

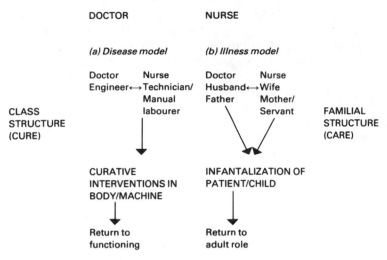

Figure 5.1   *Simplified representation of doctor–nurse–patient relationships under biomedical model and sick role*

threat it poses to entrenched white and male class structures, professionalizing movements compromise by seeking to offload socially undesired or undervalued elements of the nurse role. It is the latter in particular that also (across both 'models') leads to divisions of class, 'race' and gender within nursing. Attempts to reform aspects of nurses' role may seek also to reform, but not fundamentally to challenge the role of the 'patient'.

More recent and radical challenges to the status quo seek to challenge class, gender and 'race' roles from the outside as part of a wider attack on subordination. They may also seek to undermine the internal basis for health care hierarchies by challenging both the disease and sickness models, as ways of ordering relations between doctors, nurses and other 'paramedicals', and users of services.

The case of British nursing

The theoretical model that I have outlined suggests that nurse subordination is not an established fact, but something that has to be constantly recreated, capable of challenge as a result of internal developments and trends in health care and the weight of social forces in the wider society. I now wish to consider this relatively briefly in the context of the development of British nursing, where health care has been shaped by the creation after 1945 of a universal system of socialized health care under a system of professional dominance. I want to suggest that the crisis in medicine and the challenge to class, gender and 'race' forms of subordination especially since the late 1960s are factors which favour a challenge to such subordination. However, the linked crisis in the welfare state and the coming to power of the new right in the 1980s are leading to attempts to impose neo-liberal solutions to this crisis, which if successfully implemented will tend to heighten rather diminish patterns of domination and subordination in health care.

The 'facts' concerning the development of British nursing are readily available (Abel-Smith, 1960; Dingwall et al., 1988). This is therefore an attempted interpretative account which inevitably glosses over important details. My starting point is the distinction made in the USA by Habenstein and Christ (1955) between three 'types' of nurses with rather different ideological orientations: 'traditionalizers', 'professionalizers' and 'utilizers'. Very briefly, while the 'traditionalizer' is focused on the needs of the patient, and deferent to the doctor, the 'professionalizer' is skills-focused and more self-assertive. The 'utilizer', on the other hand, is just concerned to do the job, fulfil the labour contract, and get home. Habenstein and Christ recognized that these 'ideal types' might not be found in their pure form. I want to use them as a way of analysing, within a social divisions approach, how nurses themselves have sought to shape their destiny according to different sets of ideals and aspirations, and how these have been shaped by both 'technical' factors and changes in the labour process, and wider social movements.

I would argue that British nursing has been subjected to three main attempted transformations by occupational elites which have been constrained by changing social divisions in the health-care system and the weight of social forces in the wider society. The first two stages are characterized by the growing ascendancy of both professionalized medicine and the welfare state. The third stage emerges during a period when both are in crisis, and nursing's occupational future is likely to be conditioned by the direction in which these are resolved. The three stages are:

Stage one   The Nightingale era, which lasted from the mid-nineteenth century to around the time of the First World War. This was characterized by subordination to medicine, but involved an attempt to create a sphere of autonomy for the occupation within the hospital, the 'nursing structure'. It was a 'localist' strategy of control which was careful not to trespass against the managerial needs of the local hospital. This was a pre-feminist movement which sought to expand the social position of women within prevailing male definitions of their role, through the social creation of the 'traditionalizer' nurse.

Stage two The attempted 'professionalization' or social closure of care as an exclusively middle-class occupation, which was initiated in the late nineteenth century by Mrs Bedford Fenwick. This sought professional autonomy for the nursing structure from the state and local managements, an extension of the domination of general nursing over the nursing universe, and a complementary but still subordinated position of nursing to an ascendant medicine – a 'cosmopolitan' or occupation-wide strategy of control.[4] It was a movement which emerged from the 'first-wave' feminist movement of the late nineteenth century, involving an attempt to socially construct a 'professionalizer' nurse.

Stage three The new professionalism, characterized by a number of different currents, all of which seek in a more concerted way to establish cosmopolitan autonomy in relation to the state. However, for the first time, in any serious way, there is an attempt to renegotiate, and even challenge, the traditional subordinate relation of nursing to medicine. It has been strengthened by the growing problems and limitations of the medical model, and influenced by a number of social movements since the 1960s, but most significantly by trade unionism (speaking up for the 'utilizer' nurse) and a professionalism linked to 'liberal' feminism (rather than its more radical currents). It represents the attempt in part to create a type of nurse synthesizing 'professionalizer' and 'utilizer' elements, but perhaps also to create something new which is not encapsulated by any of the three models of Habenstein and Christ.

I will now look at each of these three stages in a little more detail, focusing finally on the third stage, and its potentialities and problems.

Stage one: the Nightingale era
The first reform movement, based on the vocation/womanly ideal of the nurse, influenced the phase of nursing development which lasted from around the middle of the nineteenth century to the beginning of the twentieth. It largely achieved its goal (though to a much lesser degree in the Poor Law hospitals and asylums), which was, under Nightingale's influence, to transform the nurse according to the ideal of the Victorian 'good woman'. Yet though nurses were born rather than made, it was still seen as necessary to add certain nursing skills through an apprenticeship training. So gender definitions were

fundamental to the definition of what constituted a 'good nurse', even though they did not completely define its limits. Hence nursing was a womanly 'vocation' for which the prime qualities were a high moral character ('decency'), willingness to carry out menial tasks necessary to patient welfare, and a readiness to offer unswerving obedience to the doctor, acting as a subordinate but necessary female counterpoint. This system led to the subordination of the patient through a process of infantalization within the triad doctor (father, decision-taker), nurse (mother, nurturer), patient (compliant child) (see Garmanikow, 1978). Nursing was organized very much along bureaucratic and hierarchical lines under the matron, and organized by ward tasks rather than around the needs of individual patients, typically the sick poor, who were also regulated by this bureaucratic authority (Dean and Bolton, 1980).

Strictly speaking, the system predates the full-scale development of the biomedical model, as indeed does medical professionalization itself (which was granted in 1858 more in anticipation of its future promise than demonstrable therapeutic results). Nursing reform itself, under Nightingale's influence, was based on the dominant 'miasmatic' theory of disease, which assumed that disease was carried by particles in the air signified by smells: hence the emphasis in nursing practice on hygiene and fresh air. This theory, which was a driving force behind public health reform during the nineteenth century, placed considerable emphasis on the environment as a cause of disease, so that the emphasis in early nursing is as much on regulating the ward environment as the needs of the individual patient (Woodward, 1974).

It was a localist strategy, focused in managerial terms on the needs of the particular hospital, and strongly articulated in terms of the social divisions of the day, of both class and gender. The division of labour in health care reflects the wider social division of labour in that the middle-class woman is superordinate in the household and has her sphere of autonomy over the servants. However, she must still respect the authority of her husband over the crucial issues about the survival of the household in the wider world. In other words it involves power within a system of dependence. The key internal divisions of the time which emerged were class ones between the lady pupils and ordinary probationers, once the working-class women (the 'Sarah Gamps' who formerly did the care) were either resocialized or expelled.

Stage two: the professionalization of care
The second reform movement, whose emergence overlapped with the end of the first phase of nursing development, and persisted until

around the end of the 1960s, sought to define nursing skills as more scientifically than intuitively based, and attempted on this basis to erect an exclusive occupation based on state registration. Nursing skills were not exactly seen as separate from gender, but needed to be acquired – this was, after all, the era in which 'domestic science' also emerged, which emphasized that girls needed to be trained in womanhood. Nursing also began to embrace more technical as well as caring skills, some of which had been handed down by doctors. Though nurses were still largely 'good' women, they were thus to be made rather than born through a system of academic training. Since this applied to both caring and technical skills, nursing should be a wholly trained profession.

This movement was initiated by Mrs Bedford Fenwick in the era of 'first wave' feminism, in opposition to Nightingale and her allies. It was spearheaded by the elite Lady Pupils who sought autonomy from the hospital, and private duty nurses (Dingwall, 1986). Its 'cosmopolitanism' – the attempt to create a universally transferable system of training – was in part an attempt to improve the 'marketability' of nursing skills as a commodity.

The knowledge base was therefore partly still rooted in hygiene and housekeeping, but the professionalizing movement also sought to attach medical knowledge and tasks to nursing. In other words, it sought to hitch its fortunes to the ascendant biomedical model, increasingly capitalizing on its increasing therapeutic success as a result of the germ theory of disease. In nursing this reinforced the passivity and objectification of the patient already pronounced within the Nightingale system, but added a more rational 'technical' basis to the familial system of control over the patient. In no way was the intention to challenge nursing's subordination to medicine, even though some doctors were worried nurse professionalization might lead to their own substitution, particularly in private practice.

The retention of the task system of work organization in nursing protected medical prerogatives. There is some mileage in the psychoanalytically influenced notion that it helped to protect nurses from the anxiety generated by disease and suffering, by limiting contact with patients (Menzies, 1963). However, it was also an ideal way of ensuring that doctors retained control over the diagnostic and treatment process as a whole, while parcelling out fragmented bits of the labour process to nurses (Carpenter, 1978).

The movement's main aim was to achieve exclusivity, as well as autonomy from hospital and nursing managements, through a scheme of state registration modelled very much on that achieved by doctors in the mid-nineteenth century. Its subsidiary aim was to achieve domination for general hospital nursing within the constellation of occupations which had become attached to it, some more willingly than others. The movement's acceptance of professional dominance on the one hand, and the only partial success of its other avowed aims, have together conditioned a semi-professional form of organization in nursing, which has set the context for a prolonged struggle for occupational control which continues to this day. The movement's greatest victory was the 1919 Nurse Registration Act, though that perhaps should not be attributed solely to its efforts. External forces were also extremely powerful in the initial shift to state registration, and also in blunting its impact in subsequent years. The oft-cited desire to reward women for their contribution to the war effort may have been a factor, but so too was the Liberal government's original intention to create a national health system after the War, which demanded some rationalization of nurse training (Dingwall et al., 1988). The collapse of plans for social reform, in the face of growing economic difficulties and diminished threat of working-class revolution (Navarro, 1978), also by implication led to a dilution of professionalizing moves. Governments, also under pressure from employing authorities, intervened consistently to restrain professionalizing moves by nurses on the General Nursing Council (GNC), which had been set up in 1919 to supervise registration (Abel-Smith, 1960).

The eventual nationalization of the health-care system, initially during the Second World War, and confirmed by the creation of the NHS as part of the welfare state after it, might have been expected to alter this situation. As we saw, Armstrong (1976) argued that nationalization was leading to greater recognition for semi-professions in health care that in the long run might also threaten medical dominance. The capacity of this development to enhance nurses' position was limited for three main reasons. First, the creation of the NHS, though enacted by a 'socialist' government, was based on unswerving support of the principle of professional dominance as the fundamental organizing principle for the new service (Foot, 1973; Klein, 1989), which served to legitimate medical rule over other occupations in the health-care division of labour. Second, even during an expansionist period the demands placed upon state expenditure always outstripped the resources available, and the NHS was particularly affected as a service largely financed out of general taxation rather than contributions or charges. Third, and not unconnected, despite the hopes of its creators the NHS did not work itself out of business by creating a healthier population. The costs of the intensified technological revolution in health care, as well as the growing need for care, led to a continuing squeeze on nursing expenditure as the largest part of the budget.

The 'grade' system (as you will recall Bellaby and Oribabor called it) eventually emerged as a response to such pressures, leading to firmly established divisions by the 1960s between untrained nursing auxiliaries and assistants, enrolled nurses with a two-year practically based training, and registered nurses with a three-year, more 'academically' focused training. As a result caring and curing responsibilities were redistributed within nursing, with a greater concentration of registered grades in the high-status acute sector, and unqualified and enrolled grades in the lower-status, more caring sectors.

The other failure of the professionalizing movement was its desire to create a generic nursing occupation in 1919. Instead separate registers became established for general nurses on the one hand, and mental illness, mental handicap and children's nurses on the other. Health Visiting and midwifery retained a separate occupational identity from general hospital nursing but entry to them depended increasingly on state registration (see Dingwall et al., 1988 for more details). This partial unification of nursing contrasted markedly with the medical profession, part of whose system of professional control was based on the principle that all entrants to specialist branches approached them through a common professional entry point.

Part of the reason for this situation in nursing was the jealously guarded autonomy of the 'sub-occupations' themselves. Mental nursing in particular, where larger numbers of working-class men were concentrated, resented and resisted the incursion of middle-class professionalizing women. In turn this was reflected in ideological conflict, with mental nurses and to some extent nurses in Poor Law (later local authority) hospitals being more likely as a result of the work itself (its closer association with basic care and/or custodialism), as well as their own working-class predispositions, to develop a 'utilizing' ideology. This led them to identify more with trade-union concerns with pay and conditions, and the rising labour movement, than professional concerns with status and occupational autonomy (Abel-Smith, 1960; Carpenter, 1988).

By the late 1960s, the grade system was one factor which was leading to a reorientation of outlook among many nurses. Among unqualified and enrolled nurses, there was a growing concern with pay and conditions as the prime focus for collective organization. Registered nurses were being pulled in two directions, some more towards union concerns to address the effects of subordination and low pay, others more towards addressing thwarted professional ambitions. This also affected the masculinization of the nursing authority structure associated with the grade structure, leading to a new group of highly mobile nursing leaders who could be called 'managerializers' (see Carpenter, 1977). At the same time, though there was some suggestion that the racialization of care created some opportunities for upward mobility for black nurses, grade and specialty discrimination ensured a strong 'instrumental' orientation among them (*Race Today*, 1974). Restrictions on NHS expenditure, managerial changes including the 1974 reorganization of the NHS, the growth in numbers of part-time women workers, and the general favourable political culture for 'instrumental' trade unionism, led initially to an explosion of militancy in the 1970s. Meanwhile, however, and almost unnoticed, the professionalizers were marshalling their forces for a renewed campaign, in some ways similar to, but in others rather different from, the past.

Stage three: the new professionalism
The third phase, which emerged (or was introduced into Britain from the USA) in the early 1970s, in part involves a renewed attempt to achieve longstanding goals of professionalization. Thus 'Project 2000' of the United Kingdom Central Council for Nursing and Midwifery (UKCC),[5] which is currently being implemented, aims to separate nurse training from the hospital and grant 'proper' student status to learner nurses by taking them out of the workforce. It also seeks to create a generic system of training and a single register. There are two new features that characterize this phase of professionalization. First, whereas previous movements have sought initially to professionalize the whole occupation, this time around the aim is primarily to turn 'clinical' nursing into an exclusive occupation. Basic care, carried out previously by untrained or enrolled nurses (often black) after a two-year practical training, and students as 'pairs of hands', is now being gradually assigned to an army of 'support workers' or 'health-care assistants' who are likely only to receive a limited training. Thus, though it will be supervised by an elite corps of trained nurses, a significant amount of basic nursing care is now being defined as the work of 'others', and nursing itself is increasingly being redefined to mean primarily clinical nursing.

The second break with the past is the attempt to redefine the position of clinical nursing (and hence trained nurses) within the health-care division of labour. Linked to this is an attempt to 'intellectualize' clinical nursing. An integral part of the 'new' nursing is an attempt to establish a new knowledge base independent of medicine and other health-care professions (see Armstrong, 1983). In the past 'nursing knowledge' has often involved a cut-down version of medical training. The development of intellectual nursing systems, many imported from the USA, is reflected, for example, in the current popularity of 'nursing models'. These attempt to devise a systematic and intellectually rigorous approach to the definition of patients' health-care needs, in order to improve health-care delivery (Salvage and Kershaw, 1986, 1990). However, these models might also be seen as attempts to stake out a sphere of occupational autonomy, redefining nursing as intellectual rather than manual labour in order to acquire the 'attributes' of a profession. The widespread adoption of another American 'import', the 'nursing process', which emulates medical professional practice through individual nursing histories, diagnosis and care plans, could similarly be seen as an attempt to mark out a sphere of occupational independence, as well as placing nursing care on a more rational, rigorous and individualized basis.

There is no doubt that the implementation of such 'models' and 'processes' involves attempts to produce dramatic shifts in the organization of health-care delivery. For example, 'primary nursing' has become closely linked to the implementation of the nursing process, under which a trained nurse becomes the 'key' and responsible worker for a group of patients/clients. Processes of patient participation are in theory built into the new system, on an individual nurse-to-patient basis. Individualization of care, rather than organization of nursing care by task (such as dressings, injections and so on), is integral to the 'new' nursing. Another closely allied development, particularly in the community sector, is the development of the 'nurse practitioner' role, with a semi-independent diagnostic as well as treatment role (Department of Health and Social Security, 1986; Austin, 1979). The 'new' nursing implies a challenge to patterns of traditional subordination of registered clinical nurses, to both medicine and higher nurse management (Beardshaw and Robinson, 1990).

In the USA, where after all many of these developments originate, the reform movement initiated by nursing leaders has been portrayed by Reverby (1989) as strongly influenced by 'liberal feminism'. It involves an attempt to move nursing away from the dominant ideology of the past, which imposed on nurses, as women, an 'obligation to care', to a situation in which they still serve others but without being subservient. The new professionalism and its associated intellectualization of nursing seek to resolve traditional dilemmas between caring and self-determination by promising greater benefits to the patient as a result of greater nurse autonomy, through more personalized care for the patient, and the extension of the role of the nurse to encompass that of becoming the 'patient's advocate'.

It is easy to see how much of this draws upon radical critiques of health care and the dominant medical model, including doubts about medical effectiveness, disregard of the patient's subjectivity and the overbureaucratization and routinization of care. In the process, the 'new nursing' also critically distances itself from many traditional nursing approaches to care. Yet the radical potential of the new nursing can easily be exaggerated. For one thing, it will tend to widen the social divisions within the nursing workforce, marking out sharper divisions between clinical and basic care, with the dangers of creating a white, middle-class nursing elite (Baxter, 1988). In most instances it will involve less of a direct challenge to medical power than an attempt to reform it, a renegotiation of traditional patterns of subordination and a claim for greater 'responsible autonomy' within it. While the benefits for patients that may well in many instances be associated with the new nursing are undeniable, individual advocacy seems to fall a long way short of collective patient or user empowerment.

The restructuring of health care under Conservative governments in the 1980s has in some senses been favourable to the demands of the new professionalism in British nursing, but in ways that on the whole help to curtail its 'progressive' potential. In part the tacit encouragement of professional associations like the Royal College of Nursing represented an attempt to divide and weaken support for more militant trade unionism. In addition, the uplifting and separation of an elite of clinical nurses from basic carers fits in broadly with a managerialist rationalization of the health service, in which 'skilled' workers will obtain higher rewards and autonomy, while basic care is generally cheapened. This process has been reinforced by the implementation of a 'clinical grading' pay structure since 1988. The whole process of 'substitution' and delegation of tasks, often referred to as the 'skill-mix', has also become a live issue. An increasing amount of basic care is being transferred to health-care assistants, which may well lead to a shrinking number of qualified nurses in the future.

Other aspects of the 'new right' approach to health policy could be seen as congruent with the new professionalism. For example, the individualist focus of the nursing process, and its desire to promote patient 'self-care' and early mobility might be regarded as 'cost-effective'. Others have argued that primary nursing fits in with a new right decentralized approach to management, in which ward sisters become increasingly budget holders and primary nurses are held responsible for the care they give (Bowers, 1989). The emphasis on decentralized systems of power also gives strength to the new professionalism at a time when nursing managerialism has been largely eclipsed in the wider managerial structure (Robinson and Strong, 1987). The 'demographic time bomb' – an increased need to recruit nurses to care for an ageing population – also put pressure on the government to enhance the attractiveness of nursing, both to attract and retain trained nurses. On the other hand, it also potentially strengthens the labour market position of the large numbers of those who need to be recruited to perform more basic care. One way that this might be resolved relatively cheaply after 1992, in the context of the single European market, might be to recruit large numbers of staff from southern Europe (Beardshaw and Robinson, 1990: Ch 7).

Other aspects of the new right rationalization of health care, however, particularly the attempt to intensify working conditions in the search for better 'value for money', are likely to inhibit the progress of the new professionalism. Cost pressures are already delaying the implementation of Project 2000. The increased managerialist emphasis on quantity – which is likely to be reinforced by the introduction of an 'internal market' in the NHS (involving pricing and competition between health providers through a system of contracting) under the 1990 NHS and Community Care Act – might force nurses to sacrifice quality, and will inhibit the ability to implement individualized systems of care fully. Matching changes in staffing levels to increased throughput of patients, Moores (1987) estimated that there had been an overall increase in nursing workload of 32 per cent in the years 1962–84. This suggests that there are growing pressures to deliver higher standards of care at a time when the means available to deliver it are diminishing and when also, if the radical critique is correct, curative medicine is itself in crisis. This is likely to increase stress levels of nurses, not only because of 'pressure' of work, but because holistic nursing adds to the load of 'emotional' labour carried by nurses. In other words, implemented in a managerialist context, the new nursing may well heighten rather than resolve caring dilemmas. The demanding Code of Professional Conduct developed by the UKCC in 1984, and backed up by a firm disciplinary machinery, may well be adding to these pressures, by magnifying nurses' sense of vulnerability. Nurses are being asked to take on added responsibilities, with limited resources and no real power, and at the same time expected to be more accountable for the quality of care.

Conclusions

The theoretical perspective developed in this chapter, and applied to the specific context of British nursing developments, has suggested that nurses' position within the health-care system is partly technically determined from within the health-care system, but also socially by the cleavages associated by the wider society, and the extent to which these are challenged by social movements. In some senses this is an optimistic analysis. The development of curative medicine as a complex labour process, and its growing crisis, both present possibilities for a reordering of social relationships in health care that might enhance the position of nurses within it. Since health care is also politically determined from the outside, this also creates possibilities by which political challenges might modify or transform hierarchical relationships.

In other senses the analysis is pessimistic, in that it challenges the notion that professionalizing movements, particularly those associated with subordinated groups of workers, can easily break free of their constraints, unless they can lend their weight to wider struggles for social change. Especially during the last decade, when social divisions have been widening in all industrialized countries, insular occupational strategies will at best benefit an occupational elite, and their progressive potential will be weakened. This is not to argue that the attempts to shift towards a new nursing have no positive features. Rather it is to agree with Reverby's view that 'the dilemma of nursing is too tied to society's broader problems of gender and class [and 'race'?] to be solved solely by the political or professional efforts of one occupational group' (1989: 482).

A 'solution' to nurses' particular problem of subordination can only therefore occur in a political context favourable to addressing social subordination in general. However, nursing has a great deal to contribute to that solution if it can also develop a strategy which addresses not only its own subordination to medicine but nursing's internal division of power, and its role in controlling rather than empowering users. This would also need more nurses to begin to see common ground and forge new alliances with all those seeking to change the present class-bound, racist and sexist health-care system and its distorted system of priorities.

There are many possibilities on which to build, from critiques of medical effectiveness, to feminist challenges to male medical supremacy, from abundant evidence on the social causes of ill-health and their links with the same inequalities of 'race', gender and class which also permeate the health system, to the so-called 'demographic crisis' – the growing social need for care in a society which does not value it. These are the kinds of 'political' issues which have enormous implications for nurses and nursing and building them into occupational strategies in my view offers a more hopeful long-term way of resolving the fundamental problems of the health system, at the same time as it addresses the position of nurses within it, than an isolated pursuit of occupational autonomy.

Notes

1 The analysis in this chapter does not try to account for the changing position of nurses in developing countries, though such an analysis is certainly needed.

2 Other social divisions, including age, disability and sexual orientation could also have been highlighted, and my neglect of them does not mean I regard them as of less significance.

3 It may be that the claims of direct ruling-class intervention to socially construct medical professionalization, through the Flexner Report, is stronger in the USA than, for example, Britain.

4 The meaning and significance of distinctions between 'locals' and 'cosmopolitans' are discussed by Gouldner (1957).

5 The body which in 1979 replaced the General Nursing Council (GNC).

References

Abel-Smith, B. (1960) *A History of the Nursing Profession*. London: Heinemann.

Abercrombie, N. and Warde, A. (1988) *Contemporary British Society: a New Introduction to Sociology*. Cambridge: Polity Press.

Armstrong, D. (1976) 'The decline of medical hegemony: a review of government reports during the NHS', *Social Science and Medicine*, 10: 157–63.

Armstrong, D. (1983) 'The fabrication of nurse–patient relationships', *Social Science and Medicine*, 17: 457–60.

Austin, R. (1979) 'Practising health care: the new practitioner in health', in P. Atkinson, R. Dingwall and A. Murcott (eds), *Prospects for the National Health*. London: Croom Helm. pp. 145–58.

Baxter, C. (1988) *The Black Nurse: an Endangered Species*. Cambridge: National Extension College.

Beardshaw, V. and Robinson, R. (1990) *New for Old? Prospects for Nursing in the 1990s*. London: Kings Fund Institute.

Bell, D. (1961) *The End of Ideology*. New York: Free Press.

Bellaby, P. and Oribabor, P. (1977) 'The growth of trade union consciousness among general hospital nurses', *Sociological Review*, 25: 801–22.

Bellaby, P. and Oribabor, P. (1980) 'The history of the present – contradiction and struggle in nursing', in C. Davies (ed.), *Rewriting Nursing History*. London: Croom Helm. pp. 147–74.

Bond, J. and Bond, S. (1986) *Sociology and Health Care*. Edinburgh: Churchill Livingstone.

Bowers, L. (1989) 'The significance of primary nursing', *Journal of Advanced Nursing*, 14: 13–19.

Brent Community Health Council (1981) *Black People and the Health Service*. London: Brent Community Health Council.

Carpenter, M. (1977) 'The new managerialism and professionalism in nursing', in M. Stacey, M. Reid, C. Heath and R. C. Dingwall (eds), *Health and the Division of Labour*. London: Croom Helm. pp. 165–93.

Carpenter, M. (1978) 'Managerialism and the division of labour in nursing', in R. Dingwall and McIntosh, J. (eds), *Readings in the Sociology of Nursing*. Edinburgh: Churchill Livingstone. pp. 87–103.

Carpenter, M. (1988) *Working for Health: the History of COHSE*. London: Lawrence and Wishart.

Davies, C. (ed.) (1980) *Rewriting Nursing History*. London: Croom Helm.

Davies, C. and Rosser, J. (1986) 'Gendered jobs in the health service: a problem for labour process analysis', in D. Knights and H. Willmott (eds), *Gender and the Labour Process*. Aldershot: Gower.

Davis, F. (ed.) (1966) *The Nursing Profession: Five Sociological Essays*. New York: Wiley.

Dean, M. and Bolton, G. (1980) 'The administration of poverty and the development of nursing practice in nineteenth-century England', in C. Davies (ed.), *Rewriting Nursing History*. London: Croom Helm. pp. 102–22.

Department of Health and Social Security (1986) *Neighbourhood Nursing – a Focus for Care: Report of the Community Nursing Review* (Cumberlege). London: HMSO.

Devereux, G. and Weiner, F.R. (1950) 'The occupational status of nurses', *American Sociological Review*, 15: 628–34.

Dingwall, R. (1986) 'Training for a varied career', *Nursing Times*, 26 March: 27–8.

Dingwall, R., Rafferty, A.M. and Webster, C. (1988) *An Introduction to the Social History of Nursing*. London: Routledge.

Doyal, L. (1979) *The Political Economy of Health*. London: Pluto Press.

Doyal, L., Hunt, G. and Mellor, J. (1981–82) 'Your life in their hands: migrant workers in the National Health Service', *Critical Social Policy*, 2: 54–71.

Ehrenreich, B. and English, D. (1973) *Witches, Midwives and Nurses: a History of Women Healers*. London: Compendium.

Ehrenreich, J. (ed.) (1978) *The Cultural Crisis of Modern Medicine*. New York: Monthly Review Press.

Etzioni, A. (1969) *The Semi-Professions and Their Organisation: Teachers, Nurses, Social Workers*. New York: Free Press.

Evers, H. (1981) 'Care or custody? The experiences of women patients in long-stay geriatric wards', in B. Hutter and G. Williams (eds), *Controlling Women: the Normal and the Deviant*. London: Croom Helm.

Foucault, M. (1973) *The Birth of the Clinic*. London: Tavistock.

Foot, M. (1973) *Aneurin Bevan*. Vol 2. London: Davis-Poynter.

Freidson, E. (1970a) *Profession of Medicine: A Study in the Sociology of Applied Knowledge*. New York: Dodd, Mead and Co.

Freidson, E. (1970b) *Professional Dominance*. New York: Atherton.

Freidson, E. (1977) 'The futures of professionalisation', in M. Stacey, M. Reid, C. Heath and R. C. Dingwall (eds), *Health and the Division of Labour*. London: Croom Helm. pp. 14–38.

Garmanikow, E. (1978) 'Sexual division of labour: the case of nursing', in A. Kuhn and A. Wolpe (eds), *Feminism and Materialism*. London: Routledge and Kegan Paul. pp. 96–123.

Gittins, D. (1985) *The Family in Question*. London: Macmillan Education.

Goffman, E. (1961) *Asylums: Essays on the Social Situation of Mental Patients and other Inmates*. Garden City, NY: Anchor/Doubleday.

Gorz, A. (ed.) (1976) *The Division of Labour: the Labour Process and Class Struggle in Modern Capitalism*. Brighton: Harvester.

Gouldner, A. W. (1957) 'Cosmopolitans and locals: toward an analysis of latent social roles', *Administrative Science Quarterly*, December: 281–92.

Graham, H. (1983) 'Caring: a labour of love', in J. Finch and D. Groves (eds), *A Labour of Love: Women, Work and Caring*. London: Routledge and Kegan Paul.

Habenstein, R. W. and Christ, E. A. (1955) *Professionalizer, Traditionalizer and Utilizer*. Columbia, Mo.: University of Missouri.

Hughes, D. (1988) 'When nurse knows best: some aspects of nurse/doctor interaction in a casualty department', *Sociology of Health and Illness*, 10: 1–22.

Illich, V. (1976) *Limits to Medicine*. London: Marion Boyars.

Jeffrey, R. (1979) 'Normal rubbish: deviant patients in a casualty department', *Sociology of Health and Illness*, 1: 90–107.

Johnson, M. M. and Martin, H. W. (1965) 'A sociological analysis of the nurse role', in J. K. Skipper and R. C. Leonard (eds), *Social Interaction and Patient Care*. Philadelphia: J B Lippincott. pp. 29–39.

Johnson, T. (1972) *Professions and Power*. London: Macmillan.

Katz, F. (1969) 'Nurses', in A. Etzioni (ed.), *The Semi-Professions and Their Organization: Teachers, Nurses, Social Workers*. New York: Free Press. pp. 54–81.

Klein, R. (1989) *The Politics of the National Health Service*. London: Longman (second edition).

Kuhn, T. (1962) *The Structure of Scientific Revolutions*. Chicago: University of Chicago Press.

Larson, M. S. (1977) *The Rise of Professionalism: a Sociological Analysis*. Berkeley and Los Angeles: University of California Press.

Lewin, E. and Olesen, V. (eds) (1985) *Women, Health and Healing: Towards a New Perspective*. New York and London: Tavistock.

Mauksch, H. O. (1965) 'The nurse: coordinator of patient care', in J. K. Skipper and R. C. Leonard (eds), *Social Interaction and Patient Care*. Philadelphia: J B Lippincott. pp. 251–65.

McNaught, A. (1988) *Race and Health Policy*. London: Croom Helm.

Menzies, I. E. P. (1963) 'A case study in the functioning of social systems as a defence against anxiety', *Human Relations*, 13: 95–121.

Moores, B. (1987) 'The changing composition of the British hospital nursing workforce', *Journal of Advanced Nursing*, 12: 499–504.

Navarro, V. (1976) *Medicine Under Capitalism*. New York: Prodist.

Navarro, V. (1978) *Class Struggle, the State and Medicine: an Historical and Contemporary Analysis of the Medical Sector in Great Britain*. London: Martin Robertson.

Navarro, V. (1988) 'Professional dominance or proletarianisation?: neither', *The Milbank Quarterly*, 66, suppl. 2: 57–75.

Oakley, A. (1984) 'The importance of being a nurse', *Nursing Times*, 12 December: 24–7.

Parkin, F. (1979) *Marxism and Class Theory: A Bourgeois Critique*. London: Tavistock.

Parsons, T. (1951) *The Social System*. London: Routledge and Kegan Paul.

Race Today (1974) 'Black Women and Nursing: A Job Like Any Other'. August.

Reverby, S. (1989) 'A caring dilemma: womanhood and nursing in historical perspective', in P. Brown (ed.), *Perspectives in Medical Sociology*. Belmont, Ca: Wadsworth. pp. 470–85.

Robinson, J. and Strong, P. (1987) *Professional Nursing Advice After Griffiths*. Warwick University, Coventry: Nursing Policy Studies Centre.

Salvage, J. (1985) *The Politics of Nursing*. London: Heinemann.

Salvage, J. and Kershaw, B. (1986), (1990) *Models For Nursing 1, 2*. London: Scutari Press.

Savage, J. (1987) *Nurses, Gender and Sexuality*. London: Heinemann.

Scheff, T. (1970) 'Control over policy by attendants in a mental hospital', in O. Grusky and G.A. Miller (eds), *The Sociology of Organizations: Basic Studies*. New York: Free Press. pp. 329–40.

Stacey, M. (1988) *The Sociology of Health and Healing*. London: Unwin Hyman.

Stein, L. (1978) 'The nurse–doctor game', in R. Dingwall and J. McIntosh (eds), *Readings in the Sociology of Nursing*. Edinburgh: Churchill Livingstone. pp. 107–17.

Strauss, A. et al. (1963) 'The hospital and its negotiated order', in E. Freidson (ed.), *The Hospital in Modern Society*. London: Collier-Macmillan. pp. 147–69.

Strauss, A. et al. (1982) 'Sentimental work in the technological hospital', *Sociology of Health and Illness*, 4: 254–78.

Townsend, P., Davidson, N. and Whitehead, M. (1988) *Inequalities in Health, and the Health Divide*. Harmondsworth: Penguin Books.

Turner, B. S. (1987) *Medical Power and Social Knowledge*. London: Sage.

Twaddle, A. C. and Hessler, R. (1977) *A Sociology of Health*. St Louis: C.V. Mosby Company.

Versluysen, M. C. (1980) 'Old wives' tales? Women healers in English history', in C. Davies (ed.), *Rewriting Nursing History*. London: Croom Helm. pp. 175–99.

Watson, T. J. (1989) *Sociology, Work and Industry*. London: Routledge.

Williams, F. (1987) 'Racism and the discipline of social policy', *Critical Social Policy*, 7: 4–29.

Williams, F. (1989) *Social Policy: a Critical Introduction*. Cambridge: Polity Press.

Woodward, J. (1974) *To Do the Sick No Harm: a Study of the British Voluntary Hospital System*. London: Routledge and Kegan Paul.

6

A cross-national view of the status of midwives

Raymond G. DeVries

Why study midwives? The almost absolute obscurity of midwives in some countries and their secondary status in others can easily lead to the conclusion that the study of midwifery is simply an esoteric exercise. After all, what good can come from investigating the practices of a group of women who stubbornly cling to old-fashioned practices in a world of bright technological promise? In fact, study of the fate of this occupational group offers much. Because nearly all midwives are women, the exploration of midwifery helps us understand the import of gender in the occupational structure of medicine. More generally, the history of midwifery demonstrates that medical systems are not rational and predictable applications of science, but are instead social products subject to the influence of structural arrangements and cultural ideas. If health care is to be more effective, it is essential that its social nature be understood.

My concern here is with the nature of midwifery practice, not with measures of outcome. My goal is to learn why the work of midwives is organized in so many different ways. To that end I explore how different approaches to midwifery evolved (and are evolving). I examine how different organizational structures and cultures influence midwives' niche in the health-care system, the way midwives view their profession, how midwives do their work, and how midwives are viewed by others. How do structural arrangements and cultural values affect the meaning and practice of midwifery? How does midwifery influence structure and culture?

Several accounts of midwifery around the world are provided by anthropologists, sociologists and others. To compare these accounts is to be struck by the great diversity in the status of midwives. While midwives share the common tasks of assisting at birth and caring for the health of women, they do *not* share a common status. In some cultures people genuflect and kiss the hand of a midwife when she passes (see Sargent, 1982); in other places midwives are seen as 'polluted' (see Jeffery et al., 1989); in still other cultures midwives are accorded the middling status of 'semi-professional'. These accounts also reveal a wide diversity in recruitment, training, styles of practice, the midwife's place in the community and in the medical system, and the rewards of practice. If we organized midwives along a continuum, with those who use all the tools of modern technology at one end and those who are non-technological in orientation at the other, those on the extreme ends of the continuum would not recognize each other as members of the same occupation.

This diversity extends to the terms used to denote a midwife. The World Health Organization (WHO) would like to distinguish midwives from traditional birth attendants. According to the WHO, the term 'midwife' should be reserved for those with professional training and formal education. Some cultures make similar distinctions, using different words for indigenous midwives and formally educated midwives. In some places distinctions are made *among* indigenous midwives, separating those who assist at birth only occasionally from those who assist regularly (see Voorhoeve et al., 1984a, 1984b). To settle this confusion, Cosminsky offers a generic definition: 'The term midwife refers to a position which has been socially differentiated as a specialized status by the society. Such a person is regarded as a specialist and a professional in her own eyes and by her community' (1976: 231).

Most accounts of midwives note the on-going evolution of this occupation. Titles of books and articles call attention to this aspect of midwifery. Consider: *Midwives in Passage* (Benoit, 1991), 'Midwives in Transition' (B. Rothman, 1983), *Labor Pains: Modern Midwives and Home Birth* (Sullivan and Weitz, 1988). Throughout its history the encounters between midwifery and modern culture left midwifery changed, but, not unexpectedly, these changes have not been consistent across cultures.

To understand the evolution of midwifery and its diverse manifestations, we must consider several factors. In their study of contemporary midwives in Great Britain, Australia and New Zealand, Sullivan and Weitz conclude: 'The current status of midwives in each country is a product not only of physician status and interests but also of economic development, social stratification, government structure, the timing of regulation, the degree of integration with British medicine, and geographic barriers to health-care delivery' (1988: 167). Browner provides a comparable list:

> The social position of midwives varies according to the status of women in society; the status of healers who are not midwives; the amount of technical or other skill that midwives possess, including whether they are responsible for complicated deliveries or whether in such cases they are expected to call upon the other specialists; and whether midwives are

chosen by divine selection, self-selection, inheritance, or in other ways. (1989: 69)

These rather long lists of influences on midwifery can, I think, be reduced to four factors. These are first, geography; second, technology; third, the structure of society (included here are occupational structures and the arrangements between medical organizations and other institutions – political, legal, economic, religious, educational); and fourth, the culture (meanings and values) of the people served by the midwife. These categories overlap. Technology is to a certain extent the product of the interaction between culture and structure. And the meanings given to gender (a cultural variable) have a great influence on the way occupations are arranged (a structural variable). Note that technology and geography are physical things that influence the way midwives work. Social structure and culture are less tangible, but no less important, influences on midwifery.

In the following pages, I direct my attention to the impact of technology, social structure and culture on midwifery. This is not to underestimate the influence of geography. Geographic arrangements play an important role in the transmission of technology and culture. Sullivan and Weitz (1988) detail the ways the geography of New Zealand and Australia influenced the regulation and practice of midwifery there. Benoit (1991) makes similar observations about granny midwives in rural Canada. In the United States, granny midwives persisted in the rural south largely because of geographic isolation. But further analysis of this phenomenon takes us beyond the scope of this chapter and is best left to medical geographers.

Technology

For better or worse, technology changes the character and the meaning of work. Essayist Wendell Berry (1990: 170–7) calls our attention to this fact when he explains his refusal to use a personal computer. He is certain that the move from pencil and typewriter to computer will diminish his relationships with his editor, his typist and the local community. Unlike most of us, he is unwilling to make that sacrifice.

The history of midwifery suggests that Berry is right. Technology has changed, and continues to change, midwifery. It is conventional wisdom that midwifery forceps were the 'technological breakthrough' that led to the decline of midwifery in most western nations. But how does technology diminish midwifery? It is obvious that midwives suffer because they lack access to new tools and techniques, but this is just part of the story. New (and successful) technology challenges the legitimacy and authority of midwifery. As technology replaces tradition, patterns of recruitment are changed and doubts about existing techniques, definitions and sources of knowledge that surround birth are created.

In traditional societies a midwife's authority comes from her 'call' (see, for example, Cosminsky, 1976; MacCormack, 1982; Buss, 1980; Laderman, 1983). Traditional midwives become midwives because of a 'call' that comes either supernaturally or through tradition (that is, biological or social heredity). Their training follows from this 'call' coming at the hands of another experienced and accepted midwife or, occasionally, in the form of visions or dreams. Technology changes this traditional pattern. In technological societies recruitment is not the basis of legitimacy. No one is concerned with the reasons a midwife chooses her occupation. Training and certification are the primary sources of authority. As Cosminsky notes, 'training is offered as an alternative to a divine mandate, opening up the role to others who want to practice'(1982: 209).

Technology brings in its wake ideas, definitions and approaches to childbirth that supplant traditional patterns. Laderman calls our attention to the way technology alters concepts of 'trained' and 'untrained': 'Every active village midwife [in rural Malaysia] . . . has been fully trained. . . . Characterizing *bidan kampung* [local midwives] as untrained is an expression of cultural bias in favor of formal schooling over apprenticeship. It is not an objective description of fact' (1983: 119). The World Health Organization shares this technological bias when it observes that 'two-thirds of the babies in the world are delivered without a *trained* attendant'. This statement invalidates all non-formal modes of education (Cosminsky, 1976).

Formal training discounts *all* other sources of knowledge, including traditional midwifery and the unique information a client possesses (about her body, previous births, and so on). This attitude is evident to traditional midwives in Benin. Sargent reports that a midwife there 'would have appreciated learning from clinic staff and had hoped to work together, as in the past, when the indigenous midwife would accompany her client to the dispensary in the event of complications. Now, she said, the "heart" of the nurses is unwelcoming' (1989: 217). In their collection of statistics on childbirth in rural Kenya, Voorhoeve and his colleagues (1984a) demonstrate this lack of faith in the knowledge of indigenous midwives. Note the tone of the following comment: 'none of the midwives ever *admitted* that any of their patients had a total perineal tear' (Voorhoeve et al., 1984a: 319, emphasis added). Specialized instruments and machinery 'provide a kind of knowledge of the event that is privileged' (Jordan and Irwin, 1987: 197).

Kirkham summarizes the tremendous impact of technology on midwifery:

> Previously all pregnancies were seen as normal until judged otherwise, a judgement usually made initially by a midwife. The reverse is now true, as all pregnancies now fall under medical management and are 'normal only in retrospect'. By this logic the midwife as practitioner in her own right is defined out of existence. (1986: 37)

The possibility of being 'defined out of existence' is very real. Unlike other traditional healers, who can find a niche in modern medical systems by treating native diseases peculiar to their area, diseases outside the ken of modern medicine, indigenous midwives find their services exactly duplicated by other, 'modern' birth attendants. For this reason Laderman (1983) is concerned about the future of traditional midwives in Malaysia. Technology is able to create a uniform culture and it is a culture that makes midwifery obsolete. Jordan makes the interesting observation that the instruments of high technology are more portable between cultures than are indigenous, low-technology items: 'Although one imports a fetal monitor to do electronic fetal monitoring, it would not make sense to import ropes from Africa so that women could hold onto them during labor' (1987: 39).

Technological culture seems able to overwhelm other cultural influences. Holland and McKevitt (1985) suspected that childbirth in the Soviet Union might be more humane and tender because the majority of Soviet physicians are female. They hypothesized that the nurturing values learned by little girls might translate into more gentle care than that given by the male-dominated profession of obstetrics in western nations. But they discovered this was not the case. The Soviet Union had a technologically advanced system where the few remaining midwives served as obstetrical nurses. Laboring women were treated much as they would be in any hospital: often left alone and forced to fit their labours into the hospital schedule. The hegemony of technology, the unwillingness to consider other sources of knowledge, is evident in this statement by a Soviet physician:

> The doctor cannot put the question of the desirability of this or that therapeutic measure before the woman in labour and establish this right to choose treatment measures. You see, if we establish this right for women in labour then, whether we like it or not, it automatically shifts responsibility for the outcome of the birth onto the childbearing woman. *Therefore such a position is incorrect.* (Holland and McKevitt, 1985: 173, emphasis added)

Social structure

Although it is somewhat artificial to separate culture and structure, it is useful to look at the ways social structure influences midwives. Most important for our analysis is the organization of the system that delivers health care and its relation to other parts of the society. In some societies midwives are a regular and accepted part of the health-care delivery system. In other places midwives either do not exist or play only a marginal role.

In her comparison of the roles of midwives in five western countries (Sweden, Netherlands, Britain, United States, Canada), Benoit (1991) distinguishes 'midwifery' and 'medical' models of care. According to Benoit, the health-care systems of Sweden and the Netherlands have midwifery models of care that allow midwives to play an important and independent role (see also Van Teijlingen, 1990). Britain, the United States and Canada have medical models of childbirth care. In the medical model midwives have little autonomy and often function as assistants.

Why do these differences exist? The success of midwifery as an autonomous occupation is closely tied to the structural arrangements for the payment of services. Decisions by governments and private insurance companies determine the terms of existence for midwives. It is informative to contrast the situations of midwives in three countries that have national health insurance: Britain, Sweden and the Netherlands. Sullivan and Weitz comment on the effect of the establishment of the National Health Service (NHS) in England in 1946:

> The immediate effect of the NHS was to discourage the dwindling number of independent, fee-for-service midwives in Britain. These women could not compete with the free care provided by the government. The NHS not only removed the cost differential between midwives and physicians, but also removed the economic barrier that kept many high risk, low-income mothers out of hospitals. In addition, the program paid general practitioners for obstetric cases whether or not they attended the delivery. The latter provision created a resurgence of interest in routine prenatal care among general practitioners. (1988: 173)

In Sweden midwifery is not diminished by nationalized health care because of the creation of a decentralized maternity care system. Most maternity care is provided at 'mothercare centres' staffed by midwives. Complicated cases are referred by midwives to general practitioners at 'Type II Clinics' or obstetricians at 'Type-III Clinics'. The Dutch also have a decentralized maternity system that promotes independent midwifery. In the Netherlands midwives are remunerated on a fee-for-service system, and they are allowed to supervise normal deliveries at home and in hospitals.

My research of licensed and unlicensed lay midwives in the United States underscores the importance of insurance plans for midwives. Government recognition in the form of a licence does not guarantee the flourishing of midwifery. A midwife might be licensed, but if insurance companies do not pay for her services her viability is uncertain. Parenthetically, I should note that this relation between insurance and midwives in the United States could work in favour of the occupation. With the coming 'corporatization of medical care', (see Starr, 1982: 420–49; McKinlay and Stoeckle, 1988) insurance companies, looking for more economical approaches to health care, might begin to favour the services of midwives.

The structure of the midwife's work setting also influences the nature of her practice. Benoit (1991) suggests that, even though midwives in Sweden and the Netherlands have a great deal of independence, their different work settings create very different types of midwifery. In particular she claims that the professional status of Dutch midwives is hindered by the fee-for-service system because it isolates midwives, forces them to compete for clients, provides little opportunity for career advancement, and forces them into an unpredictable round-the-clock work schedule. By way of contrast, Sweden's midwives have regular hours, a steady flow of clients, interaction with colleagues and well-defined career ladders.

Political structure plays a part in the fate of midwifery. Government regulations that control the practices of midwives are hammered out in political settings. Several researchers have commented on the legislative access physicians have by virtue of their professional associations and the significant sums of money spent on lobbying and campaign contributions. I witnessed this close association in the legislative houses of several states in the United States where bills concerning the licensing of midwives were being considered (DeVries, 1985).

The larger social structure also affects midwifery. For instance, opportunities afforded by the occupational structure can influence the flow of women into midwifery. Sargent (1989) observed this in Benin. In that country, becoming a midwife was a route to enhanced prestige for women. But with modernization, many other avenues for prestige enhancement are now open to young women. She goes on to point out that this fact and other structural and cultural forces (government policies, the need for certified birth certificates unavailable from traditional midwives, and increasing scorn and harassment of home birth women) are directing women away from using and becoming indigenous midwives. 'Although maternity remains central to the concept of the successful woman, the accretion of other possibilities in the public domain, such as salaried worker, provide alternatives – both symbolic and actual – to traditionally acceptable options, principally that of midwife' (Sargent, 1989: 218).

Culture

How does culture influence the acceptance of midwifery as a practice and as a system of belief about women and birth? It is no exaggeration to say that midwifery will not long survive if it does not 'make sense' in terms of the local culture. A midwife's place in society is affected by cultural ideas about pregnancy and birth, about the role of women, about religion, about technology.

Perhaps the clearest example of culture's influence on midwives is found in India. The religious system there specifies that the touching of bodily fluids is 'polluting'. Given the fact that a birth attendant inevitably comes into contact with bodily fluids, the status of an Indian midwife (known as a *dāi*) is very low. In fact, Jeffery and her colleagues suggest *dāis* should not be known as midwives:

> It is inappropriate to regard the *dāi* as an expert midwife in the contemporary Western sense. Even in the absence of medically trained personnel, the *dāi* does not have overriding control over the management of deliveries. Nor is she a sisterly and supportive equal. Rather, she is a low status menial necessary for removing defilement. (1989: 108)

My study of lay midwives in several states in the United States also revealed connections between religion and midwifery. Religious beliefs were often a primary factor in seeking the services of a midwife. For example, many Jehovah's Witnesses, anxious to avoid hospital procedures that violated their beliefs (for example, they believe that it is wrong to accept a blood transfusion), solicited the services of lay midwives for home births. Religious groups, when correctly situated, can influence legislation. A legislator in Arizona, one of the few states where lay midwives gained the legal right to practise, explained that a large Mormon constituency with a preference for midwife-attended home birth 'encouraged' a positive vote on the part of many members of the legislature.

Secular values can have a similar effect on legislation. In explaining the success of a bill that favoured lay midwives in New Hampshire, a midwife pointed to the Yankee tradition of independence and self-reliance. In the state whose automobile licence plates proclaim, 'Live Free or Die', it would seem incongruous to deny the freedom for midwife-attended home birth. She claimed that a group of wizened old Yankee men (most born at home themselves) were not about to let the representatives of medical organizations deny this basic freedom to New Hampshire citizens.

Cultural values determine the nature of the midwife's role and the prestige it possesses. Browner (1989) says that few women in the village of San Francisco in Oaxaca choose to become midwives. Why? Because 'the role offers little advantage'. Information on childbirth is widely shared, families attend their own births, and consequently midwives have little 'esoteric' knowledge.

Culture also plays an important part in the relation between midwives and clients. Sargent notes: 'Clients and indigenous midwives [in Benin] are found to be homophilous in that they share concepts of causation, beliefs, values and role expectations' (1982: 62). She goes on to point out that the absence of homophily deters prospective clients from using the obstetrical services of government-provided nurse–midwives. These practitioners do not share the world view of their clients, often speak to them only in French, and are quick to criticize client behaviour.

In her study of midwives in Malaysia, Laderman (1983) describes a situation similar to the one found in Benin. In one village, a government-provided midwife, unfamiliar with the local culture, had an uneasy relationship with the residents she served. But (and this is an important *but*), Laderman noticed this midwife was respected for her knowledge of, and connections to, the bureaucracy. She was especially valued because she was the only one who could summon the ambulance in emergencies. Laderman's study reminds us of the subtle ways culture can change. Local culture was powerful enough to make an 'outside midwife' feel out of place, but not powerful enough to resist the new definitions and new possibilities offered by this midwife. The villagers distrusted the government midwife, but they recognized the utility of her view of birth and her treatments and valued access to 'her' technology. Gradually, the 'taken for granted' definitions of birth changed.

Cultural change can promote midwifery. The renaissance of independent midwifery in the United States (and to a lesser extent in Canada) in the 1960s and 1970s offers an example of cultural change encouraging a revival of traditional birth techniques. The nearly simultaneous emergence of the anti-Vietnam War movement, the civil rights movement, the feminist movement and the ecology movement called into question a number of American cultural values and challenged all forms of institutionalized authority. David Rothman asserts that the 'rights orientation' that emerged in the mid-1960s 'dramatically reduced the discretionary authority of a number of social actors' (1990: 196). This was certainly true in medicine, where many questioned the institutionalization and 'medicalization' of birth. As a result of this cultural change, independent midwives flourished in several areas and there was a small but significant rise in home births (see DeVries, 1984; Reid, 1989).

Structure and culture

Structure and culture interact in significant ways to shape the practice of midwifery. For example, consider the fate of midwifery in the United States where the demise of midwifery was quite rapid. Physicians were able to exploit their structural advantage (in other words, connections to the political system) to promote legislation that eliminated or effectively reduced the practice of midwifery (see DeVries, 1985; Devitt, 1979). This structural advantage created a cultural advantage. Denied the credibility of licences, midwives lost their place in the reimbursement system and gradually lost their legitimacy in the eyes of the public. The structural advantage that allowed physicians to promote legislation that prohibited midwifery also allowed them to modify the cultural definition of midwives. Where once midwives were the only birth attendant women trusted, now they are defined as ill-trained, dirty and dangerous. Hospital birth, once considered odd, is now 'safer', 'more fashionable', 'easier'. The structural and cultural advantage of physician organizations remains visible in those states where lay midwives are seeking licensing. Susie (1988) describes the situation in the state of Florida where physicians used their political and economic influence to overturn a 1982 law that allowed licences to lay midwives.

Laderman's (1983) study of Malaysian midwives offers a good example of the interaction between the occupational structure of a society and its culture. She observes that in some areas the availability of a government midwife reduced the duties of the traditional midwife to 'laundry, cooking, cleaning, bathing the baby, and massaging the mother. Stripped of her obstetric role and reduced to the status of household help, the traditional *bidan's* calling will no longer ring so loudly in the ears of the village girls'(1983: 123). As technology influences the work of the midwife, the meaning of the occupation changes and it becomes a less attractive occupation.

The interaction of culture and structure can also be seen in the rise of alternative birth settings in the United States. The cultural challenge presented to the medicalization of birth in the 1960s and 1970s resulted in structural changes in the delivery of care in childbirth. The new meanings given birth (as 'natural', not 'medical'; as a family experience, an opportunity for 'bonding') caused associations of medical professionals to recommend change and to endorse nurse–midwives. Hospitals responded by creating new environments for birth and by hiring nurse–midwives to staff them. Providers of health-care equipment contributed to this change by mounting marketing campaigns to sell products designed for these new birth environments. The Borning Corporation has a well-crafted presentation on 'natural birth' intended to promote sales of a bed made to facilitate combined labour and delivery rooms in hospitals.

Midwifery as a profession: risk, knowledge and power

Our analysis of midwifery leaves us with a final question: can midwives survive in the modern world without sacrificing their tradition, their identity and their unique body of knowledge? To answer this question we must consider two things: first the structural, cultural and technological constraints that operate on midwives, and second the way midwives wish to define their profession in a changing medical culture.

How does the 'culture of midwifery' suit it for survival in the midst of cultural and social change? The essence of midwifery is low-technology, one-to-one supportive care. When midwives reflect on their tradition they celebrate the simple and practical wisdom of their forebears. But this low-technology tradition is not ideally suited to the modern world. By way of contrast consider the more pragmatic culture of allopathic medicine. When allopaths look back on their forebears, whose therapies (such as bleeding and purging) would now be seen as 'quackery', they celebrate the *pragmatic spirit* embodied there. The culture of midwifery stresses being *practical* and *simple*, the culture of medicine stresses being *pragmatic*.

Being practical and simple does not necessarily help an occupational group survive societal change. For example, the wisdom of midwifery suggests that only one who is 'called' should become a midwife; several lay midwife groups in the United States, when establishing criteria for granting credentials, made some effort to ascertain the reasons for pursuing this occupation. This makes practical sense. Those who are called have a reason to withstand the hardships of midwifery; they have a larger sense of the importance of their task. Buss (1980) illustrates the way a call translates into commitment when she describes the tireless Jesusita, a *partera* in rural New Mexico, who attended the births of 11,924 babies and is willing to care for women who cannot pay her. But this approach to recruitment is not pragmatic. It does not ensure 'enough' midwives, it does not promote the profession, it does not ensure that all candidates have certain minimal qualifications, and, in societies that equate technological mastery with credibility, it does not establish midwifery as a credible occupation.

In thinking about the survival of midwifery (or any profession) it is important to recognize that at least three different types of interests are at stake: the interest of midwives as *persons*, the interests of midwifery as a *profession*, and the interests of midwifery as a *service* (interested in the health and wellbeing of women and babies). It is too often assumed that all three of these are of one piece, that an improvement in any one brings an improvement in all the others. This has been the assumption of physicians: 'what is good for us (personally and professionally) is good for our clients'. But this is decidedly not true. Often the interests of the profession are at odds with the interests of clients.

In the Netherlands the organization of midwifery care has been good for the profession of midwifery. Advocates of midwifery in the United States point to the Netherlands as a model for midwifery care. They note that Dutch midwives have a good deal of autonomy, that they are free to work with little supervision. But, as Benoit (1991) points out, these situations are not good for midwives as people. The hours are gruelling and family life becomes impossible. In Sweden, midwives as people benefit from the government organization of midwifery clinics – hours are regular and predictable and they have a certain degree of autonomy. But the independent profession of midwifery is compromised; they are not as free as their colleagues in the Netherlands.

And what of the third element: the interests of clients? Where are clients best served? If the criterion of choice is used, clients are best served by a more autonomous profession because it offers a choice between *true* alternatives. In places like the Netherlands, clients have the opportunity to benefit from the independent tradition of midwifery. In places where midwives have gained legitimacy by affiliation with technological medicine, clients have less choice. Midwife care looks much like physician care. In the long run clients benefit from having more than one medical tradition. When strong and vital approaches to health care can interact, they learn from each other. There are several instances where physicians learned valuable techniques from midwives, including approaches to avoiding perineal tears and the importance of immediate contact between parents and babies (see DeVries, 1984).

Many midwives believe that it is in the best interest of midwifery to define itself as a profession. What makes an occupation a profession? Must midwifery establish itself as a profession to survive? Reid (1989: 220) suggests that midwifery is best thought of as a 'semi-profession' because it has some of the trademarks of a profession, but lacks all the features. 'Although [midwives] work with some independence, they are restricted from attending high-risk labors and deliveries and from using a number of medical technologies. Ultimately they are accountable to others, most notably, physicians'.

Social scientists disagree about defining features of a profession. Some claim a list of traits (prolonged training, a professional association, a code of ethics, etc.) separates a profession from other occupations. Others assert that there is one defining feature of a profession: power (see Abbott, 1988: 3–31 for a summary of this literature). Our analysis of the varied statuses of midwives helps us rethink the criteria that establish an occupational group as a profession.

I suggest that an occupational group gains power to the extent that it can reduce risk and uncertainty for clients. Doctors are valued because they help their clients deal with sickness, an unscheduled and uncertain status transition. Lawyers gain prestige and power because they handle unnerving and uncertain problems like divorce and litigation that threaten our material possessions. Members of the clergy help people deal with the uncertain fate of their souls. The most highly rewarded members of society (in terms of money, prestige and power) are those that reduce the most frightening risks. In a less secular age, priests were the most important risk-reducers and were among the most powerful members of society. Today our concerns are more existential, our bodies and our material possessions are more important than our souls, hence physicians and lawyers are the primary risk-reducers.

My thesis suggests that professional groups can gain power by 'creating' risk – that is by *emphasizing* risk, by redefining life events as 'risky'. Perhaps the best example of this is the promotion of prenuptial contracts by lawyers, intended to avoid the risks of divorce. Medicine encourages us to see once-normal life experiences such as eating, exercise and ageing as fraught with risk.

We can understand the occupational status of midwives by considering the way they relate to risk. How do midwives gain power (status, prestige and respect)? Cross-cultural study shows that midwives are respected to the extent that they can offer some way (be it technological spiritual, or some combination of these) to reduce risk and uncertainty. Although birth has a more regular and predictable trajectory than sickness, it is still a risky event, especially in traditional societies where the mortality rates are high. Where they are the primary managers of the risk of birth, midwives have high status. Where other practitioners offer 'better' means of risk reduction *or* where birth is redefined as a less risky event, midwives lose status. Landy (1978: 239) notes that the traditional healer's role faces the greatest challenge 'as the course of disease becomes more controllable (prevention, public health measures), more predictable (medical intervention with miracle drugs, scientific surgery), and less uncertain'. Midwives were bound to lose status as birth became less risky and as other 'better' practitioners appeared who could help manage this uncertain time. By the same logic, obstetricians enhance their status by increasing the number of surgical deliveries (in other words, Caesarean sections) they do.

Gender is a factor here. In most societies, women care for the sick. But the care they give is palliative care. They are a presence during the uncertain episodes of sickness, but they do not alter its course or reduce its impact through intervention. Historically men often played the more 'heroic' role (with all its good and bad connotations) with regard to sickness. Their ministrations were seen as reducers of uncertainty, as the hope of salvation. This is how midwifery forceps were perceived when they were introduced by the Chamberlens in the seventeenth century. Midwives, whose less interventive tradition led them to eschew forceps, became less desirable attendants.

My analysis of the relationship between risk and professional status leads to the unfortunate conclusion that the attempt by some midwives to seek a niche in modern medical systems by claiming to be experts in 'low-risk' birth threatens their credibility as a professional group. Prestige and power are given to those who manage high-risk situations, not to those who attend to low-risk births. But midwives face an unusual predicament: to enhance their status it seems they must renounce their tradition. They can earn their niche in the system only if they cease to be recognizable as midwives. In seeking to survive, midwives must ask: survive for whom? For the good of the profession? For their own good as practitioners? Or for the health of the women and babies they serve?

Acknowledgements

This paper benefited from comments and editorial assistance given by Terry Hoops and C. A. DeVries.

References

Abbott, Andrew (1988) *The System of the Professions*. Chicago: University of Chicago Press.

Benoit, Cecilia (1991) *Midwives in Passage: a Case Study of Occupational Change*. St. John's, Newfoundland: ISER Press.

Berry, Wendell (1990) *What Are People For?* San Francisco: North Point Press.

Browner, Carole H. (1989) 'The management of reproduction in an egalitarian society', in C. S. McClain (ed.), *Women as Healers: Cross-cultural Perspectives*. New Brunswick, NJ: Rutgers University Press. pp. 58–72.

Buss, Fran Leeper (1980) *La Partera, Story of a Midwife*. Ann Arbor: The University of Michigan Press.

Cosminsky, Sheila (1976) 'Cross-cultural perspectives on midwifery', in F. X. Grollig and H. B. Haley (eds), *Medical Anthropology*. The Hague: Mouton. pp. 229–48.

Cosminsky, Sheila (1982) 'Childbirth and change: a Guatemalan study', in C. P.

MacCormack (ed.), *Ethnography of Fertility and Birth*. New York: Academic Press. pp. 205–30.

Devitt, Neil (1979) 'How doctors conspired to eliminate the midwife even though scientific data supported midwifery', in D. Stewart and L. Stewart (eds), *Compulsory Hospitalization or Freedom of Choice in Childbirth?* Marble Hill, MO: NAPSAC. pp. 345–70.

DeVries, Raymond (1984) 'Humanizing childbirth: the discovery and implementation of bonding theory', *International Journal of Health Services*, 14: 89–104.

DeVries, Raymond (1985) *Regulating Birth: Midwives, Medicine and the Law*. Philadelphia: Temple University Press.

Holland, Barbara and McKevitt, Teresa (1985) 'Maternity care in the Soviet Union', in B. Holland (ed.), *Soviet Sisterhood*. Bloomington: Indiana University Press. pp. 145–76.

Jeffery, Patricia, Jeffery, Roger and Lyon, Andrew (1989) *Labour Pains and Labour Power: Women and Childbearing in India*. London: Zed Books.

Jordan, Brigette (1987) 'The hut and the hospital: information, power and symbolism in the artifacts of birth', *Birth*, 14: 36–40.

Jordan, B. and Irwin, S. (1987) 'A close encounter with a court-ordered Cesarean section: a case of differing realities', in H. A. Baer (ed.), *Encounters with Biomedicine*. New York: Gordon and Breach. pp. 185–200.

Kirkham, Mavis (1986) 'A feminist perspective in midwifery', in Christine Webb (ed.), *Feminist Practice in Women's Health Care*. New York: John Wiley and Sons. pp. 35–50.

Laderman, Carol (1983) *Wives and Midwives: Childbirth and Nutrition in Rural Malaysia*. Berkeley: University of California Press.

Landy, David (1978) 'Role adaptation: traditional curers under the impact of Western medicine', in M. H. Logan and E. E. Hunt (eds), *Health and the Human Condition*. North Scituate, MA: Duxbury. pp. 217–41.

MacCormack, C. P. (1982) 'Biological, cultural and social adaptation in human fertility and birth: a synthesis', in C. P. MacCormack (ed.), *Ethnography of Fertility and Birth*. New York: Academic Press. pp. 1–23.

McKinlay, John and Stoeckle, John (1988) 'Corporatization and the social transformation of doctoring', *International Journal of Health Services*, 18: 191–205.

Reid, Margaret (1989) 'Sisterhood and professionalization: a case study of the American lay midwife', in C. S. McClain (ed.), *Women as Healers: Cross-cultural Perspectives*. New Brunswick, NJ: Rutgers University Press. pp. 219–38.

Rothman, Barbara Katz (1983) 'Midwives in transition: the structure of a clinical revolution', *Social Problems*, 30: 262–71.

Rothman, David (1990) 'Human experimentation and the origins of bio-ethics', in George Weisz (ed.), *Social Science Perspectives on Medical Ethics*. Dordrecht: Kluwer Academic Publishers. pp. 185–200.

Sargent, Carolyn (1982) *The Cultural Context of Therapeutic Choice: Obstetrical Care Decisions among the Bariba of Benin*. Dordrecht: D. Reidel.

Sargent, Carolyn (1989) 'Women's roles and women healers in contemporary rural and urban Benin', in C. S. McClain (ed.), *Women as Healers: Cross-cultural Perspectives*. New Brunswick, NJ: Rutgers University Press. pp. 204–18.

Starr, Paul (1982) *The Social Transformation of American Medicine*. New York: Basic Books.

Sullivan, D. and Weitz, R. (1988) *Labor Pains: Modern Midwives and Home Birth*. New Haven: Yale University Press.

Susie, Debra Anne (1988) *In the Way of Our Grandmothers: a Cultural View of*

Twentieth-Century Midwifery in Florida. Athens, GA: University of Georgia Press.

Van Teijlingen, Edwin (1990) 'The profession of maternity home care assistant and its significance for the Dutch midwifery profession', *International Journal of Nursing Studies*, 27: 355–66.

Voorhoeve, A. M., Kars, C. and van Ginneken, J. K. (1984a) 'Modern and traditional antenatal and delivery care', in J. K. van Ginneken and A. S. Muller (eds), *Maternal and Child Health in Rural Kenya*. London: Croom Helm. pp. 309–22.

Voorhoeve, A. M., Kars, C. and van Ginneken, J. K. (1984b) 'The outcome of pregnancy', in J. K. van Ginneken and A. S. Muller (eds), *Maternal and Child Health in Rural Kenya*. London: Croom Helm. pp. 223–40.

Health-manpower planning or gender relations? The obvious and the oblique

Arminée Kazanjian

Owing to their concentration in selected occupations within the health sector, women, in general, operate in a very different employment context from men. Current literature on sex stratification in the workplace has identified at least five measures of positional inequality which partly explain male/female differences in occupational attainment (Roos, 1981). Most of these measures are applicable to women in health occupations: first, these jobs are low-paid, regardless of sex; second, they are predominantly female (for example, nursing occupations). A third characteristic is that working women are less likely than men to control the means of production, as in hospital management occupations. Fourth, women are less likely than men to exercise authority over others, such as in physician–patient interaction, and finally, women are segregated by industry, as demonstrated by the concentration of registered nurses in public hospitals relative to their numbers in private practice. There is, furthermore, ample evidence to suggest that structural factors play an important role in the occupational attainment process (Duncan et al., 1972). Empirical evidence from this field of research indicates that certain socioeconomic characteristics such as family background and education foster occupational achievement which, ideally, should be based solely on an individual's technical competence.

It is, therefore, rather curious that most efforts in health human-resources planning have focused solely on the economic determinants of labour force participation. Despite acute shortages in predominantly female occupations, planning and policy initiatives do not appear to even acknowledge the impact of changing sex roles in society on the health labour market. Thus, taking into account the social as well as the traditional economic factors influencing the health labour market and the particular organizational context within which it operates should certainly contribute to a better understanding of recurring episodes of personnel imbalances.

However, in order to appreciate fully the magnitude of current and past health human-resources problems, particularly in systems that are publicly funded, the historical development of current regulatory and public policy environments from a gender relations perspective must be taken into consideration (Blumberg, 1984; Chafetz, 1984; Acker, 1989). More specifically for the health sector, the impact of regulatory and public policies on human resource supply and requirements, as well as on organizational structures that traditionally favour occupational attainment for males, warrant more extensive and careful study than they have had in the past. The interrelatedness of the three areas of professional dominance, human-resource planning, and system structure provides a clear example of how the macro-political inequality of men and women is reflected – and perhaps even magnified – in the micro-political health human-resources market. The thrust of this study is that most of the norms of inequality of professional status (Freidson, 1970) merely serve to perpetuate the more fundamental norms of inequality of the sexes, and that the exercise of professional power rests equally on structural and cultural legitimacies.

As health falls under provincial jurisdiction in Canada, all public policies and professional governance legislation are administered by provincial governments. However, the Hospital Insurance and Diagnostic Act (Canada), the Medical Care Act (Canada) and the Canada Health Act have set national standards for all provincial funding of health services which render each province generally comparable to others regarding its delivery system.

First, the hierarchy of health professions in the province of British Columbia, Canada, is described, and the main regulatory policies perpetrating this hierarchy are discussed. Then, a brief historical overview of policy development – in particular public policies related to health human resources, including health professions legislation – sets the context for explaining current health human-resource situations. This approach provides a macro-structural perspective by allowing a more thorough examination of the 'external' environment of the health-care delivery system (Light, 1989). In addition, it demonstrates that gender inequalities are not simply 'internal' to this sector but form part of and are affected by the macro-political inequality of men and women in society. This macro-structural approach also facilitates comparative studies at the national and international level, enabling the examination of the relative contributions made by cultural and structural factors as well as economic variables in explaining health labour market behaviour. While there may be vast differences in economic conditions and health insurance payment systems between regions or countries, there appears to be uncanny similarities in their health human-resource markets. That these may largely be due to similarities in the macro-political inequalities of men and women in modern western society warrants serious consideration. Ultimately, comparative systems analysis from a gender relations perspective is essential for empirical verification.

The gender hierarchy of health occupations and professional distance

The situation in British Columbia is described in this analysis as an illustration and not because it is a unique situation. A case study approach provides sufficient detail for elaborating the postulated relationship between professional status and gender stratification.

Facets of the health occupations hierarchy
The dominant professions, comprised of physicians, dentists and, to a lesser extent, pharmacists and optometrists, are and have been among the main stakeholders in the health-care market. The regulatory statutes bestow upon them powers and privileges unattainable by most others. It is not pure coincidence that the top three in the professional hierarchy happen to be male-dominated professions (Table 7.1). Recent statistics show that the proportion of women in medicine, optometry, dentistry and podiatry is very low (19%, 18%, 11% and 4%, respectively) but more equitable in psychology (43%)

Table 7.1 *Women as percentage of total personnel in selected health occupations in BC, Canada 1989–90*

	Total*	Male	Female	% Female
Certified Dental Assistants	3,606	6	3,585	99.8
Dental Hygienists	880	24	855	97.3
Dentists	2,002	1,780	218	10.9
Licensed Practical Nurses	6,387	394	5,992	93.8
Occupational Therapists	448	15	433	96.7
Optometrists	227	187	40	17.6
Pharmacists	2,379	1,312	1,067	44.9
Physicians	6,421	5,202	1,219	19.0
Physiotherapists	1,575	187	1,240	86.9
Podiatrists	54	52	2	3.7
Psychologists	788	448	340	43.1
Registered Nurses	30,140	715	29,420	97.6
Registered Psychiatric Nurses	2,087	545	1,524	73.7

* Includes those with missing gender information

Source: Cooperative Database, HHRU, University of British Columbia

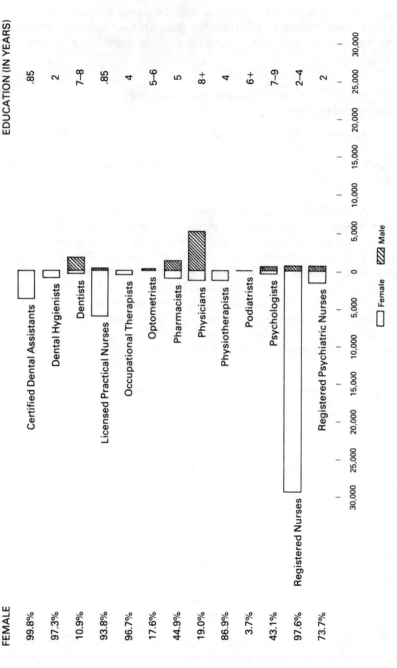

Figure 7.1   *Years of education and gender for selected health personnel in BC, Canada 1989/90*
Source: Cooperative Database, Health Human Resources Unit, University of British Columbia

and pharmacy (45%). As previously documented in other jurisdictions, women are overrepresented in the psycho-social healing occupations and, to a lesser degree, in some somatic-diagnostic occupations that have limited autonomy and control over other workers. Thus, specific job functions in health care have become associated with traits perceived to be male or female attributes, and the traditional division of labour between men and women in the family has been transferred to the health labour force.

The non-competitive, complementary aspect of the division of labour in the family is also reflected in the labour market in the form of non-competing gender groups: 'feminine' occupations in supportive roles and 'masculine' professions in dominant roles (Butter et al., 1985). Complementarity rather than competition governs the placement of men and women in different fields of work and creates a labour market for predominantly male or female occupations. Superimposing a gender hierarchy onto an occupational hierarchy characteristic to the health labour force (Mick, 1978; Fuchs et al., 1970) creates differential entry barriers and mobility blockages for men and women. One way in which professions clearly differentiate themselves from other groups is by claiming a set of distinguishing attributes (Warburton and Carroll, 1988). Key among these is a claim to prolonged specialized training in a body of scientific knowledge that is exclusive to the profession, providing a significant factor in occupational stratification and professional power. A brief analysis of level of education for health personnel in British Columbia indicates a systematic gender bias. Figure 7.1 shows that the female-dominated, supportive occupations are those with the lowest levels of post-secondary education; male professionals dominate occupations ranked in the four top levels.

Another dimension of the health occupations hierarchy is shown in Figure 7.2. Extreme income inequality is indicated by these data on average annual earnings, regardless of years of education. The two most lucrative occupations represent a very small proportion of the total health workforce in the province (approximately 12%); women are severely underrepresented in these two groups. Disparities in income become even more pronounced when the self-reported nature of the data is taken into consideration (from the 1986 National Census Survey). While pharmacy is among the dominant professions, it ranks much lower on the income distribution measure; women are more equitably represented in this profession. The recent 'feminization' of pharmacy explains its very low income – especially in the retail sector. Physiotherapy, a predominantly female occupation with four years of post-secondary education, ranks lower than pharmacy with similar number of years of education. It is interesting

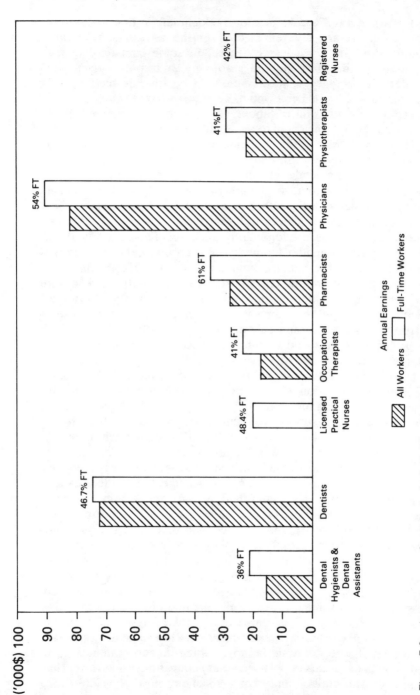

Figure 7.2   Average annual earnings of selected health personnel in BC, 1986
Source: Job Futures British Columbia, Employment and Immigration Canada, 1989

to note that in developing countries physiotherapy remains a medical specialty and is male-dominated. However, historical evidence in the western world indicates that, in an effort to deal with the problem of escalating specialized labour costs, policy-makers at the operations as well as government levels sought to rationalize the system by breaking down work roles into component parts and assigning the simpler functions to workers with less formal training. Thus, new engineering and laboratory technologists emerged from functions previously defined to be those of physicians; in contrast, other roles such as those of physiotherapist, dietitian and health record technician grew out of the nursing role (Bullough, 1988). More recently, large-scale differentiation of the nursing role occurred following the Second World War, delegating some of the work role of the registered nurse to less expensive workers such as the licensed practical nurse or the nursing aide. Both situations illustrate the theory of women's access to devaluated occupational streams (Reskin, 1988).

The gender hierarchy among health professionals is also shown in the differential earnings structure and career opportunities by occupation. Dominant professions such as physicians and dentists which are remunerated on a fee-for-service basis can increase earnings through specialization; specialists are paid at higher rates than generalists for similar services. For physicians in a publicly funded health insurance system, the rates are set by a fee-negotiating mechanism determined by government and the professional association. Others, who have much narrower scopes of practice, such as chiropractors, optometrists and podiatrists, are reimbursed at specialist rates – albeit for a very limited number of fee items. The situation for the semi-professional groups is quite different. The earnings structure in place for general duty registered nurses does not promote either the acquisition of additional nursing education, at the certificate or degree level, or the development of career ladders. For example, the academic bonus which is paid to baccalaureate-prepared nurses was increased slightly in 1990, after remaining at the 1980 amount throughout the decade; the bonus for specialty certification still remains at the 1980 level.

Furthermore, the six-step increment system that has been in place for general duty RNs for the last ten years has preserved, throughout that period, the same 15-percentage-point difference between entry-level and maximum-level hourly wages for all classifications. Despite acknowledged problems of workforce retention, the range of possible earnings for general duty nurses has never expanded beyond 15 per cent in a decade. The same increment range applied equally uniformly to the head nurses; for supervisors, the nurses classified in the highest category, that increment range was compressed in the mid-1980s and then returned to the previous level of the beginning of the decade. For licensed practical nurses, the number of steps was limited to four, increased to five and compressed again to four steps in the past ten years. The extent of the difference between the lowest and highest steps for LPNs was at its highest in 1980, at about 11 per cent; in 1991 it has reached its lowest at less than 7 per cent.

Finally, the percentage difference between the minimum and maximum earnings for general duty nurses actually exceeds the percentage difference between entry-level staff and head nurses. This does suggest at least a static view of career advancement incentives for staff nurses: both to remain in the field throughout their working life, and to aspire to greater responsibility in leadership positions. Negotiated salary differentials for different grades of rehabilitation therapists are somewhat more favourable, in terms of both within- and between-position increments.

The possession of autonomy is another key feature which professions use to differentiate themselves from other groups (Freidson, 1970). The professions may exercise autonomy by determining standards of education and practice, by licensing professional practice and by shaping relevant legislation. Using the framework of autonomy, expertise and social value is useful in the consideration of status relations between health occupations. Physiotherapy, occupational therapy, medical social work and dietetics are, like nursing, professions with overwhelming majorities of female members. Yet, each group has a higher status relative to nurses. Members of the aforementioned professions have greater autonomy than nurses because they have better defined, specific fields of practice and are considered to be more knowledgeable about that practice than anyone else. Nurses have a much less clearly defined field of practice, one that incorporates skills from a number of other disciplines. While nurses are often responsible for providing 'continuity of care' and coordinating the care delivered by other health personnel, they lack the authority conferred by clear autonomy and expertise to exercise that coordinating role to its fullest. Nurses also suffer in status relative to the others due to their more limited educational preparation; while university preparation in nursing degrees is possible, the vast majority of the registered nurses are trained at the diploma level and are graduates of college-based programmes. All aforementioned health professions require at least baccalaureate for entry to practice; two- and three-year diplomas do not ascribe the same status to the practitioner. The greater autonomy and perceived expertise of the other professional groups are reflected in their work schedules (day shift only) and in the absence of uniforms.

For the last twenty years nurses have struggled against physician-dominated definitions of autonomy, expertise and social value. The steep power gradient of the system has consequences for the roles of the care-givers, and their interaction patterns. Status clearly defines these roles to be more superordinate and subordinate than collegial. Thus, while physicians encourage a form of 'team work' in which nurses are subordinate, nurses seek mutual collegiality with physicians (Campbell-Heider and Pollock, 1987). In their efforts to define their field of practice, nurses have on the one hand attempted to determine a field of practice that incorporates non-medical roles and tasks, and on the other advocated the development of an expanded scope of practice, emulating the medical model. While new knowledge and the expanded use of technology have made health-care delivery a complex phenomenon, nurses have been unsuccessful in their push for increased status and responsibility, manifested particularly in their failure to institutionalize nurse practitioner roles. It has been suggested (Dibble, 1963) that the ideology of higher-ranking occupational groups will often be more widely diffused throughout society. It follows, then, that the parochial concerns of the nurses' association to improve the status of nursing may have greater impact if they are linked to the values held by society at large.

Some observers see the doctor–nurse game, the role-playing and managed interactions integral to the maintenance of an uncontested hierarchical relationship, as adapting to a changing world (Stein et al., 1990). Yet, there is ample evidence to support the viewpoint that dominant groups invoke their powers to exclude competing groups and the exclusory tactics are intimately connected with powers legitimated by the state (Giddens, 1982).

Table 7.2 provides a synopsis of selected provincial statutes. It is shown that the dominant professions have the earliest statutes and the most revisions, regardless of date of first enactment, reflecting in part the culturally embedded gender bias of policy-makers/legislators. Physicians and dentists have not only the statutory powers of defining and controlling their exclusive scopes of practice, but also the power to define the standards and scope of practice of their 'ancillary' groups, the predominantly female 'semi-professions'. For these 'ancillary' groups, statutory privileges are limited to a system of registration or certification, whereby practitioners have to meet the standards set by their professional associations and, at best, are permitted to maintain exclusive use of title. Although their statutory titles refer either to 'Registered' or 'Licensed', certification is often the intent of the statute. Legally, these groups receive an endorsement of competence and exclusive use of statutory title. Excepting nurses, no exclusive right to practise

Table 7.2   *Selected provincial health personnel legislation, BC,*
Canada (1989–90)

Current statute	Date of initial statute	Number of revisions	Most recent applicable statute
Chiropractors Act, 1979	1934	4	1989
Dentists Act, 1979	1908	8	1988
Medical Practitioners Act, 1979	1886	9	1979
Nurses (Licensed Practical) Act, 1979	1951	2	1988
Nurses (Registered) Act, 1979	1918	7	1988
Nurses (Registered Psychiatric) Act, 1979	1951	4	1988
Optometrists Act, 1979	1921	7	1989
Pharmacists Act, 1979	1891	9	1979
Physiotherapists Act, 1979	1946	4	1989
Podiatrists Act, 1979	1929	4	1989

Note: Amendments are made all the time, but the entire volume of all statutes is published only once every 15–20 years.

Source: Revised Statutes of BC, 1979.

in their particular field exists for most 'supportive' occupations; practice by an uncertified person who does not use an exclusive title is not prohibited by law and is not a punishable offence.

Registered Nurses, Registered Psychiatric Nurses and Licensed Practical Nurses are the largest groups in this supportive category who have just recently expanded their definition of exclusive use of title to restrict the practice of nursing to those registered with their respective associations/licensing bodies (the Nursing Statutes Amendment, 1988). While they possess the sound training, exceptional knowledge and rare expertise required of 'professionals' (Brown et al., 1987; Wuthnow, 1986; Fagin and Diers, 1983), they lack the autonomy to control the nature and conditions of their work.

The current efforts and success of the Registered Nurses Association of BC to amend the Nurses (Registered) Act (which has had significant implications for the other two nursing groups as well), draws its strength largely from the gains made by the women's movement in general. As a professional association, this body is well organized, has able leadership, is financially solvent and is suitably conversant with strategic planning. However, its ability to bring about significant legislative changes remains unproven. While more statutory power is generally associated with better access to public funding, that does not appear to be a great benefit to this group, given current fiscal structure.

The preservation of professional distance
The recently enacted amendment is by and large explained by the political gains nurses have attained due to their enhanced self-image and their desire to take a more assertive role in the delivery of primary prevention (as well as their traditional role in secondary and tertiary prevention). However, despite the government's recent commitments to health promotion, and the research evidence indicating that nurses are skilled in patient education and counselling and a cost-effective alternative to physician services (Spitzer, 1984), there have been no policy initiatives to facilitate the use of nurses in primary settings. Independent nursing practice and fee-for-service payment appear to be somewhat incongruent with society's – and in particular the policy-makers' – stereotype of appropriate labour market behaviour for women. Such 'innovative' action would have serious ideological repercussions, especially in the current market situation of physician surplus. Physician opposition notwithstanding, could the state afford the social as well as the economic costs of placing highly educated members of a dominant profession – mainly male – in the ranks of the unemployed, replacing them with less trained and lower paid but more effective primary care professionals? It is doubtful that such action could ever be envisaged by any government, especially if the substitute professionals are predominantly female.

Registered Nurses do have control over entry to practice as well as the newly acquired increased control of their own licensing process; the Nurses (Registered) Act (RSBC, 1979: Ch. 302) under section 13 charges the Registered Nurses Association with the right to approve all nursing education programmes that prepare nurses for registration. Since much of the control over a profession's ideology accrues from the control over the education process (Olmsted and Paget, 1969), entry-to-practice restrictions tend to be defined in terms of stringent educational qualifications. In 1982, the Canadian Nurses Association, following in the earlier footsteps of its American counterpart, resolved to require nurses to have a baccalaureate degree in nursing in order to enter practice by the year 2000. Activities in this regard are part of the larger effort to improve the status of nursing among the health professions, and also to define nursing vis-à-vis other health professions. For the time being, though, nurses cannot diagnose, prescribe or initiate technical procedures. It is somewhat paradoxical, however, that during the night shift these restrictions are somehow lifted (although only implicitly), and the nurse on duty shoulders enormous patient responsibilities. In nursing circles this phenomenon is jestingly referred to as 'the reverse Cinderella syndrome', but there is no humour in an ideology that 'allows' women into male territory only when it becomes less attractive to men.

Similarly, the collaboration of dental hygienists and certified dental assistants with dentists is another interesting example of an unequal professional relationship. The council of the College of Dental Surgeons of BC has statutory powers to make rules respecting persons to whom a dentist may delegate duties, including 'providing different rules for different classes of persons and different classes of registration', and 'setting out requirements as to training, experience, character and registration in a class', among many others (RSBC, 1979: Ch 92).

Dentists have generally delegated tasks to Certified Dental Assistants, the less professional of the two semi-professional ancillary groups, when it would have been more logical to delegate expanded functions to Dental Hygienists. The latter's formal training and preparation make them excellent candidates for independent practitioner roles in both preventive and curative dental care. In fact, there is some overlap in the functions of hygienists and periodontists, especially in BC, where hygienists may administer local anaesthetic. Supply statistics indicate that while the number of CDAs increased fourfold between 1975 and 1985, the ratio of hygienists to dentists in fact decreased during this time. The number of periodontists, small as it may be, almost tripled.

Since the practice of dentistry is largely in the private sector (the government pays dental care costs for only a small segment of the population – those on social assistance) public policy in dental resources supply or service organization is virtually non-existent. Thus, the impact of professional governance statutes has been much more pronounced on the internal differentiation of dental personnel and the professional dominance of dentistry than of medicine; dentists in BC have more control over their work and the work of their 'ancillary' groups because these latter are totally dependent on the former for the creation of a labour market.

Nurses or dental hygienists comprise a category of personnel who can 'substitute' for physicians or dentists in a number of settings and fields. As such, they are doubly threatening to the dominant professions because of their gender and their possible assumption of the professional role. Other health professionals, initially excluded from providing services that would be considered impingements on physician 'turf', were later recognized. This acceptance by the medical brotherhood was achieved for a price: a much restricted field of practice and only limited powers of self-regulation. According to Wardwell (1981), the marginal status of chiropractic has had important implications for the practice of chiropractic and for its survival as an occupation. In order to cope with their marginal status, chiropractors adopted an 'ideology of the oppressed' and attempted to improve their position by lobbying and attacking medical orthodoxy. The fact that chiropractic is 'scientifically unverified' presented a serious obstacle to its full professionaliz-ation. Chiropractors, therefore, rejected its more metaphysical or philosophical aspects in favour of a focus on chiropractic science and technique (Baer, 1984; Willis, 1983). They have redefined their role from comprehensive drugless practitioners to neuro-muscular specialists in the process of becoming legitimized (Biggs, 1988).

Gender in the middle ranks
The status hierarchy among a subset of professionals immediately below the two elite professions is also gender-based. Among pharmacists, optometrists, chiropractors, podiatrists and physical therapists, the latter are on the bottom rung. Physiotherapists are mostly hospital-based, and in that setting can work only with physician referrals. By statute, they have to be Chartered Physio-therapists. Registered Physiotherapists, on the other hand, for whom entry-to-practice requirements are less stringent, can be independent practitioners and their services are remunerated by the provincial Medical Services Plan on a fee-for-service basis. It is interesting to note that, in British Columbia, while overall 13 per cent of physiotherapists are male, only 9 per cent of Chartered Physiotherapists are men; males comprise 30 per cent of Registered Physiotherapists. In terms of the health occupations hierarchy, however, the group comprising rehabilitation personnel provides an interesting example of inter-professional status relations. As with nurses, status relations among physiotherapists, occupational thera-pists, audiologists/speech pathologists, psychologists and medical social workers, and between each of them and the other health professionals, are shaped by societal perceptions of autonomy, expertise and social value. Each of the above named five groups has a more or less defined body of knowledge that is specific to its practice, and each is permitted to practise in conditions of greater autonomy than exists for nurses, although none approaches the degree of autonomy belonging to physicians or dentists. In addition to this attribute, their more extensive educational preparation for entry to practice and their ability to command higher levels of remuneration than nurses, rehabilitation therapists, medical social workers and psychologists are seen as possessing considerable social value. However, among this selected grouping, it appears that the overall value of each of their services is directly related to the relative proportion of female workers in each group. Furthermore,

both chiropractors and podiatrists – predominantly male professionals – have attained recent gains in statutory power: the latter in the area of exclusive scope of practice, the former in a more powerful licensing body; but not without eliciting strong reaction from organized medicine.

The gender dimension of regulatory and public policies and professional dominance

Consistent with the individualistic ethic of the times, the Canadian health-care delivery system at the turn of the century 'was characterized by the primacy of the physician in a structure that provided care largely in terms of services to individuals in a doctor–patient relationship' (Weller and Manga, 1983). Thus, professional governance policy was formulated with the objective of protecting the public from incompetent practitioners. The governance structures that were consequently established were presumably designed to achieve this objective. The practice environment then consisted mainly of small groups of independent male generalists, with no overlaps in scope of practice. In the course of the next decade, when the emergence of other professionals made possible such overlaps, the relationships among groups were clearly defined in terms of dominant and subordinate status, reinforced by the formal delegation of acts, as in the case of physicians and nurses, dentists and dental assistants, and so on. The development of the health sector into the major industry it is in modern times has culminated in an elaborate occupational structure that continues to legitimize and maintain the historical position of the dominant professions. An analysis of this stratification system from a gender relations perspective indicates that the relations of dominance among health occupations are merely reflections of gender inequalities present in society at large, manifested through regulatory and other public policies at all levels of the health sector.

Professional governance policies
Since neither government nor patients had the knowledge or funds to judge the competence of the provider and monitor the practice settings, the professions themselves were given the power to define the standards of practice and to enforce those standards (Lomas and Barer, 1986). Thus emerged self-regulation, which granted to the profession the apparent power to act as an agent of the state in protecting the patient from the evils of incompetent practitioners and as an agent of the individual patient in ensuring quality care. The right of a profession to self-regulation comes through discussion

between the professional association and government policy-makers. Hall (1969) describes this as the process of procuring 'community sanction'; the community at large thus believes it will benefit by granting this power to a profession. Through this effort of the professional association a monopoly is, therefore, granted to all members of the profession. As described in the previous section, powers of professional self-regulation comprise not only professional autonomy but also the privilege to define the conditions of work of other personnel associated in that profession's division of labour. These professional privileges are legitimized through the use of an ideology which rationalizes this extraordinary imbalance of power to be in the public interest. The intensity with which professional ideological perspectives are held is in direct proportion to the perceived threats to relations of dominance, and indicates the political essence of the ideology.

Thus, it is interesting to note changes in professional governance statutes for dentists in the last decade, as the role of women in society underwent significant changes. The 1979 statutes (Dentists Act, Chapter 92, Section 26, subsection 4) stipulated that the council of the College of Dental Surgeons of British Columbia may make rules and bylaws:

(a) providing for the definition, establishment, development, regulation and control of ancillary bodies to the profession of dentistry, which may include dental hygienists, certified dental assistants and other ancillary bodies established by the council;
(b) regulating the conditions of and establishing qualifications for admission to ancillary bodies; and
(c) establishing the conditions under which the registration of resident, non-resident and non-practising members may be erased from the register.

A recent amendment to the Act (1988) repeals this Section and redefines these same powers of making rules and bylaws in terminology that is more deferential toward the knowledge and competence of the ancillary groups. The new Section 26, subsection 1.1 states that council may make rules respecting:

(a) persons to whom a dentist may delegate duties and procedures related to the treatment of the dentist's patients including
    (i) providing different rules for different classes of persons and different classes of registration,
    (ii) setting out requirements as to training, experience, character and registration in a class,

    (iii) providing discretionary powers to register a person in a class including the power to refuse registration, and to impose terms and conditions on registration or the continuation of registration,

    (iv) designating the duties and procedures which may be delegated by a dentist to a member of a class or to a registered member of a class, and

    (v) setting out procedures to be followed by the dentist in delegating some or all of the designated duties and procedures.

Furthermore, while the division of labour is initially established by professional associations and government regulation, continuous political activity is required to maintain and/or improve the profession's position in the labour market and in the hierarchy of health occupations. Much of the control over a profession's ideology accrues from the control over the education process (Olmsted and Paget, 1969); thus self-governance produces entry-to-practice restrictions defined in terms of stringent educational qualifications. Although the profession does not biologically produce the next generation of professionals, it does so socially through control over the careful selection of professional trainees (Goode, 1957).

The effect of professional governance policies was that various degrees of monopoly power were vested in a few professionals: physicians and dentists, primarily; pharmacists, chiropractors and optometrists, to a lesser degree. As discussed in the previous section, they are viewed as elites in a power hierarchy of occupations. In short, professional governance initially ensured self-regulatory rights in order to set standards for the content of medical practice. However, by the end of the First World War, medicine, through professional governance policies and 'scope of practice' clauses, had gained control over the conditions within which care would be delivered as well as control over the roles of and relationships between other health personnel (Coburn, 1988). To protect their 'turf' under the very commendable banner of optimal quality of care provided to each individual, the elite professions proclaimed an ethic that was in full accord with the individualistic ethic of the times.

The 'turf protection' ensured a broad definition of the practice of medicine, and thus excluded potential competition from a large number of other professions. Statutes state (Medical Practitioners Act, Chapter 254, Section 72, subsection 2) that a person practises medicine who:

(a) holds himself out as being, or by advertisement, sign or statement of any kind, written or oral, represents or implies that he is qualified, able or willing to diagnose, prescribe for, prevent or treat any human disease, ailment, deformity, defect or injury, or to perform an operation to remedy a human disease, ailment, deformity, defect or injury, or to examine or advise on the physical or mental condition of a person;

(b) diagnoses, or offers to diagnose, a human disease, ailment, deformity, defect or injury, or who examines or advises on, or offers to examine or advise on, the physical or mental condition of a person;

(c) prescribes or administers a drug, serum, medicine or a substance or remedy for the cure, treatment or prevention of a human disease, ailment, deformity, defect or injury;

(d) prescribes or administers a treatment or performs surgery, midwifery or an operation or manipulation, or supplies or applies an apparatus or appliance for the cure, treatment or prevention of a human disease, ailment, deformity, defect or injury; or

(e) acts as the agent, assistant or associate of a person in a practice of medicine as set out in paragraphs (a) to (d).

Under Section 73, however, exceptions are noted:

(a) practises chiropractic while registered under the *Chiropractors Act;*

(b) practises dentistry while registered under the *Dentists Act;*

(c) practises naturopathy while registered under the *Naturopaths Act;*

(d) practises optometry while registered under the *Optometrists Act;*

(e) is an orthoptic technician acting as provided in section 23 of the *Optometrists Act;*

(f) practises pharmacy while registered under the *Pharmacists Act;*

(g) practises, under the supervision of a person registered under this Act, as a physiotherapist or dietician;

(h) practises podiatry while registered under the *Podiatrists Act;*

(i) practises psychology while registered under the *Psychologists Act;*

(j) performs emergency procedures as authorized by the *Health Emergency Act;*

(k) is registered and acts under the *Dental Technicians Act;*

(l) engages in the usual business of opticians, vendors of dental or surgical instruments, apparatus or appliances, or bath attendants or proprietors; or

(m) engages in the ordinary calling of nursing.

All of these practices, of course, were either negotiated by the medical association to entail specialized services, or were delegated tasks.

This ethic represented, however, only the male ideology of the times, since power politics – including professional power – was an exclusively male domain. It is not surprising, therefore, that the ideologies of the dominant groups were widely diffused throughout Canadian society. This implicit approval can be explained by the theory that 'parochial' concerns of a professional association may have greater impact if they are linked to 'ecumenic' values held by society at large (Dibble, 1963); both professionals and government officials (representing the public) were predominantly (if not exclusively) male.

System structure and financing policies
The Depression era somewhat slowed the increasing dominance of the elite professions, especially medicine. Provincial and national political ideologies were increasingly supportive of the tenets of broad social reform, including socialized medicine, despite some attempts from organized medicine to institute profession-designed health insurance plans (Coburn, 1988). After the Second World War pressures and politics culminated in major health-care reforms, implemented through new federal regulatory policies in the areas of system structure and financing. Briefly identified, these were: the Hospital Insurance and Diagnostic Services Act in 1958 which provided all Canadians with comprehensive coverage for in-patient or out-patient care in any of Canada's hospitals and clinics, as well as limited insurance when travelling; the Medical Care Act of 1966 (which came into effect on 1 July 1968 and had full provincial participation by 1971) covered all medically required services provided by licensed physicians; the Canada Health Act in 1984, which replaced the Hospital and Medical Insurance Acts, remaining true to the principles of the original Acts but changing the formula for the federal and provincial share of the costs, based on block funding. While it is too soon to analyse the full implications of this latter, the two former regulatory policies, developed and enacted for the betterment of Canadian society, evidently did not greatly promote the upward movement of women workers in the hierarchy of health occupations. In these situations, policies pertaining to system structure and financing were again being formulated by public officials who were predominantly male.

Physicians and other male administrators holding management positions were in control in hospitals, when the publicly funded hospital insurance of 1954 ensured the economic viability of this sector which was facing serious economic crisis in the private market. But this created a most unfavourable situation for nurses and other hospital personnel: a market characterized as a 'monopsony' (a situation where there is a single buyer for a product or service). Without competition from a for-profit sector, hospitals do not compete for nurses and have a comparative advantage in their negotiations with all salaried personnel, but especially nursing personnel. Wages and benefits are determined through the collective bargaining process, and apply uniformly to all hospital nurses regardless of geographic location or type of hospital. Although nurses are the single most important category of health personnel, both in numbers and role, for the provision of hospital-based care, the absence of incentives to increase their labour-force participation, and of initiatives to improve workplace conditions, appears particularly shortsighted. Nursing services are provided 24 hours of the day and hospitals are staffed around the clock. This is a universal phenomenon and applies to all countries, regardless of payment systems, cultural values or levels of economic development. Working late shifts and the rotating aspect of these shifts are incompatible with family responsibilities that are still assigned to women in most societies. The inevitability of such structural impediments is not in question; however, it is difficult to understand why hospital management has been so negligent in its human resources function. Grounding it in a theory of predominant gender relations, however, provides a plausible explanation for the conspicuous lack of staff retention policies and practices in most western systems. A global shortage of nurses, regardless of fiscal or cultural subsystems, provides an empirical verification of this phenomenon.

In addition, nurses' work situation in hospitals is usually structured along bureaucratic lines of production which are often in conflict with the professional ethic. Feelings of powerlessness and role stress are experienced by nurses who have to reconcile yet another subordinate passive role, vis-à-vis the predominantly male health-care executives, with that of professional clinical practice. In the hospital setting, nurses have almost no direct involvement in managerial or administrative decisions, despite their pivotal role in the delivery of care: most hospital boards do not have nurse representatives, few formal mechanisms exist for nursing input regarding organizational decisions, and very rarely, if ever, are staffing levels based on nursing diagnoses of patient load. While evidence of the merits of such involvement of nurses does exist (Halloran and Halloran, 1985), it is rarely considered necessary or even desirable by management. Changing gender roles in society and the implied change in employment opportunities for women remain unacknowledged by the patriarchal setting of the hospital culture. Publicly funded medical insurance has also created serious limitations for women in the health labour force through extending this mode of remuneration to only a few professions. Fee-for-service payments to chiropractors, naturopaths, podiatrists and physiotherapists, as well as to physicians, are part of the publicly funded insurance scheme. Except for physiotherapists, these professionals are predominantly male; male physiotherapists licensed to practise outside hospitals are overrepresented relative to the overall distribution of males in physiotherapy. Nursing services are not eligible for fee-for-service payments and, therefore, render independent nursing practice an unviable career. Very few nurse practitioners exist in the province and none work in a medical group practice setting. Fee-for-service remuneration is an attribute of professional autonomy and provides better incentive for labour market participation, as indicated by the literature on women in medicine and dentistry (Wilson et al., 1988; Lorber, 1984; Langwell, 1982).

On the other hand, the imposition of hospital and then medical insurance in Canada did accelerate and accentuate a different level of public interest awareness, the general public interest, which incorporated the twin concepts of allocative and technical efficiency. Allocative efficiency refers to social decisions about the best use of available resources (such as health care vs. welfare or highways) and is separate from technical efficiency, which refers to the best use of health-care resources in attaining a stated health status. This public awareness emerged when third parties came to have a stake (as had private insurers, earlier) in the resources consumed by the aggregation of the 'specific' public interests. While an increasing reliance on technology resulted in a proliferation of new categories of health personnel (mainly hospital-based) and an increasing specialization of existing categories, cost containment and fiscal restraint has begun to be understood and accepted by the consuming public. However, so far this public awareness, which is at least partly attributable to government involvement in health insurance, has not posed a threat to professional dominance. Furthermore, it is suggested that the public is becoming more knowledgeable about health and medicine, sceptical about the overmedicalization of contemporary life (Stevenson and Williams, 1988), and generally less deferential toward medical professionals. Deprofessionalization has been defined and debated at length (Haug, 1973; Haug and Lavin, 1983); yet this phenomenon, and that of corporatization (McKinlay and Stoeckle, 1988), have neither changed the overall situation of professional dominance by the predominantly male professions, nor decreased the gender gap among the health occupations.

Human resource planning and supply policies
When the Canadian government acknowledged its social responsibility to ensure efficiently delivered health services in the mid-1950s
(after the introduction of health insurance), it did generate some
human resource supply policies. These included increasing the
capacity of medical schools, and were mainly designed to alleviate
concerns about possibly inadequate physician supply in the face of an
anticipated increase in the demand for health services. Since both
health and education are provincial jurisdictions, these policy
measures were developed and implemented at an uneven rate across
the country (Lomas and Barer, 1986). The outcomes of these few
policies were also uneven, often resulting in the opposite of what was
originally intended and merely accentuating the existing power
structure – especially since the expected increase in demand for
health services did not materialize.

Some years later, when the provincial government in British
Columbia (as well as in some other provinces) realized the adverse
effect of its physician supply policies in the light of negligible additional
demand, the only corrective policy measures that it initiated were
indirect ones aimed at curtailing provincial medical expenditures by
freezing or rolling back public hospital budgets (where all in-patient
care is delivered). The adverse effects of such budget constraints
included reduced nursing staff, higher reliance on casual staffing, less
accommodating rotation of schedules, and more overtime for regular
staff, further exacerbating conditions of employment which are
incompatible with family life. While these phenomena have been
documented and studied as unfavourable workplace conditions, they
have not been overtly or explicitly linked to the specific policy measure
which should have focused on the correct target group. Numerous
symbolic gestures, such as Royal Commissions and studies about the
use of substitute personnel and about alternative organizational
structures, have been undertaken by almost all provincial governments and were intended to signal the government's concern to the
dominant professions. However, these have never been accompanied
by any public policy which would allow the implementation of
necessary changes in the organizational and financial structures
required to integrate these new categories into the mainstream
delivery system. All past and present health human-resource planning
efforts assume the status quo will be maintained in the area of
inter-professional relations; gender-based professional dominance
remains, therefore, implicitly condoned. The absence of explicit
supply policies to promote women's participation in the labour force
and to provide women with opportunities for satisfying professional
careers is clearly indicative of such condonation.

Conclusion

Thus, the three areas of health policy development – professional governance, human resources planning and supply, and system structure and finance – have had varying, and sometimes contradictory, influences on health labour markets in Canada. It is not the intention of this study either to review exhaustively all health policy developments in Canada – that has been done by others (Hastings and Vayda, 1986; Vayda and Deber, 1984) – nor to examine the changing role of the medical profession (Coburn, 1988; Taylor, 1960). It is postulated here, and the historical evidence is confirmatory, that all early governance policies and most current public policies have been defined and developed by policy-makers who have defined each situation from a male perspective, resulting in a delivery system that favours male patterns of labour market participation and rewards male life-cycle activity patterns, and perpetrates the gender gap in the hierarchy of professionals. While women comprise the majority of workers in the health labour market, the description, analysis and especially the interpretation of this market situation have not, traditionally, taken into consideration the female experience. The slowly changing sex composition of the elite professions is likely to have some influence on the relations of these to the so-called semi-professions.

A detailed examination of the implications of such changes in another system already exists (Riska, 1988). Certainly, the traditional nurse–doctor game with all its elements that reflect stereotypical roles of male dominance and female passivity, will no longer appear as quaint as before (Stein et al., 1990). However, given the historical perspective, gender equality in the health labour market is more likely to happen if women participate more actively in the 'definition of the situation' at the policy level in health as well as in other power constellations. Until this century, women were not allowed to vote or to stand for federal or provincial election in Canada; women were not permitted to be jurors, lawyers or judges. Therefore, women had no say in the making of statute law, in the interpretation or application of such law, or in the development of common law. As well, women did not hold public office or rise to top bureaucratic positions in government. Women are still underrepresented in hospital management positions (Kazanjian and Pagliccia, 1993). If the society within which the health system or its legal subsystem is nested is one in which male dominance is the norm, policies and statutes developed by legislators and policy-makers will work to the advantage of men only. The Council of Europe's Seminar on Equality between Men and Women, held in 1989, concluded: 'that humankind is dual and must be represented in its dual form if the trap of an asexual abstraction in which "human being" is always declined in the masculine is to be avoided' (Smith, 1990). The culturally embedded stereotype of the role of women in society has been a factor in designing a health-care system and in defining professional governance through policies that have a strong gender bias. This stereotype also presents a significant impediment to the implementation of effective organizational and fiscal structure changes in the health delivery system. The reason for this inertia, this chapter demonstrates, is due to the almost total exclusion of women from policy-making roles in the areas of public service, administration and law. Male health policy-makers and legislators develop and implement policies and statutes that are fundamentally self-serving, albeit designed to serve the public interest. Thus, predominantly female occupations continue to have low status in the hierarchy of health occupations, male-defined health systems maintain the status quo – inefficiencies included – and gender stereotypes are reinforced from one generation to the next.

References

Acker, J. (1989) 'Making gender', in R.A. Wallace (ed.), *Feminism and Sociological Theory*. Newbury Park: Sage.

Baer, H. (1984) 'A comparative view of heterodox health systems: chiropractic in America and Britain', *Medical Anthropology*, 8: 151–68.

Biggs, L. (1988) 'The professionalization of chiropractic in Canada: its current status and future prospects', in B. S. Bolaria and H. D. Dickinson (eds), *Sociology of Health Care in Canada*. Toronto: Harcourt Brace Jovanovich. pp. 328–45.

Blumberg, R.L. (1984) 'A general theory of gender stratification', in R. Collins (ed.), *Sociological Theory*. San Francisco: Jossey Bass Inc. pp. 23–101.

Brown, W., Knight, J., Patel, K. and Pilat, D. (1987) 'Is nursing a profession?', *Evaluation and the Health Professionals*, 10(2): 206–26.

Bullough, B. (1988) 'Stratification' in M. E. Hardy and M. E. Conway (eds), *Role Theory: Perspectives for Health Professionals*, 2nd Edition. Norwalk, Connecticut: Appleton & Lange. pp. 289–308.

Butter, I., Carpenter, E., Kay, B. and Simmons, R. (1985) *Sex and Status: Hierarchies in the Health Workforce*. American Public Health Association, Public Health Policy Series.

Campbell-Heider, N. and Pollock, D. (1987) 'Barriers to physician–nurse collegiality: an anthropological perspective', *Social Science and Medicine*, 25(5): 421–5.

Chafetz, J. S. (1984) *Sex and Advantage: a Comparative Macro-structural Theory of Sex Stratification*. New Jersey: Rowman & Allanheld.

Coburn, D. (1988) 'Canadian medicine: dominance or proletarianization?', *The Milbank Quarterly*, 66(Suppl. 2): 92–116.

Dibble, V. K. (1963) 'Occupations and ideologies', *American Journal of Sociology*, 68: 229–41.

Duncan, O., Featherman, D. and Ducan, B. (1972) *Socioeconomic Background and Achievement*. New York: Seminar Press.

Fagin, C. and Diers, D. (1983) 'Nursing as metaphor', *New England Journal of Medicine*, 309: 116–17.

Freidson, E. (1970) *Profession of Medicine*. New York: Dodd, Mead & Co.

Fuchs, V., Rand, E. and Garrett, B. (1970) 'The distribution of earnings in health and other industries', *Journal of Human Resources*, 5(3): 382–9.

Giddens, A. (1982) *Profiles and Critiques in Social Theory*. Berkeley: University of California Press.

Goode, W. J. (1957) 'Community within a community: the professions', *American Sociological Review*, 22: 194–200.

Hall, R. M. (1969) *Occupations and the Social Structure*. Englewood Cliffs, NJ: Prentice-Hall.

Halloran, E. and Halloran, D. C. (1985) 'Exploring the DRG/nursing equation', *American Journal of Nursing*, October: 1093–5.

Hastings, J. and Vayda, E. (1986) 'Health services organization and delivery: promise and reality', in R. G. Evans and G. L. Stoddart (eds), *Medicare at Maturity*. Alberta, Canada: The Banff Centre for Continuing Education.

Haug, M. (1973) 'Deprofessionalization: an alternative hypothesis for the future', *Sociological Review Monographs*, 20: 195–211.

Haug, M. and Lavin, B. (1983) *Consumerism in Medicine: Challenging Physician Authority*. Beverly Hills: Sage.

Kazanjian, A. and Pagliccia, N. (1993) 'Health managers in B.C.: Who manages our system? A socio-demographic and professional profile of middle and high level managers in B.C.', *Health Care Management Forum*, 6(1): 19–24.

Langwell, K. M. (1982) 'Factors affecting the incomes of men and women physicians: further exploration', *Journal of Human Resources*, 2: 261–75.

Light, D. W. (1989) 'Social control and the American health care system', in H. Freeman and S. Levine (eds), *Handbook of Medical Sociology*. Englewood Cliffs, NJ: Prentice-Hall. pp. 456–74.

Lomas, J. and Barer, M. L. (1986) 'And who shall represent the public interest?' in R. G. Evans and G. L. Stoddart (eds), *Medicare at Maturity*. Alberta, Canada: The Banff Centre for Continuing Education.

Lorber, J. (1984) *Women Physicians: Careers, Status, and Power*. New York: Tavistock.

McKinlay, J. B. and Stoeckle, J. D. (1988) 'Corporatization and the social transformation of doctoring', *International Journal of Health Services*, 18: 191–206.

Mick, S. S. (1978) 'Understanding the persistence of human resource problems in health', *Milbank Memorial Fund Quarterly*, 56(4): 463–99.

Olmsted, A. G. and Paget, M. A. (1969) 'Some theoretical issues in professional socialization', *Journal of Medical Education*, 44: 663–9.

Reskin, B. (1988) 'Bringing the men back in: sex differentiation and the devaluation of women's work', *Gender and Society*, 2: 58–86.

Riska, E. (1988) 'The professional status of physicians in the Nordic countries', *Milbank Quarterly*, 66 (Suppl. 2): 133–47.

Roos, P. A. (1981) 'Sex stratification in the workplace: male–female differences in economic returns to occupation', *Social Science Research*, 10: 195–224.

RSBC (1979) Selected chapters and sessional volumes. Queen's Printer for British Columbia.

Smith, L. (1990) 'Women and the law', *The Vancouver Sun*, 25 May: A17.

Spitzer, W. O. (1984) 'The nurse practitioner revisited: slow death of a good idea', *New England Journal of Medicine*, 310: 1049–51.

Stein, L. I., Watts, D. T. and Howell, T. (1990) 'The doctor–nurse game revisited', *New England Journal of Medicine*, 322(8): 546–9.

Stevenson, H.M. and Williams, A.P. (1988) 'Physicians and medicare: professional ideology and Canadian health care policy', in B. S. Bolaria and H. D. Dickinson (eds), *Sociology of Health Care in Canada*. Toronto: Harcourt Brace Jovanovich. pp. 92–103.

Taylor, M. G. (1960) 'The role of the medical profession in the formulation and execution of public policy', *Canadian Journal of Economics and Political Science*, 25: 108–27.

Vayda, E. and Deber, R. (1984): 'The Canadian health care system: an overview', *Social Science and Medicine*, 18: 191–7.

Warburton, R. and Carroll, W. K. (1988) 'Class and gender in nursing', in B. S. Bolaria and H. D. Dickinson (eds), *Sociology of Health Care in Canada*. Toronto. Harcourt Brace Jovanovich. pp. 364–74.

Wardwell, W. (1981) 'Chiropractors, challenges of medical domination', *Research in the Sociology of Health Care*, 2: 207–50.

Weller, G. R. and Manga, P. (1983) 'The development of health policy in Canada', in M. Atkinson and M. Chandler (eds), *The Politics of Canadian Public Policy*. Toronto: University of Toronto Press.

Willis, E. (1983) *Medical Dominance: The Division of Labour in Australian Health Care*. Sydney: Allen & Unwin.

Wilson, A. A., Branch, L. G. and Niessen, L. C. (1988) 'Practice patterns of male and female dentists', *Journal of the American Dental Association*, 116(2): 173–7.

Wuthnow, S. (1986) 'Nurses and the new class: a comparative study of values and attitudes among professionals and semi-professional occupations', *Sociological Inquiry*, 56(1): 125–48.

PART IV
CONCLUSIONS

Katarina Wegar

As noted in the introduction, the gendered division of labour in health care is a largely neglected topic in the literature on health-care occupations. The contributions to this book primarily describe and provide explanations for the position of women health-care professionals. The concept of gender is employed to draw attention to social processes that naturalize and depoliticize the different positions of women *and* men in the organization of health care. Drawing upon cross-national, inter- and intra-occupational data, the contributors all note a marked sex segregation of health-care occupations. The studies not only contribute to the empirical knowledge of gender in the division of labour in medicine, they also challenge existing sociological approaches to the study of professions.

Considerations of the specific and universal features in the medical division of labour in different countries and occupations enable an expansion and correction of previous sociological assumptions about the state, the professions and gender. Knowledge of the dynamics of gender in predominantly female health-care occupations, such as nursing, can clarify women's position in male-dominated elite professions, and vice versa. The international approach calls into question some underlying assumptions in existing studies of the relation between professional dominance and state intervention in health care. The contributors furthermore touch upon a number of theoretical issues that illuminate the subordinate position of women in the social division of labour.

The authors' theoretical perspectives and conclusions complement, diverge, and are in some respects even contradictory. The purpose of this chapter is therefore to comment on differences as well as convergences in findings and perspectives. First, I will examine the gender basis of the medical division of labour and the social mechanisms that have contributed to such a division. Second, I will explore the role of the state in maintaining and perpetuating the power hierarchy of health-care systems. Third, I will discuss women's occupational choices and present various explanations for how their choices are shaped and articulated. Fourth, I will consider the prospect that women health-care professionals will change the nature and organization of health care.

The gender basis of the division of labour in health care

The contributions to this book lend support both to pessimistic and to optimistic interpretations of women's future professional position in health care. All studies point to a marked sex segregation of the division of labour in health care: the largest proportion of women is found in occupations or in professional niches characterized by comparatively little prestige and vocational autonomy. While women have entered the public sphere previously mainly inhabited by men, their tasks have remained subordinate. This is the case in particular in traditionally female health-care occupations. In contrast to the male-dominated and more prestigious 'curing' aspects of medicine, the female-dominated 'caring' functions of medicine have been perceived to require capabilities that women are assumed to possess. Hence, the functions performed by women health-care workers have not been recognized as professional skills (Davies and Rosser, 1986: 103; Bradley, 1989: 188). Although statistical data on the medical division of labour show a growing number of women in the medical profession, there is no reverse trend in low-paid health-care occupations such as nursing (Beller, 1984: 18). As Carpenter argues (p. 124), women's occupational choices in the division of labour in health care are also circumscribed by class and ethnic divisions. Recently, professionalization efforts within female-dominated occupations have tended to increase even further the internal status differentiation among women health-care workers.

The four chapters on women physicians explore institutional factors that have affected the sex segregation of medical work. First, the entry of women into the medical profession has in many countries been propelled not only by decisions internal to the profession but by external needs and pressures. In Britain the First World War (Elston: p. 31) and in Finland the Second World War (Riska and Wegar: p. 82) necessitated an increase in the number of women admitted to medical schools since men were serving at the front. In the United States as well, the Second World War impelled medical schools to accept more female medical students than before. In these countries, the two world wars challenged the sex segregation of medical work by revealing the social construction of the division of labour. Moreover, as Bradley (1989: 48) has noted, the wartime experience of women physicians has provided 'a salutary example of how rapidly change can occur if the "national will" and governmental power is behind it'.

In India, the actions of western 'social reformers', who opposed the religiously motivated lack of health care for Indian women by male physicians, supported the acceptance of women doctors (Chidambaram: p. 16). In all countries, however, these early concessions were later opposed by male physicians.

In the 1960s, governmental demands for increased health manpower and/or affirmative-action legislation led to an expansion in the intake of women medical students in the United States, Britain and Finland. Since then, the proportion of women physicians in these countries has grown steadily. Not only commentators who have been critical of the growing number of women physicians, however, but also feminist researchers who have welcomed this development have tended to overestimate the actual influx of women into the medical profession. The notion of the 'feminization' of the medical profession has often been prematurely applied to describe the situation in countries where women still constitute a relatively small percentage of medical students and practising physicians.

As Elston demonstrates, a continuing rise in the proportion of women physicians, especially in influential positions, cannot be taken for granted. She shows that an increasingly rigid hospital career structure in Britain has in fact expanded the possibilities of overt and covert gender discrimination over the past two decades. Because of problems in hospital staffing, the medical leadership has also recently proposed reforms that would create a new category of 'second-class niches' for 'doctors with extensive domestic responsibilities (code for women)' (Elston: p. 49). Furthermore, structural changes in British medicine might cause financial disadvantages for part-time practitioners, who are mostly women. The situation in the United States indicates that the current trend towards increasing corporatization and privatization of health care might further hamper women physicians' chances of exerting influence over policy decisions (Lorber: p. 69). Nor does the case of Finland provide grounds for optimism. Despite the comparatively large proportion of women physicians in Finland, data on specialty choices and practice settings indicate a sex segregation similar to, and in some cases even greater than, that which prevails in countries where women constitute a much smaller segment of the profession (Riska and Wegar: p. 84).

A second common finding is the similar kinds of explanations provided by women physicians in different countries about their tasks and position in medicine. Despite the considerable cultural differences between India and Finland, both Indian and Finnish women physicians interviewed saw their vocation as an extension of their domestic roles as wives, mothers and carers (Chidambaram: p. 24;

Riska and Wegar: p. 88). In both countries the women were also aware of existing institutional patterns of sex segregation. The relation between women's choices and the social context in which choices are made will be further discussed later in this chapter.

A third observation is about the changing character of the medical profession and the gender distribution of its practitioners. Among American scholars, the increasing number of women in formerly male-dominated occupations has often been explained by the faltering social status of these occupations: as the status of an occupation decreases, the percentage of women has been expected to increase (Carter and Carter, 1981; Reskin, 1988). In this volume, Lorber (p. 72) presents a similar conclusion in her assessment of the future of women in the American medical profession. However, as Elston observes (p. 37), this explanation does not hold true for the increasing proportion of women physicians in Britain. Elston does not view the increase as a result of a proletarianization of physicians due to governmental intrusion, but rather as the 'perhaps unintended' consequence of the medical profession's own collaboration with the state in increasing medical school intake. Furthermore, she examines in some detail the conventional assumption that the growing number of women in medicine will automatically downgrade the profession. She argues that the same 'syndicalist organization' that has circumscribed women's professional opportunities in the past can be expected to guarantee a continuation of collective professional privileges, despite the 'feminization' of the profession (p. 38). However, because of the internal division of labour in medicine, women will probably have less opportunity than their male colleagues to exercise or regulate their professional privileges.

The medical profession is, of course, not the only occupation in which skills and tasks tend to be sex-typed (Fox and Hesse-Biber, 1984; Reskin, 1988; Crompton and Sanderson, 1990; Reskin and Roos, 1990). In this volume, Carpenter argues that the social processes that regulate the subordination of nurses in Britain reflect gender inequalities in the wider society. He also underscores the necessity of including class and race divisions in the analysis. Kazanjian (p. 159) observes that the social worth and the degree of expertise attributed to the skills of nurses, physiotherapists, occupational therapists, speech therapists, psychologists and medical social workers in British Columbia is inversely related to the proportion of women in each occupation. And in his comparative analysis of midwifery in different countries, DeVries explores the complex social mechanisms that determine the status and autonomy of midwives, mechanisms that are intrinsically related to women's position in society. A central theme throughout this volume is that the gendered division of labour reflects the social construction and evaluation of skills required in medical work, and that these evaluations mirror women's position in society.

The studies of women physicians by Chidambaram, Elston, Lorber, and Riska and Wegar show that women physicians are concentrated in specialties related to the caring aspects of medicine. As noted earlier, these are aspects of medical work that tend not to be acknowledged as skills but as qualities inherent or natural to women (Davies and Rosser, 1986: 103). Work in these niches can be characterized as relatively routinized and as lacking the kind of autonomy considered distinctive of professional work. The authors explain the high proportion of women working in these specialties by institutional factors such as informal and formal processes of closure. These structural or institutional explanations of inter- and intra-occupational sex segregation challenge voluntaristic interpretations that assume that the concentration of women in certain niches reflects the women's own attitudes and preferences. Furthermore, as Riska and Wegar suggest (p. 89), medical practice in specialties which are viewed as reflecting women's particular interests tends to maintain their lack of influence over policy decisions – that is, their chances of setting the terms of their work.

According to Carpenter (p. 112), the traditional medical and sociological representation of nursing as a low-skilled occupation is neither accurate nor static. A characterization of nurses as relatively low-skilled and lacking responsibility is socially ascribed rather than technically determined by their tasks. The lifting of restrictions on nurses' activities during the night shift is a telling illustration of the social construction of skills required in nursing (Kazanjian, p. 157). Kazanjian (p. 154) argues that the relatively low status of nurses in the health-care hierarchy of British Columbia is related to the fact that their skills are less well defined than the skills of elite health professionals. Yet, it is not because nursing skills cannot be clearly defined, but because they are considered undefinable in the vocabulary of the dominant medical model. To gain legitimation for their claims and professional autonomy, occupational groups have to frame their activities to fit the medical–scientific framework. This strategy has been chosen by chiropractors, who have 'redefined their role from comprehensive drugless practitioners to neuro-muscular specialists' (Kazanjian, p. 159). Against this background one can understand DeVries's conclusion that occupational groups gain authority to the extent that they can reduce risk and uncertainty for clients. Professional groups seeking to enhance their status are thus advised to emphasize or redefine life events as 'risky' (p. 143). This poses a serious dilemma for midwives who wish to gain professional autonomy at the same time as attempting to demedicalize pregnancy and birth.

However, a cross-national perspective on the division of labour in health care reveals that the involvement of a large number of women is not a sufficient explanation for the comparatively low autonomy or prestige attributed to predominantly female health occupations. The social standing of an occupational group is also defined by its particular position within the national organization of health care. The organization of health care has significantly affected, for example, the work of midwives. In countries such as Sweden and Netherlands where the maternity-care system is decentralized, midwives have retained aspects of autonomy that their colleagues in the more centralized systems of Britain, Canada and the United States have lost (DeVries: 136). Since 'continuous political activity is required to maintain and/or improve the profession's position in the labour market and in the hierarchy of health occupations' (Kazanjian: 162), the occupational autonomy of 'semi-professionals' is crucially determined by their relation to more powerful occupational groups (Halpern, 1992). This is clearly demonstrated in the case of British Columbia where tasks that should logically have been delegated to dental hygienists have been assigned to dental assistants instead, primarily because the latter group has been perceived as less threatening to the privileges of physicians or dentists (Kazanjian: 158).

Professional autonomy, gender and the state

American studies of the medical profession have suggested that government or corporate intrusion in health care will lead to diminished professional power and autonomy (McKinlay and Arches, 1985; McKinlay and Stoeckle, 1988). The situation in Britain, Canada and Finland indicates that reduced professional autonomy might be a particularly American phenomenon, which challenges the assumption that a high degree of professional autonomy is necessarily inversely related to the extent of state intervention in health care. Furthermore, the American debate on the changing character of the medical profession has neglected to take into account the increasing proportion of women physicians and the sex segregation of tasks within the medical profession.

The organization of health care in Britain, Canada and Finland reveals that various avenues for professional freedom of action remain open despite a high degree of state involvement in health care. In the analysis of the relation between professional autonomy and state involvement, it is thus important to distinguish between different types of professional autonomy. State intervention might have double-edged consequences: some aspects of professional self-regulation may be circumscribed while other aspects may prevail and even be heightened. Inter- and intra-occupational tactics of closure are not static but are modified as the external conditions for self-regulation change. These modifications may be legitimated by agreements of sheltered markets between professional organizations and government policy-makers, and institutionalized by insurance and third-party payment arrangements. For example, the occupational independence of midwives is largely determined by insurance policies (DeVries: 136).

Because of their reliance upon government policy-makers, health-care professionals can be characterized as 'relatively autonomous' agents of the state (Carpenter: 108; Kazanjian: 160). In Britain, Finland, the United States and Canada, the enduring and even enhanced clinical autonomy granted to the medical profession continues to have a profound impact on the situation of women physicians and other health-care workers. In Britain, the state-funded health-care system has during the past two decades actually enhanced physicians' control over decision-making in the workplace both with regard to their own work and health-manpower policy-making in general (Elston: 29). The creation of the National Health Service (NHS) in fact 'served to legitimate medical rule over other occupations in the health-care division of labour' (Carpenter: 120). For midwives the development of the NHS meant a decline in autonomy under the medical model (DeVries: 136). In Finland, physicians have maintained control over positions in health administration that guarantee them the power to determine the parameters of their work – that is, their professional dominance. In 1990, this right was challenged but later confirmed by the Mayor of Helsinki as the result of an administrative dispute between the city and the physicians employed in the health districts in the capital (Riska, 1993). Also, in Canada, the government's lack of funds and need for pertinent expertise has led to a health-care system in which jurisdiction over various health-care occupations has been confined to the hands of a few professionals, primarily physicians (Kazanjian: 162).

Some commentators have regarded bureaucratic organizational structures which emphasize formal criteria for employment and advancement as inducive to women's advancement in professions formerly dominated by men (Carpenter, 1977). The formal legal rules applied in bureaucratic organizational structures require that formal gender equality be observed – that similarly situated women and men be treated alike. Both Elston and Lorber note, however, that a more rigid – more hierarchical – hospital career structure does not necessarily minimize the potential for patronage and gatekeeping. Furthermore, feminist legal scholars (MacKinnon, 1989) have argued that existing gender inequalities stem to a large extent from principles of formal equality. Since the dominant legal principles are based on a male-dominated gender order that obscures women's concrete life situation, the state both legitimates and perpetuates gender inequalities.

Feminist scholars have characterized the state or welfare institutions as reflective of a male-dominated gender order in that their laws and policies suppress or neglect women's interests (Sassoon, 1987; Walby, 1990). According to this view, professional privileges and sources of social control are legitimated by a 'patriarchal' ideology sanctioned by the state. In her chapter, Kazanjian notes that although the welfare state has created new jobs for nurses and for female primary-care physicians, planning and policy alternatives have continued to establish female-dominated niches as complementary or subordinate to male-dominated elite professions. Her analysis of the health-care system of British Columbia reveals that, even when there is empirical evidence that female health-care professionals can be more effective in delivering health services formerly provided by the male-dominated professions, culturally embedded stereotypes enforced by governmental policies can present a sizeable barrier to changes in the organization of health care (p. 157).

In this context the case of Britain and the policies of the so-called neo-liberal state deserve particular mention. Neo-liberal policies, aimed at the 'explicit rationing' of health services, are not affecting male and female health-care workers equally. Demands for greater efficiency of the health services call for a more hierarchical division of labour, which is likely to heighten existing social divisions, including those drawn along class and ethnic lines. As an unintended consequence of nursing professionalization, the new nursing not only caters to the demands of increasingly hierarchical health-care organizations but also lowers the potential for collective bargaining by intensifying social divisions among nurses. The process might in particular increase the importance of class and race divisions in occupational attainment, and further devalue the work of women involved in more traditional patient-oriented forms of nursing (Carpenter: 113). The restructuring of nursing management in both Britain and the United States has transformed the previous gender disadvantages of male nurses into advantages as men in nursing are perceived to possess distinctive 'managerial traits' (Bradley, 1989: 107; Williams, 1989: 95). As noted earlier, attempts to solve the 'health-care crisis' have also created within the British medical profession new divisions that tend to have more negative effects for women physicians than for men. The same reforms – for example, part-time work – that are declared to help women 'with extensive domestic responsibilities' are those that threaten crucially to restrict their rights to options in the sphere of work (Elston: 49).

To explore further the sex-segregated character of the division of labour in health care, the next section will consider a theme that appeared in several of the chapters in this volume: the personal preferences of women health-care workers and the social context in which choices are shaped and articulated. This perspective also allows for a recognition of women not as 'structural dopes' (Giddens, 1979) but as active agents in the struggle against occupational inequality.

Women's choices and structural constraints

Institutional explanations of the sex segregation of occupations have questioned the assumption that women are concentrated in certain occupations only because these occupations are compatible with women's domestic roles or because they reflect preferences formed during gender socialization (Crompton and Sanderson, 1990: 28; Reskin and Roos, 1990). The tendency for women to cluster, however, in medical specialties lacking the characteristics generally attributed to professional work cannot be attributed solely to overt or covert discrimination. In the interviews with Finnish and Indian women physicians, many women maintained that their choice of specialization had been guided by a personal preference for certain types of tasks. For example, the high proportion of women physicians working at municipal health centres in Finland was accounted for by women's gender-specific abilities to handle the work involved (Riska and Wegar: 88). The choice of specialty was often the outcome of a skilful balancing of professional and family demands and by informed evaluations of obstacles and opportunities in the profession (see also Elston: 54). This notion of women's occupational choices as strategies based on knowledgeable assessments of the opportunity structure fits the human-capital theory of career paths selected by gender (Crompton and Sanderson, 1990: 28). In this section, I will first discuss how women health-care workers have used claims to gender-specific competence to advance their own professional interests. Second, I will consider various theoretical explanations for the division of labour in health care, in particular the debate over the relative importance of agency and structure in explaining human behaviour, and the recent 'poststructuralist' critique of essentialist tendencies in sociological and feminist theory.

Recent professionalizing movements in nursing and midwifery

illustrate that women health-care professionals cannot be characterized exclusively either as autonomous subjects (as proponents of the
individual-oriented approach propose) or as structural or cultural
dopes (as some of their sociological critics seem to suggest). The
history of nursing (Carpenter: 117) and of women's entry into the
medical profession (Riska and Wegar: 88) shows that women have
referred to their gender-specific competence for 'emotion work'
(Hochschild, 1979) in order to claim the work related to the caring
aspect of health care. While male-elite physicians represent the
technical and capital-intensive aspects of medical expertise, the ethos
of service and altruism, which Parsons (1951) identified as central to
the practice of medicine, has today become the prerogative primarily
of women. Although this 'indeterminate' dimension (Atkinson and
Delamont, 1990: 106) of health-care work has been overpowered and
to some extent also conditioned by the dominant medical model, the
professional strategy of female health-care workers has been anal-
ogous to that of male physicians. In short, not only male-elite
physicians but also women health-care workers have tended to
'mystify the skills required to sanction the "social closure" of the
occupation' (Carpenter: 107).

The mastery of medical uncertainty has been seen as a central
organizing principle in the legitimation of the power of the medical
profession (Light, 1979; see also DeVries: 143). But the gender-
based division of labour in medicine is characterized by different
claims of managing medical uncertainty. While the male-dominated
areas of medicine are characterized by efforts to expand the scientific
and technical mastery of the body, the female-dominated areas are
characterized by the mastery of patients' emotions. Today, women
physicians in primary care can appeal to a management and mastery
not only of patients' feelings but also to the whole array of
uncertainty related to what Armstrong (1983) has called the illness
related to social spaces. This area of medicine approaches illness
from the viewpoint of social relations and the social and cultural
factors embedded in these relations. The effort to master these
factors has led to the establishment of a variety of specialty fields in
primary care. By claiming the role of interaction or communication
experts, women have been able to enter these new niches in
medicine. Ultimately, however, such stereotyping of expertise might
restrict women's occupational choices, and also intensify the occupational hierarchy in health-care organizations. The clustering of
women in positions as lower-paid 'communications technicians' is a
common phenomenon not only in the health-care field, but in many
other occupations (Reskin and Roos, 1990: 75).

The contributors to this book explain the sex segregation of health-care work primarily by social processes of closure. In the literature on health-care professions, the gendered division of labour in health care has also been attributed to more subtle processes of socialization that shape women's preferences. Much research on gender-specific traits and preferences among medical students and physicians has explicitly or implicitly relied upon the individualistic framework of sex-role theory (Riska and Wegar: 79). This approach explains gender differences in attitudes by the different role expectations that women and men face during periods of socialization. However, as critics have pointed out, socialization and role theory is basically voluntaristic and excludes issues of power and social interest (Connell, 1987: 50–3; Walby, 1990). Hence such interpretations fail to take into account the social character of motives. To regard motives as socially constituted means that motivational processes are internalizations of existing social rules and power relations, and that people's motivations are mediated by the socially constructed vocabularies of motive they employ (Mills, 1940). While the view that motives are internalizations of social relations stems from the classical Meadian tradition of social psychology, the idea that motives cannot be grasped except through an understanding of socially constructed vocabularies of motive has only recently been rediscovered by 'poststructuralist' researchers (Silverman, 1989).

The poststructuralist approach to the analysis of gender-specific preferences of occupation raises a number of questions that are of interest for the study of the division of labour in medicine. Most important, this approach questions the view that women's choices are direct manifestations of their 'inner nature' as well as the assumption that this 'inner nature' is a static entity that can be grasped in its pure form. Although certain occupations are more appealing to women than others, given the structure of their experiences, their choices should not be mistaken for expressions of a given female 'nature'. This essentialist tendency is both empirically and politically problematic. Future research on gender and the social division of labour need to take into account that women's perceptions and explanations of their occupational choices are indistinguishable from culturally sanctioned and socially constructed gender identities.

The extent to which women's occupational choices are seen as circumscribed by structures of domination is largely guided by the researcher's own theoretical perspective. While structural explanations focus on institutional barriers to advancement, interactionist studies of the micro-politics of power (Carpenter: 98) are more likely to recognize women's emancipatory strategies. The debate between proponents of the structural approach and theorists who emphasize women's interests and occupational choices reflects a fundamental disagreement over the relative importance of agency and structure in explaining human behaviour. As Wharton (1991: 381) has argued, this theoretical dilemma can be resolved only by taking into consideration the 'processes through which interests are defined and recognized by actors'. The situation of women health-care professionals also indicates that structural constraints can be discerned in the unintended consequences of actions (see Giddens, 1984: 294). Further examination of the unintended consequences of women's occupational strategies (such as those noted by Carpenter and by Riska and Wegar in this volume) is central to expanding the knowledge of how inequalities in the wider society affect the medical divison of labour and how health-care systems in turn perpetuate these inequalities. In the next section, the assumption that women health-care workers share common concerns will be discussed further and the consequences of the new professionalism in nursing and the growing number of women physicians for the collective empowerment of patients will be explored.

The future of health care: providers and users

Although the concept of gender was originally generated to call into question the naturalization of sexual difference (Haraway, 1991: 131), some work of women health-care professionals has nevertheless tended to reinforce an essentialist notion of 'female interests' (Altekruse and McDermott, 1987: 85). In his study of nursing subordination in health care, Carpenter argues that women health professionals cannot be assumed to share a common interest merely because they are women. Social divisions drawn along class and ethnic lines must also be considered, including those related divisions that stem from the separation and segregation of work tasks (such as specialties among nurses and physicians). Hence it is erroneous to assume 'the existence of a common occupational nursing "interest" in relation to outside agencies like the medical profession or the state' (p. 97). In the mid-nineteenth century the professionalization of nursing was already strongly affected by class distinctions, as the new middle-class nurses aspired to distinguish themselves from the 'drunken old dames' who had earlier cared for the sick at the infirmaries (Bradley, 1989: 192).

Carpenter's criticism parallels a debate among feminist scholars about the misuse of gender as a universalizing explanatory concept (Harding, 1991). While proponents of the dual-systems theory have attempted to include the combined impact of class and gender in their analyses, few feminist theorists have successfully interwined race, class and gender (Haraway, 1991: 129). So far critical studies of the medical division of labour have tended to focus mostly on gender. The neglect of other social divisions has largely been due to the exclusive focus on physicians and the failure to take into account other health-care occupations and the larger health-care system.

The feminist critique of medical dominance has mainly centred on the social control and construction of gender and women's bodies by medical men. Medical knowledge has been exposed as part of the means by which gender divisions in society are maintained (Ehrenreich and English, 1978; Martin, 1989). Not only do social divisions have an impact upon nurses, according to Carpenter (p. 97); nursing and nurses also have an impact upon social divisions among lay carers and the users of health services. This is an important addition to a literature that has tended to romanticize the work of women health professionals and to see women professionals as 'natural' allies with users of services. Although the characterization of women's work as 'emotional labour' (James, 1989) has cast a new light on this type of labour and the standard sociological definition of work, it has also led researchers to neglect as well as to underestimate how much women health-care workers in their daily work serve as functionaries of the medical gaze (Carpenter: 101). In the latter capacity they reproduce the same power imbalances vis-à-vis patients that have shaped their own working conditions. Furthermore, while the recent professionalization effort in nursing on the one hand challenges the subordination of nurses vis-à-vis physicians, such efforts also curtail the loyalties that facilitate collective bargaining in the workplace. The new nursing is less a direct challenge to medical power than an attempt to reform it, a tendency that limits nurses' potential to act as the patient's advocates (Carpenter: 124).

Carpenter's argument challenges the optimistic viewpoint presented by feminist scholars who have projected that the increasing number of women physicians will change the nature of health care and promote the interests of female patients (Altekruse and McDermott, 1987: 85). While the existence and consequences of race-, class-, and specialty-based divisions among women physicians is a largely neglected research topic, it would be a mistake to assume that women's interests are unaffected by such differences. Access by a few women to prestigious positions in the organization of health care is not enough to guarantee changes in the nature and organization of health care or in the position of female patients or health-care workers. The argument that the equal promotion of women and men physicians would mean that 'those presumed qualities of womanhood – nurturance, community and relational abilities – were as valuable to those in positions of authority as they are to those who give primary care' (Lorber: 66) cannot be put forward without qualification. For this reason it is doubtful whether the changing sex composition of the elite in health-care professions will diminish women's experiences of gender inequalities in the less prestigious 'semi-professions', as Kazanjian (p. 169) assumes.

The assumption that women physicians will change the quality of medicine is also questioned by Elston (p. 38), who argues that the 'feminization' of the profession *per se* cannot be expected to downgrade or transform the character of medical work. Furthermore, professional socialization and the structure of medical practice might well be more influential than gender in determining the identity and interests of women practitioners. Referring to an Israeli study, Lorber (p. 69) notes that female primary-care physicians, rather than being the patients' advocates, in fact were less willing to accept patients' initiatives than hospital-based specialists who were mostly men. The probability that women physicians would promote patient interests is lessened by the gendered division of labour that puts women in jobs where they have little control over the organization of their work. By reinforcing existing social divisions within the medical division of labour, neo-liberal policies aimed at rationalizing and rationing health care are likely further to diminish the prospect of women health-care professionals' contributing to the collective empowerment of patients.

References

Altekruse, Joan M. and McDermott, Susanne (1987) 'Contemporary concerns of women in medicine', in Sue V. Rosser (ed.), *Feminism within Science and Health Professions: Overcoming Resistance*. Oxford: Pergamon Press. pp. 65–88.

Armstrong, David (1983) *The Political Anatomy of the Body: Medical Knowledge in Britain in the Twentieth Century*. Cambridge: Cambridge University Press.

Atkinson, Paul and Delamont, Sara (1990) 'Professions and powerlessness', *Sociological Review*, 38: 90–110.

Beller, Andrea H. (1984) 'Trends in occupational segregation by sex and race, 1960–1981', in Barbara F. Reskin (ed.), *Sex-segregation in the Work Place: Trends, Explanations, Remedies*. Washington: National Academy Press. pp. 11–26.

Bradley, Harriet (1989) *Men's Work, Women's Work: a Sociological History of the Sexual Division of Labor in Employment*. Minneapolis: University of Minnesota Press.

Carpenter, Eugenia S. (1977) 'Women in male dominated professions', *International Journal of Health Services*, 7: 191–207.

Carter, Michael J. and Carter, Susan Boslego (1981) 'Women's recent progress in the professions or, women get a ticket to ride after the gravy train has left the station', *Feminist Studies*, 7: 477–504.

Connell, Robert W. (1987) *Gender and Power: Society, the Person and Sexual Politics*. Cambridge: Polity Press.

Crompton, Rosemary and Sanderson, Kay (1990) *Gendered Jobs and Social Change*. London: Unwin Hyman.

Davies, Celia and Rosser, Jane (1986) 'Gendered jobs in the health service: a problem for labour process analysis', in David Knights and Hugh Willmott (eds), *Gender and the Labour Process*. Aldershot: Gower. pp. 94–116.

Ehrenreich, Barbara and English, Deirdre (1978) *For Her Own Good: 150 Years of Expert Advice to Women*. New York: Anchor Press.

Fox, Mary Frank and Hesse-Biber, Sharlene (1984) *Women at Work*. Palo Alto: Mayfield.

Giddens, Anthony (1979) *Central Problems in Sociological Theory*. Berkeley: University of California Press.

Giddens, Anthony (1984) *The Constitution of Society*. Cambridge: Polity Press.

Halpern, Sydney A. (1992) 'Dynamics of professional control: internal coalitions and cross-professional boundaries', *American Journal of Sociology*, 97: 994–1021.

Haraway, Donna J. (1991) *Simians, Cyborgs, and Women: The Reinvention of Nature*. New York: Routledge. pp. 127–48.

Harding, Sandra (1991) *Whose Science? Whose Knowledge? Thinking from Women's Lives*. Ithaca: Cornell University Press.

Hochschild, Arlie Russell (1979) 'Emotion work, feeling rules, and social structure', *American Journal of Sociology*, 85: 551–75.

James, Nicky (1989) 'Emotional labour: skill and work in the social regulation of feelings', *The Sociological Review*, 37: 15–41.

Light, Donald (1979) 'Uncertainty and control in professional training', *Journal of Health and Social Behavior*, 20: 310–22.

MacKinnon, Catharine A. (1989) *Toward a Feminist Theory of the State*. Cambridge: Harvard University Press.

Martin, Emily (1989) *The Woman in the Body*. Boston: Beacon Press.

McKinlay, John B. and Arches, Joan (1985) 'Towards the proletarianization of physicians', *International Journal of Health Services*, 15: 161–95.

McKinlay, John B. and Stoeckle, John D. (1988) 'Corporatization and the social transformation of doctoring', *International Journal of Health Services*, 18: 191–205.

Mills, C. Wright (1940) 'Situated actions and vocabularies of motive', *American Sociological Review*, 5: 904–13.

Parsons, Talcott (1951) *The Social System*. New York: Free Press.

Reskin, Barbara F. (1988) 'Bringing the men back in: sex differentiation and the devaluation of women's work', *Gender and Society*, 2: 58–81.

Reskin, Barbara F. and Roos, Patricia A. (1990) *Job Queues, Gender Queues: Explaining Women's Inroads into Male Occupations*. Philadelphia: Temple University Press.

Riska, Elianne (1993) 'The medical profession in the Nordic countries', in Frederic Hafferty and John McKinlay (eds), *The Changing Character of the Medical Profession: an International Perspective*. Oxford University Press.

Sassoon, Anne Showstack (ed.) (1987) *Women and the State: the Shifting Boundaries of Public and Private*. London: Hutchinson.

Silverman, David (1989) 'The impossible dreams of reformism and romanticism', in David Silverman and Jaber F. Gubrium (eds), *The Politics of Field Research: Sociology beyond Enlightenment*. London: Sage. pp. 30–48.

Walby, Sylvia (1990) *Theorizing Patriarchy*. Oxford: Basil Blackwell.

Wharton, Amy S. (1991) 'Structure and agency in socialist–feminist theory', *Gender and Society*, 5: 373–89.

Williams, Christine L. (1989) *Gender Differences at Work: Women and Men in Nontraditional Occupations*. Berkeley: University of California Press.

Index

Achieving a Balance, 48–9, 52
administration, women in, 85–7, 89–90,
    165
Allen, I., 52, 53, 54
American Medical Association, 71
American Medical Women's
    Association, 62
anaesthetics
    as shortage specialty, 50
    women in, 17, 20–2, 40, 53, 78, 87
Arches, Joan, 3
Armstrong, D., 104, 107, 120, 182
Atkinson, Paul, 5
autonomy, medical
    in Britain, 27–8, 30–8, 40, 55, 117
    in bureaucratized medicine, 84
    female, 174, 177–8, 182
    in general practice, 45–6
    in hospital medicine, 47, 49, 52
    loss of, 28–9, 31, 35, 36–8, 41
    of midwives, 136, 142, 176, 178, 179
    in nursing, 117, 121, 123–4, 154–6,
        166, 177
    and professionalism, 3, 154
    and state, 8, 27, 178–81
    in USA, 28, 63, 65, 68–9, 71, 81
Ayuraveda medicine, 14

Bedford Fenwick, Mrs, 117, 119
Bell, Daniel, 105
Bellaby, P., 109–10, 120–1
Benoit, Cecilia, 133, 136, 137, 142
Benokraitis, Nicole V., 68
Berry, Wendell, 133
birth, medicalization, 6, 134–5, 139, 140,
    143–4
Bradley, Harriet, 174
Britain
    gender segregation, 29–30

and medical autonomy, 29, 30, 178–9
    midwifery, 136, 178
    neo-liberalism, 8, 180–1
    nursing in, 10, 97, 115–25, 180–1
    women in medical profession, 9, 10,
        27–57, 78, 174–6
    see also National Health Service
British Medical Association (BMA),
    and nursing, 104
Browner, Carole H., 132–3, 139
bureaucratization
    of medicine, 3, 5–6, 43–4, 73, 81, 85,
        90, 179
    of nursing, 118, 165
    in USA, 9, 30, 63, 68–9
Buss, Fran Leeper, 141

Canada
    division of labour, 10, 148–69
    gender hierarchies, 149–60, 176
    midwifery, 136, 139, 178
    and professional autonomy, 178–80
Canada Health Act 1984, 148, 164
Canadian Nurses Association, 157
Candib, Lucy, 65
care
    as female role, 100, 182
    medical models, 109–12, 114, 117–19,
        123–4, 136
    professionalization, 118–14
    as role of nurse, 100, 111–12, 113–14,
        122, 124, 174
careers
    in community health, 42–3
    and family role, 14, 20–1, 24–5, 52,
        64–8, 73, 79–80, 181
    female, 5, 9, 40, 56
    in general practice, 44–7
    in hospital medicine, 51–5

careers – *cont'd*
  and pyramidal structure, 47–50, 175
Carpenter, Mick, 10, 95–126, 174,
    176–7, 179, 182, 184–5
Chicago School, 2
Chidambaram, S. Muthu, 5, 8–9, 13–25,
    177
chiropractors
  regulation, 163
  status, 153, 158–60, 166, 177
Christ, E.A., 116, 117
class
  and professions, 108, 111, 180
  and social divisions, 97–8, 112–13,
    115, 118, 174, 176, 184
client relationships, in India, 14
clinical assistants, women as, 52
closure, social, 2, 29, 112–13, 117, 177,
    182–3
Cohen, May, 66
Columbia School, 2
Committee of Vice-Chancellors and
    Principals, 34–5
communication
  as female role, 182
  male/female styles, 77
Community Care Act 1990 (UK), 125
community medicine
  and health promotion, 41–2
  women in, 41–4, 46, 71, 84–5, 88
competition
  for health care, 114
  male fear of, 21, 23, 65, 70–3
  professional, 67–8, 162–3
constructivism, social, 99
consultancy, difficulties for women
    physicians, 13, 18, 21, 43
consultants
  and junior doctors, 47–50
  women as, 51–5, 84
corporatization of medicine, 3, 28, 31,
    90, 137, 166, 175
Cosminsky, Sheila, 132, 134
credentialism, 2, 34–5, 39, 70
Crompton, R., 37, 38, 39
culture
  and gender segregation, 13–14, 19,
    25
  influence on midwifery, 138–9, 140–1
cure
  as role of nurse, 112

as role of physician, 99–100, 111, 113,
    174

Davies, C., 112
decision-making
  nurses in, 103
  and professional autonomy, 29, 179
  women in, 89
Delamont, Sara, 5
Denmark, women physicians, 83
dentistry
  and dental nurses, 158, 178
  professional regulation, 161–3
  women in, 149, 153
Dentists Act 1979 & 1988 (Canada),
    161–2
deprofessionalization, 28, 39, 55, 166
desegregation by gender, 81–2
deskilling of professionals, 37–8, 108,
    110, 112
DeVries, Raymond G., 6, 10, 131–44,
    176, 177
dietetics
  as female occupation, 153–4
  regulation, 163
discrimination
  and female physicians, 30, 39, 52,
    63–4, 66, 71–3, 175
  legislation against, 9, 31, 34–5, 72
  in nursing, 112–13, 122
  positive, 33, 67
  racial, 112–13
  reverse, 67
distance, professional, 157–9
domination
  male, 29, 68, 71–2, 87, 113, 149–51,
    164, 168
  medical, 5, 27–8, 103–4, 120
  professional, 3, 107–10, 116, 120,
    147–8, 160–1, 166–7
Durkheim, Emile
  on division of labour, 1
  on professions, 107

education, medical
  in Britain, 27, 31–6
  in Canada, 167
  control of, 30–1, 162
  gender bias, 150, 151
  for general practice, 44
  in India, 14, 15

education – *cont'd*
and midwifery, 134
for nurses, 111, 117, 119–20, 122, 154,
157
part-time, 50, 53–5
postgraduate, 39, 48–50, 51
quota system, 31, 33–4, 35–6, 72
selection procedures, 34–5, 80
and sensitivity, 7
women in, 15–17, 25, 71, 80
Ehrenreich, B., 111–12
elites
medical, 3, 5, 62, 65–70, 72, 89–90,
162
nursing, 124, 126
Elling, Ray, ix
Elston, Mary Ann, 5, 9, 27–57, 175–7,
179–80, 186
employment, part-time
for doctors, 39–40, 46–7, 54, 65, 175,
181
for nurses, 122
English, D., 111–12
essentialism, 7, 18, 88, 183, 184
Etzioni, A., 107
Evers, H., 105

family
division of labour, 151
role in health care, 8, 100–1
and women's careers, 14, 20–1, 24–5,
34, 39–40, 45–6, 49, 52, 64–8, 73,
79–80, 181
family medicine, women in, 78
Feagin, Joc R., 68
feminism
and gender inequality, 180, 184–5
and nursing, 95, 110–11, 117, 119,
123, 126
feminization thesis, 36–8, 63, 65–6, 72,
151, 175–6, 186
Ferrier, Barbara M., 66
Finland
female physicians, 9–10, 78, 81–90,
174–5, 181
and professional autonomy, 178–9
Finnish Medical Association, 85, 86
Flexner Report, 70–1, 111, 127 n.3
Foucault, Michel, 96, 101–2
Fox, Renee C., 6
Freidson, Eliot, 3, 7, 69–70, 98, 106–9

functionalist approach, 1–2, 4, 98–101
critique, 102–6, 107

gatekeepers
general practitioners as, 44
and occupational structure, 5, 39,
52–3, 80, 180
'gaze', medical, 96, 101–2, 185
gender
desegregation, 81–2
hierarchy, 149–60, 168–9
neglect in research, 1–4, 6–7, 29
and occupational structure, 38–41
and power, 4, 8
preserving difference, 66
resegregation, 81–2, 86
segregation, 9, 13–14, 18, 25, 74–81,
83–4, 89–90, 173–83
and social divisions, 96–8, 109, 111,
112–13, 115, 118, 173, 184–6
and structural change in medicine, 3–4
see also inequality; labour division
general medicine, women in, 17, 18,
22–3, 78, 88
General Nursing Council (UK), 120
general practice *see* primary care
geography, influence on midwifery, 133
geriatric medicine, as shortage specialty,
50, 84
ghettoization, of women physicians,
81–2, 85–6, 88–9
glass ceiling effect, and medical careers,
5, 9, 63, 64–6
Goodenough Committee, 32–3, 36
Graham, H., 112
Grant, Linda, 65, 67
gynaecology
career opportunities, 51
and medicalization of birth, 6, 135
women in, 13, 17, 18–25, 53, 54–5, 71,
84

Habenstein, R.W., 116, 117
Hall, Oswald, 62
Hall, R.M., 161
harassment, sexual, 21–2, 67–8
health care
gender hierarchy, 149–56
as gendered, 7–8
rationing, 113–14, 125, 180
HMOs, women in, 69–70

holistic approach, 77, 88, 125
Holland, Barbara, 135
homeopathic medicine, in India, 15
Hospital Insurance and Diagnostic
    Services Act 1958 (Canada), 148,
    164
hospital medicine
    career opportunities, 50–1
    consultants and junior doctors, 47–50
    women in, 51–5, 56
Hughes, D., 103
human resource planning, 165, 167
human-capital theory, 79–80, 181

illness, as deviance, 99, 106–7
income, and gender hierarchy, 151–4
India
    female physicians, 5, 8–9, 13–25, 175,
        181
    medical practice, 14–15
    midwifery, 138
inequality, and organizational structure,
    148–69, 176, 179–80, 184
infantalization of patient, 115, 118, 119
insurance, and midwifery, 137, 179
integration of women physicians, 81–2,
    89
invisibility *see* subordination
Irwin, S., 134
Israel, women in primary care, 69, 186

Jeffery, Patricia, 138
Johnson, M., 100
Johnson, T., 107
Jordan, Brigette, 134, 135
Joshi, Anandabai, 16
junior doctors
    and consultants, 47–50
    women as, 51

Kanter, Rosabeth Moss, 9
Kars, C., 134
Kazanjian, Arminée, 10, 147–69, 176–8,
    180, 186
Kessler-Harris, Alice, 66
Kirkham, Mavis, 135
knowledge
    and control, 1, 101–2, 105–6,
        108–9
    elite, 5–6, 7
    nursing, 122–3

labour division, medical, 2–6, 7–9,
    13–25, 173–86
    cultural effects, 13–14, 19
    as gendered, 1, 4–5, 6–7, 78–81,
        149–56, 174–8
    individual approach, 78–80, 81, 86, 88
    institutional approach, 80–1, 86–8
    social divisions approach, 96–126,
        173, 184–6
    and specialization, 39–40
    see also gender
labour process, changes, 109–10
Laderman, Carol, 134, 135, 139, 140
Landy, David, 143
Larkin, G., 29
Larson, Magali S., 6, 7, 108
Light, Donald, 6
London medical schools, 32–3, 35, 36
Lorber, Judith, 5, 9, 62–73, 80, 176–7,
    179–80, 185–6

magic, and medicine, 6
Malinowski, B., 6
management roles
    in community medicine, 43–4
    in hospital medicine, 49, 164
    and nursing, 102–3, 104, 121, 124,
        165–6, 180
    in USA, 68–9
    and women, 147, 168
Manga, P., 160
manpower planning, 147–69
market, and health care, 29, 90, 165
Martin, H.W., 100
Martin, Meredith, 65
Marx, Karl, on division of labour, 1,
    4
Marxism
    and professionalization, 107–9
    on proletarianization, 81
Mauksch, H.O., 102
McKevitt, Teresa, 135
McKinlay, John B., 3, 31
Medical Care Act 1966 (Canada), 148,
    164
Medical Women's Federation, 46
medicine, corporate, 3, 28
midwifery
    and culture, 138–9, 140–1
    definition, 132
    as female occupation, 5, 10, 131

midwifery – *cont'd*
  and medicalization of birth, 6, 10, 111,
    134–5, 139, 140, 143–4
  as profession, 141–4, 181–2
  and social structure, 136–8, 140–1
  status, 131–44, 176, 177–8
  and technology, 133–5, 140
  traditional, 134–5, 137–9, 140
  training, 134
  untrained, 15, 134, 138
  see also autonomy
Moldow, Gloria, 70–1
Moores, B., 125

National Health Service
  community medicine, 41–4
  and midwifery, 136
  and professional autonomy, 36, 120,
    179
  reforms, 27, 28–9, 41–3, 44, 49, 56
  self-governing trusts, 49–50
Navarro, V., 98, 108–9, 110
neo liberalism, 8, 180–1, 186
neo-Weberian approach, 2–3
Netherlands, midwifery, 136–7, 142, 178
networks
  female, 62–3
  professional, 9, 13–14, 18, 28, 38, 52,
    80, 90
neurology, child, 84
Norway, women physicians, 10, 83, 88
nurse, clinical, 122–4
nurse practitioner, 123, 155, 166
Nurse Registration Act 1919 (UK), 120
Nurses (Registered) Act (Canada), 156,
    157
nursing
  and crisis in health care, 113–15, 116,
    125, 180–1
  and doctoring, 102–4, 111, 118, 119
  earnings, 153–4, 166
  as female occupation, 5, 37, 117–19
  grade system, 110, 120–1
  medical model, 109–12, 114, 117–19,
    123–4, 155
  men in, 180
  Nightingale model, 109, 116–18
  professionalization, 107–8, 114–15,
    117–25, 126, 180, 181–2, 184–5
  professionalizer type, 116–25
  and race, 112–13, 122

regulation, 163
  social divisions approach, 96–126,
    184–5
  sociology of, 6–7, 10, 95–6, 98–115
  subordination, 97, 98–125, 155, 165,
    176–7, 184–5
  and system structure, 165
  traditionalizer type, 116–18
  training, 111, 117, 119–20, 122, 154,
    157
  utilizer type, 116, 117, 121
  see also technology

Oakley, Ann, 95–6
obstetrics
  career opportunities, 51
  and medicalization of birth, 6, 135
  women in, 13, 17, 18–22, 24–5, 53,
    54–5, 71, 84, 135
occupation
  inequalities, 147–69, 174, 180
  structure, 38–41, 47–50, 65, 71, 80–1,
    86, 179–80
occupational health, women in, 84
occupational therapy, as female
    occupation, 154
ophthalmology, women in, 17, 20–4
optometrists
  status inequalities, 153, 159, 163
  women in, 149
organization
  and occupational attainment, 39,
    147–8
  structures, 1–2, 77–8
Oribabor, P., 109–10, 120–1
orthopaedics, as shortage specialty, 51
Osler, William, 5

paediatrics *see* pediatrics
Parsons, Talcott
  on medical profession, 1, 4, 6, 96, 105,
    107, 182
  and sociology of nursing, 98–102, 106
pathology, as shortage specialty, 50, 53
patient
  and female physicians, 7, 77, 79, 86,
    88, 186
  infantalization, 115, 118
  and nursing, 112, 123–4
  objectification, 101–2, 119
  and technology, 100

patriarchy
  in medicine, 29
  and nursing, 111, 114, 165–6
  and state control, 8, 180
patronage, extent, 52–3, 180
payment, third-party, 3, 68, 90, 153
pediatrics, women in, 17, 18–19, 22, 54,
    78–9, 84, 87
pharmacy
  regulation, 163
  women in, 151, 159
physician
  'fee-for-service', 1, 68, 71
  female, 8–10, 13–25, 27–57, 62–73,
    174–7
  future role, 68–73
  and male patients, 19–20, 21–2, 24, 25
  as new force in medicine, 7, 77–90,
    185–6
  and gender division of labour, 5–6, 7
  income, 71, 84, 153
  and midwifery, 140
  professional networks, 9, 13–14, 18,
    28, 38, 52, 80, 90
  professional role, 1–2, 5
  see also proletarianization
physiotherapy
  as female occupation, 37, 151–3, 154
  regulation, 163
  status inequalities, 159, 166
Piccone, Mary A., 63
podiatry
  regulation, 163
  status inequalities, 153, 159–60, 166
  women in, 149
policy-making, women in, 87, 89
poststructuralism, 181, 183
power
  and gender, 80
  and health care crisis, 113–14
  negotiated order, 103–4, 110
  of nurses over service users, 98,
    104–6, 126
  of physicians, 99, 182
  professional, 2–3, 4, 5–6, 30–1, 37, 47,
    68, 101–6, 143
    inequalities, 148, 164
    radical critiques, 106–13
  social, and nursing, 96–8
practitioner role
  and nurse, 123

and occupational structures, 39–40,
    42–4, 49, 56
prevention, nursing role, 105, 157
primary care
  autonomy, 45–6
  in Britain, 40, 44–7
  in Canada, 157
  contracts, 44–7
  in Finland, 9–10, 84–5, 88–9
  in Israel, 69, 186
  men in, 45
  in USA, 65, 73
  women in, 5, 7, 18, 44–7, 56, 73, 79,
    182, 186
primary nursing concept, 123, 124
private practice, women in, 13, 18, 71, 84
privatization of health care, 175
productivity
  and curative medicine, 110
  of women doctors, 77
professions
  gender hierarchy, 149–60
  nursing as, 97
  self-regulation, 160–4
  sociology of, 1–4, 6–7, 89–90, 106–7
  and training, 150, 151
'Project 2000', 122, 125
proletarianization
  of nursing, 10
  of physicians, 1, 3, 4, 28, 31, 36–7, 39,
    47, 55, 81, 176
  of professions, 108, 114
promotion of health
  and community medicine, 41–2
  nursing role, 157
psychiatry
  child psychiatry, 84
  as shortage specialty, 50, 53, 79
  women in, 149
psychology, regulation, 163
Public Health Act 1972 (Finland), 84
public health medicine, women in, 41–4,
    71, 84–5, 88
public/private spheres, 4–5
purdah system, and entry of women into
    medicine, 15, 25

race
  and nursing, 112–13, 122, 180
  and social divisions, 97–8, 103, 115,
    174, 176

radiology
  as shortage specialty, 50
  women in, 40, 53
Reddi, Muthulakshmi, 16
referral, difficulties for women
    physicians, 13, 18, 21, 80
Registered Nurses Association
    (Canada), 156, 157
registrars, 47
  women as, 51, 54, 55
regulation
  as gendered, 160–7, 168–9
  self-regulation, 27, 160–4, 179
Reid, Margaret, 142
Relman, A.S., 3
research, women in, 86, 87–8
resegregation by gender, 81–2, 86
Reskin, Barbara F., 81
resource allocation, control of, 68–9,
    71–3, 166
restratification thesis, 3–4, 9, 68–9
Reverby, S., 123, 126
risk, creation, 6, 143–4, 177–8
Riska, Elianne, 5, 9–10, 29, 77–90, 177
Robinson, J., 47
role theory, 183
Roos, Patricia A., 81
Rosser, J., 112
Rothman, David, 139
Royal College of Nursing (UK), 124
Royal Commission on Medical
    Education 1968 (UK), 33
Royal Commission on the NHS 1977
    (UK), 104
Rukmabai, 16

Saks, Mike, 2
Sanderson, K., 37, 39
Sargent, Carolyn, 134, 137–8, 139
Scarlieb, Mrs, 15–16
Scheff, T., 103, 104
Scuder, Ida, 16
Seebohm Report 1974 (UK), 122
selection procedures, 34–5, 80
sensitivity training, 7
Sex Discrimination Act 1975 (UK), 31,
    34–5
sexism
  in medical training, 64, 66–8, 72
  in nursing care, 105
Sheppard-Towner Act, 71

sick role, and nursing, 98–105
Siddha medicine, 14
Smith, L., 168–9
social interactionism, and nursing
    research, 98, 104–5
social work, medical, 154
socialization theory, 2, 6, 79–80, 86,
    100–1, 181, 183
sociology
  of nursing, 6–7, 10, 95–6, 98–115
  of professions, 1–4, 6–7, 89–90
Solomon, David, 62
Soviet Union
  childbirth in, 135
  women in medicine, 37–8
specialist *see* consultants
specialty
  female choice, 14, 17–24, 53–4, 79–81,
    83–4, 86–7, 175, 177, 181–4
  shortages, 50–1, 53–4
sports medicine, lack of women in, 84
Stacey, Margaret, 2, 4, 104
staff grade, 49, 51–2
Starr, Paul, 3
state
  and general practice, 44
  and medical training, 28–9, 31–3, 176
  and occupational structure, 39, 63
  and professional autonomy, 178–81
  role, 8, 55–6, 68, 100
  and subordination of nursing, 97
status
  inequalities, 147–55, 159–60, 174
  of medical profession, 27–8, 37–8, 176
  of midwives, 131–44, 176, 177–8
  of nursing, 154–5, 157, 177
  of primary health care, 41, 78, 84–5,
    88
  of women, 15–16
Stein, L., 103
stereotypes
  and career choice, 79
  sex, in India, 17–25, 88
  and sick role, 105
Stid, Annie J., 16
Stoeckle, John D., 3
Strauss, A. et al., 110
stress
  in nursing, 125, 165
  in primary health care, 85
Strong, P.M., 47

structure, social
    influence on midwifery, 136–8, 140–1
    and occupational attainment, 147–8,
        183–4, 186
subordination
    of nurses, 97, 98–125, 155, 165, 176–7,
        184–5
    of patients, 100, 118
    of women, 109, 174
Sullivan, D., 132–3, 136
surgery, women in, 20, 21–3, 40, 53, 54,
        86–7, 88–9
Susie, Debra Anne, 140
Swain, Clara, 16
Sweden
    midwifery, 136–7, 142, 178
    women physicians, 10, 83
symbolic interactionist approach, 2

teaching, medical, women in, 85, 87
technology, medical
    critiques, 105–6
    effects, 1, 6, 71
    influence on midwifery, 133–5, 140
    and nursing, 100–1, 109–11, 119, 155
trade union movement, influence on
        nursing, 110–11, 117, 121–2, 124
training *see* education, medical

Unani medicine, 14–15
uncertainty, in medicine, 6, 143–4, 177,
        182
United Kingdom Central Council for
        Nursing and Midwifery (UKCC),
        122, 125
USA
    Health Maintenance Organizations,
        10
    and medical autonomy, 28, 178–9
    midwifery, 133, 136, 137, 138–9,
        140–2, 178
    nursing, 111, 123

stratification of medical profession, 9,
        68–9
women in medical profession, 30, 36,
        63–73, 78, 80, 174–6

Van Ginneken, J.K., 134
Voorhoeve, A.M., 134

Walsh, Mary Roth, 80
Wardwell, W., 158
Weber, Max
    on division of labour, 1, 4
    on power, 108
Wegar, Katarina, 1, 5, 9–10, 11, 77–90,
        173–86
Weitz, R., 132–3, 136
welfare state
    financing, 164–6
    and nursing, 116–22
    and professional autonomy, 178–81
Weller, G.R., 160
Wharton, Amy S., 184
Wheeler, Rachel, 65
Williams, F., 97
women
    constraints on choice, 181–4
    devaluation of skills, 3
    as emotional experts, 7–8, 79, 88–9,
        100, 174, 182
    health issues, 77
    in health occupations, 149–60
    and ideology of domesticity, 5
    in medical education, 15–17, 25
    see also gender; physician, female;
        specialty
Women in Medicine, 46
Woodward, Christel A., 66
working hours, female, 64–5, 68, 73, 77,
        87, 165
World Health Organization, on
        midwives, 132, 134